DATE DUE

DE 16 '96		
MR 13 '97		
NO 20 '97		
MR 11 '98		
AP 2 '98		
OC 16 '00		
DE 13 '00		
FE 6 '01		
OC 3 '01		

DEMCO 38-296

The
Castles and Keeps
of Scotland

FRANK ROY FRAPRIE

BARNES
&NOBLE
BOOKS
NEW YORK

To Her,

WHO, BY THE LIGHTENING OF MY BURDENS, HAS MADE
THIS BOOK POSSIBLE.

This edition published by Barnes & Noble, Inc.

1993 Barnes & Noble Books

ISBN 1-56619-087-8

Printed and bound in the United States of America
M 9 8 7 6 5 4 3

Preface

—•—

In these pages I have tried to bring together some of the history and romance which attaches to the more important castles of Scotland, and to tell enough of their architectural peculiarities to enable the visitor to understand what he is viewing. In none of these respects is it to be hoped, at this late day, that new facts of importance could be brought forth. My task has been rather to furnish a convenient collection of facts hitherto to be found only by much reading of books often not easily accessible, adding thereto my own opinions and experiences where they seemed novel or interesting.

The book, though the outcome of three trips to Scotland, the last of which was undertaken solely to collect material for it, is less a record of travel than a companion and guide for it. It is, as the only handbook on the subject, a necessity for the visitor to the castles who would know the truth about them. The so-called facts dispensed by local guides are in most instances erroneous, and have not been used in this volume, where historical references are taken from more authoritative sources. I dare not assume, however, that entire accuracy has been attained in the transcription of the thousands of names and dates mentioned, even when a choice had not to be made between conflicting spellings and figures, elsewhere given.

It would be impossible to enumerate the sources of historical information. In many instances, they are named in the text, but to mention all would be to include most of what has been written on Scotch history. Architecturally, I am greatly indebted to the monumental work of MacGibbon and Ross, " Domestic and Castellated Architecture of Scotland." Their theory of native development as opposed to Billings' hypothesis of French origin I have adopted and expounded. In a few instances of minor castles which I have not personally visited, my account is based upon their measurements.

I have been asked what castles should first be seen by the average visitor to Scotland. Edinburgh and Stirling, I assume, will be included in every itinerary, but they are citadels and palaces rather than castles. For a single castle which will give the most satisfactory idea of Scotch feudal life, I would select Doune, which is easily included in the Trossachs trip taken by almost every visitor to Scotland. Others easily reached and well worth seeing are, for beauty of situation, Bothwell, Kilchurn, Castle Campbell; for historic interest, Lochleven, Dunnottar, Craigmillar, Hermitage, Lochmaben; for romantic story, Tantallon and Tillietudlem. These would perhaps be enough to satisfy the average traveller. The specialist could make out a more extensive list after reading the following pages.

Contents

The Castles and Keeps of Scotland

CHAPTER I

DEVELOPMENT AND STYLES OF THE CASTLES OF SCOTLAND

THOUGH the fact is not generally recognized, and may easily escape the attention even of one travelling in Scotland, if he keeps to the usual track of tourists, the castles and old mansions of this country are extremely numerous. As soon as one leaves the railroad, however, and makes excursions by road into any of the more settled parts of Scotland, the castles become a most striking and picturesque feature of the landscape. Not only are their magnificent outlines attractive in themselves and admirably fitted to adorn the rugged hills and gloomy glens which they occupy, but their historical associations lend them the added charm of in-

1

tense human interest. They revivify for us the glorious memories of Bruce and Wallace, striving for the independence of their native land. The ancient names of the daring Douglases and other great clans, the exploits of a long line of kings, the terrible sieges and struggles of the English wars, leap into our thoughts as we scan these scarred and mouldering walls. Above all, most dear to the romantic mind, the tragic memory of the beautiful and unhappy Mary Stuart is constantly present, as we travel from castle to castle, for we find traditions of her attached to nearly every important building in Scotland.

Even the most casual visitor to ecclesiastical edifices in any part of Europe soon learns to know and distinguish the various styles of architecture which prevailed at different periods, and can gauge approximately the age of a building by its prominent features. With castles and mansions the case is somewhat different. The sequence of styles is not so obviously marked, and the differences are not such as to impress the lay visitor unless he knows what to observe. It may be of value, or at least interest, therefore, to give a short sketch of the evolution of the mediæval castle and its architectural development in Scotland. The

style of domestic architecture at different
epochs is well adapted to throw a flood of light
on the manners and customs of those who lived
in them. The castles not only show forth the
comparative condition of safety, prosperity,
and neighbourly intercourse of their owners,
but make it easy for us to trace the growth
of civilization through the centuries.

Scotland possesses no remains of Roman
buildings. Rome's occupation of the country
was so partial and temporary that neither
were buildings of great strength erected, nor
were the natives civilized enough to imitate
the architecture of the invaders. The usual
fortifications of the early inhabitants of
northern Europe were formed of ditches and
mounds strengthened by wooden palisades, or
were artificial islands of piles set in the midst
of lakes. Many remains of these exist in
northern Scotland. There are also north of
the Tweed, but in not a single instance south
of it, numerous "brochs," or round towers
constructed of uncemented masonry. These
consist of a thick wall around a central well
or court. The staircase and numerous small
rooms and galleries are hollowed out of this
wall and lighted by windows overlooking the
inner court. Though strong and well adapted

to their purpose, they are all of Celtic origin and great age, and had no effect on the later development of castellated architecture in Scotland. The only exception to this statement is that some of the later castles have a series of wall chambers, whose construction may have been suggested by tradition or observation of these strongholds.

Development of the Feudal Castle in Gaul

In Gaul, the influence of the architecture of the Romans was very lasting. When they retired from that region, during the fourth and fifth centuries, they left the whole country covered with towns, houses, and castles of their building. The native inhabitants had acquired their civilization, and transmitted much of it to the Goths and Franks who gradually spread over the country. The ecclesiastical architecture never departed from Roman models. The basilica was and is the universal prototype of the Christian church. The mediæval monastery was a direct derivation from the Roman house. The pillared cloister about an open court, giving access to a series of surrounding apartments, is copied from the peristyle of the Roman city house, the *villa urbana* of the country mansion. The *villa rustica* of the Roman house became the outer court of the monastery, surrounded by its stables and storehouses, and the *tablina* was turned into the chapter house.

The country houses of the Franks retained the Roman construction, — a series of buildings around a central court. The outer defences were ditches, and palisades erected on a mound. In the centre, on another mound, was built the hall of the chieftain, thus doubly defended. These structures were of wood, and were common among both Franks and Normans on the Continent, and in England. The latter, being masons by instinct, were not satisfied with defences so easily reduced by fire, and substituted a tower of stone and mortar for the central wooden redoubt. Thus, toward the middle of the eleventh century, originated the massive and gloomy structure known as the " Norman keep." These were built of great strength and concentrated in themselves the defensive strength of the castle, the outworks being usually unimportant. After the Norman Conquest they became common in England and spread to the very borders of Scotland, one standing at Carlisle on the west, and another at Norham on the east. But not

one was ever reared on Scottish soil, which
thus is free from any mark of Norman domination.

The Norman keep, in its typical form, was a
three-story tower, quadrangular in outline, and
with walls of great thickness. The ground
floor was used for storerooms, and was lighted
only by a very few small loopholes. The entrance was on the first floor, and was reached
by a movable ladder, or later was defended by
a forework which contained a stair. The gateway opened directly into the great hall, where
chieftain, retainers and domestics lived by day
and feasted and slept by night. The chieftain
alone, with his family, had a private apartment in the room above, reached by a spiral
stair in the wall, which was continued to the
roof. The defence of the keep was made from
the parapet, which ran around the top of the
walls and was provided with embrasures
through which weapons and missiles could be
showered on the enemy below. As the walls
of the keep were from twelve to twenty feet
thick, and of the most substantial construction,
such a fortress, properly provisioned and garrisoned, was able to withstand any means of
assault known at the period. The customary
solidity of the work may be judged by the fact

that in the last century it took six weeks to pierce a doorway in the ground floor wall of the Tower of London, though the builders were aided by all the resources of modern science. Though the Norman keep was thus perfectly adapted to the needs of defence so essential to its owners in this turbulent period, it was, according to our ideas, absolutely lacking in domestic comfort. Yet for two or three centuries the nobles of England lived in such abodes.

The Crusades caused great changes in castle architecture. Military engines were introduced and improved, and the soldiers of Europe learned valuable lessons as to the attack and defence of fortresses. Miners, working under " cats," or movable sheds, found the square corners of the keeps especially vulnerable points while unprovided with flanking defences. Improved engines easily demolished the parapets by hurling huge stones and ignited wooden roofs with balls of Greek fire.

To keep these engines at a distance, the walls of the outer keep were now greatly extended and strengthened, becoming the principal strength of the castle. The keep became merely the place of last resort, and was garrisoned by the lord himself. The walls were

furnished with towers at the angles and along
the flanks, to defend the curtains by cross fires.
Each of these was an independent fortress,
with its own garrison and supplies, furnished
by the vassal whose duty it was to defend it.
This style of castle prevailed in both France
and England during the thirteenth century,
and the earliest Scotch castles are also of this
type.

First Period of Scotch Castle Building, 1100 — 1300

Until this period, the forts of Scotland consisted of the ancient wooden hall on its mound,
surrounded by a palisaded mound of earth or a
wall of stones and earth. Macbeth was slain
in 1057 at the peel of Lumphanan on Deeside,
a tower of this construction. During the
twelfth century great changes took place in
the condition of Scotland, which were reflected
in the style of building castles. The Norman
Conquest had driven out of England many
Saxon nobles. King Malcolm Canmore, having married the Saxon Princess Margaret, received them favourably, and established them
on estates. They were followed by hosts of
Norman adventurers, who were well received

by David I, and also frequently vested with lands. Desirous of firmly establishing themselves, these newcomers naturally raised towers on the plan then in fashion in the southern lands whence they came. Thus were introduced at once building with stone and mortar, and castles consisting mainly of a great wall of enceinte.

As the Norman lords were generally given fiefs on the outlying borders of the kingdom, which, during the twelfth and thirteenth centuries, was gradually extended northwards and westwards, many castles of this type were erected in these parts of the country. A number of them still survive there, while in the more accessible regions they have been either destroyed or rebuilt. Several of them will be later described, including Urquhart and Inverlochy on the Caledonian Canal, and Dunstaffnage, built to dominate the Western Islands.

Professor Cosmo Innes, in his book, " Scotland in the Middle Ages," mentions the following castles as existing in the thirteenth century: Duffus and Bocharm, in Moray; Ruthven and Lochindorb, in Badenoch; Strathbolgie, Fyvie, Inverurie, Kildrummie and others in Aberdeenshire; Kincardine, Brechin, Redcastle, Forfar, Glamis, Leuchars, Craill and

St. Andrews in the east; Dumbarton, Bothwell, Douglas, Rothesay and Turnberry in the
west; Edinburgh, Stirling, Linlithgow, Dunbar, Yester, Roxburgh, Jedburgh, Lamberton,
Morton, Dalswinton, Lochmaben, and Con-
gleton in the centre and south, as well as many
others. The majority of these have either disappeared or have been entirely remodelled, but
some have remained to show us that their general design was similar to, though smaller
than, the contemporary castles of England
and France.

The castles of this period are usually quadrilateral, with necessary changes of form in
some cases to adapt them to their sites. Some
show towers at one or more angles, but all
were defended by crenelated parapets, behind
which a walk went around the walls. Lochindorb, Inverlochy and Achencass are square
with corner towers. Duart, Skipness, Castle
Swin and Castle Roy were simple parallelo-
grams, two of them having one or two square
towers. Loch Doon Castle, Urquhart, Home
and Mingarry are built to conform to the outline of the rocky sites they occupy. Rothesay
is oval and Caerlaverock is triangular, both
being defended by moats. These castles usually had curtain walls seven to nine feet thick

and twenty to thirty feet high. Their original
towers have now mostly disappeared, as well
as parapets and rampart walks. Most of them
depended on water as their principal defence,
some being on islands, others surrounded by
wet ditches. A few only occupy high crags.
They were mostly large enough to hold the
population and herds of the tributary territory
in case of siege, but not of exceptionally fine
construction. In the central parts of Scotland, however, where good freestone abounds,
and where the influence of the church building
so frequent in Scotland at this period could be
felt, some large and finely adorned castles
arose. Remarkable among these are Bothwell,
Kildrummie, and Dirleton, the latter being as
finely finished architecturally as any castle in
Scotland.

Second Period, 1300 — 1400

During the reigns of Alexander II and
Alexander III, Scotland attained to a state
of prosperity and influence among the nations
of Europe far above what might have been
expected of so small a kingdom. Her ambassadors and merchants contracted alliances and
carried on commerce with many nations. Her

knights and soldiers were numbered with the crusading hosts. Her architecture developed to a high pitch, and not only buildings of defence, but numerous churches and monasteries were erected at this period.

In 1286 this state of prosperity came to a sudden and tragic close. King Alexander III was thrown from his horse and killed during a foolhardy night ride. His only descendant, the Maid of Norway, died in Orkney, while coming to claim her throne.

The disputes about the succession paralyzed the ordinary activities of the country, and plunged it into lasting war. Ten years later the English invaded and occupied the country, and then for eighteen years the Scotch under Wallace and Bruce struggled to free their country from the invader's yoke. Even after Bannockburn, a constant strife with the English had to be maintained until the weak reign of Richard II left the Scots finally free. This hundred years of strife left the country utterly impoverished. It had been devastated over and over again. Its castles were destroyed by the sieges of the English, and were not reconstructed on their former scale. The owners, no matter how high their rank, could not afford extensive works, and Bruce forbade the

construction of large castles, which, if taken,
afforded secure strongholds to the invaders.

Under these circumstances, the nobles fell
back on the plan of the Norman keep, abandoned in both France and England for two
hundred years. Owing to the poverty of the
country, they were all small; no large castle
was built in Scotland during the fourteenth
century. They were little more than secure
places to protect the owner's family and close
retainers from sudden attack. Being entirely
of stone, they contained little which could be
burned, and after capture by an enemy, if he
damaged them to the extent of his power, a
little cleaning and a new roof restored them to
a habitable condition.

The Scottish keep, like the Norman, usually
was a three-storied tower. The basement was
invariably vaulted and used for stores, or a
stable. Very often its only communication
with the hall above was through a trap in the
vault. The first floor was the hall, and the
entrance door opened into this, being reached
by a ladder or movable stair. In this hall retainers, guests and domestics fed and slept in-
discriminately, no privacy for man or woman
being possible. This hall was usually furnished with a wooden floor midway of its

height, forming a chamber in the vault, as is everywhere evidenced by the rows of supporting corbels to be seen in the walls. The second floor was the private apartment of the chieftain and his family, who also had a loft in the roof, as a general thing. The roof was usually formed of stone slabs laid on a pointed arch, to render the whole fireproof, but in the smaller peels was of wood. The defence was undertaken from the parapet at the roof, which ran completely around the tower, expanding into rounded angles or bartizans at the corners. The walls were of great thickness, usually carrying spiral staircases, small closets for bed places, retiring rooms, etc., in their structure.

The accommodation of these towers was so circumscribed that they often were added to by a small square projection at one corner, giving an additional room on each floor. Besides this, there is little doubt that practically all these keeps had a courtyard attached, surrounded by a high wall. This contained the stables and offices, and was an additional protection against sudden assault.

Although the accommodation of these fourteenth century castles was of the most meagre description, there was one room which they never lacked, the " pit " or prison. This was an adjunct of some importance when every chieftain possessed the power of " pit and gallows " and could confine and hang his vassals as seemed to him right. The pit was a small chamber from six to nine feet long, and three or four wide, inside the wall, and reached only by a stone hatch in the floor of the guard-room or hall above. This had no window, but was ventilated by a small diagonal shaft running up to the open air. Prisoners were never executed here, as is often alleged by guides, but were publicly suspended on a large gallows-tree near the castle, for the edification of the lord and as an example to the surrounding population.

Ornamentation was entirely absent from these castles. The parapets and bartizans sometimes were carried on corbels of the simplest kind, and these, with a few plain gargoyles to drain off the rain from the parapet walks, were the only things which broke the stern severity of the grim towers.

As the proprietors of these castles felt the need for more space, various expedients were resorted to. As mentioned before, in some cases a small addition was built on one corner, making the so-called L plan. Sometimes

these had many more low floors than the main
keep, access to these pigeon-holes being gained
from a circular stair. In other cases numerous
small rooms were hollowed out of the walls,
occasionally two tiers to a single story. Later
keeps also had a fourth story added to the
main building. Some forms of decoration
were occasionally added both to exterior and
interior.

During the whole century which succeeded
Bannockburn, all the castles erected were of
the simple keep pattern. From the smallest
proprietor to the king himself, this was the
case. At Rothesay, the keep was added to
the ancient circular wall of enceinte, and
Dundonald, in which Robert II lived and died,
is but a plain keep, about forty by eighty feet.
This is somewhat larger than the ordinary
keeps of the nobles, which vary from twenty
by forty feet to as large as forty by sixty, but
are seldom larger. Not only were these small
buildings sufficient for the nobles of this
period, but even down to the seventeenth century the keep was the ordinary pattern of
mansion built and occupied by the smaller
proprietors, who would thus seem to have paid
little more attention to the amenities of do-

mestic life than their ancestors of the time
of Bruce.

Some of the more notable castles of this
period, many of them now being of great size
by reason of later additions, are Lochleven,
Drum, Threave, Neidpath, Craigmillar, Crichton, Castle Campbell, Aros, etc.

Third Period, 1400 — 1542

By the end of the fourteenth century, the
country was more settled and beginning to
recover from the exhaustion of its wars. The
wealthier nobles began to desire better dwellings, and turned for models to England and
France. Castles began to be erected in the
form of structures surrounding a courtyard
or quadrangle. At first the buildings were
attached here and there to the walls of the
outer courtyard as convenience dictated.
Many of the older keeps were greatly added
to at this period, and others were built on the
new plan. Gradually the capricious arrangement of rooms gave place to a settled plan,
which was developed to its highest point in the
royal palaces of Linlithgow and Stirling, as
complete in arrangement as the royal buildings of other countries. The smaller castles

finally came to be built on a well-understood
plan. The great hall was in the centre, with
the kitchen, pantry and buttery at the entrance end, and beyond the dais end the lord's
solar or private apartment. Above this were
bedrooms, and below the wine cellar. In the
more magnificent castles built on this plan in
other countries, the rooms were more numerous,
banqueting halls, halls of justice, reception
rooms, etc., being added, until the building
finally became a complete quadrangle about
a central court. No complete quadrangle in
a private castle of this period exists in Scotland, but at Tantallon, Dirleton and Doune,
the courtyard buildings were doubtless much
more extensive than at present. At Doune
the large windows in the wall of enceinte
show that the intention was to completely surround the court with buildings. The great
royal palaces of Stirling and Linlithgow are
the most perfect examples of the courtyard
plan of this period. They are not only large
enough for commodious private apartments
for the Court, but also contain a parliament
hall, chapel, drawing rooms, banqueting hall,
etc. They thus prove that by the time of
James IV and V the prosperity of the country had again reached such a pitch that the

Court lived in dignified state, and was able to suitably receive and entertain distinguished guests.

On the whole the castles of this period still show that they were built for defence, in spite of the increasing amelioration of manners and decreasing fear of foreign invasion. Although the interiors begin to show ornamentation of a rude character, the exteriors are still as rugged and forbidding as in the preceding period. The use of artillery, though it came into vogue during this period, had not advanced far enough to make it evident that small castles could no longer be defended against a determined siege, and only the larger structures, notably Tantallon, show embrasures for cannon dating from this century.

During this period, as also later, many simple keeps were built. Another common plan is the L type, with a doorway or stair tower in the re-entering angle, where it was easily defensible.

The usual means of defence at this period was still from the parapet, which is machicolated in a great number of instances. The entrance doorways were often on the ground floor, for greater ease of access, and were usually defended by oaken doors secured by

bars, and iron grates or "yetts." At Doune
and Tantallon the entrance is by an archway
under the hall, easily defended by gates and
portcullises, and commanded from guard-
rooms at the sides and openings in the floor
above.

Fourth Period, after 1542

The third period of Scottish castle building
closed with the death of James V in 1542.
The long minority and troubled reign of
Queen Mary were very unfavourable for
architectural development, and few existing
buildings date from this time. This, with
other circumstances, combined to produce a
distinct break in the development of domestic
architecture. Let us briefly enumerate these
factors.

The most important was the development
of artillery until it became the principal
weapon in sieges. The use of great guns was
not unknown in the preceding period, and
large splayed embrasures had been provided
at Tantallon and one or two other castles.
Experience soon showed, however, that the ordinary castles of the nobility were entirely unable to withstand the attacks of siege artillery.
Such fortresses as Dunbar, Dumbarton, Edin-

burgh and Stirling were well equipped for the national defence, but the castles of the nobles as a general rule did not possess artillery. These proprietors henceforth contented themselves with equipping their mansions to resist sudden attack and this caused a gradual change of plan and construction.

Another event of great importance was the Reformation. This movement led to the secularization of all the lands and possessions of the Church. Those who had the power to seize and keep the lands, that is, the nobility and gentry, were suddenly enriched and began to build new houses, or enlarge their old ones. With the Union under James VI English manners and the Renaissance style began to be introduced into Scotland, and had their effect on building.

The net result of these causes during this, the final period of castle building, was the gradual evolution from fortified castles to strong mansions, and finally to country houses without defence. During most of this period, the mansions are in no sense castles, but they retain this title by courtesy, and many of them are worthy of our attention.

During this period, as well as earlier, many simple keeps were built, especially as Border peel towers. The L plan is also a favourite, as affording good protection to the entrance. A new and entirely Scotch plan is very common. This has been called the zigzag or Z plan. It consists of a central tower with smaller towers or turrets built out at two opposite corners. This created a re-entrant angle on each face of the keep, and enabled every part of the wall to be flanked by musketry fire. Numerous varieties of this plan with one or two towers attached in various ways were tried, but the rapidly diminishing necessity for defensive structures caused many of them to disappear, so that only the L plan, the T plan and the courtyard plan have survived to modern times.

A great diversity of internal arrangements may be found in these later castles and mansions. In early castles the wine cellar was invariably below the hall, and furnished with a private stair, so that its contents were always under the lord's eye, and could be brought directly into the hall at meal times. The ground floor was also used for storing large quantities of provisions, as it was necessary to be always equipped for a siege. As the security of the country became greater, and settled peace was finally the normal condition, the ground floor began to be invaded by the kitchen and offices, and finally by the living rooms also, leaving the upper floors entirely free for sleeping and private apartments.

The ornamentation of castles assumed great importance during this period. In all previous castle building, corbels to carry floors and parapet were invariable features of Scotch architecture. In the sixteenth century, while still structural necessities, they were greatly exaggerated for decorative effect. In the seventeenth century they were freely employed as decorative features without any structural utility. The open bartizans, usually provided at the corners of the parapets in earlier castles, began to be roofed in about the beginning of this period, and peaked turrets soon became a most picturesque feature of Scotch buildings, sometimes being small and used only for decoration, and again being large enough for small apartments. The parapets themselves were absorbed in the roof, the eaves being at their top, with dormer windows and crow-stepped gables rising above.

As a result of the desire for decoration of all kinds, a Scottish castle of the latest period presented a most fantastic and picturesque appearance. It usually started from the ground as a plain and simple masonry tower, but by means of jutting corbels and overhanging stories, often of quite different and much larger plan, it offered ample accommodation in the upper parts. It was beset with a multitude of angle turrets and corner towers and its sky line was a mass of crow-steps, peaked and conical roofs and iron finials.

The last stage of castellated architecture is a simplification toward the symmetry and plan of the English mansion. Possessing no means of defence it can be called a castle only by courtesy and does not come within the province of this book.

In fact, the author's task has not led him to the inspection of many houses of the later periods. Having in most cases escaped the vicissitudes of war and time, they have been continuously occupied to the present day. They have thus been modernized in many cases and fail to appeal to lovers of the picturesque. They also lack the romantic history of the older structures. When to these reasons is added the habitual unwillingness of the Scotch gentry to admit the casual traveller to their grounds, it will be apparent why the photographs and descriptions are confined mostly to those older structures which are now public property or generously opened to public inspection by the courtesy of their present owners.

CHAPTER II

Dumbarton Castle and Rock

To him who enters Scotland by her western gate, the River Clyde, there rises majestic from its low and level northern bank the cleft basaltic pile of Dumbarton Rock, crowned and walled about with a fortress which, since immemorial time, has been a stronghold of renown. Once its name was Dunbriton, "the Briton's Rock," but even before that ancient tribe gave it a name, it was a fortress; the Venerable Bede tells of the days when it was simply Alcluyd, "the Rock upon the Clyde." In his days it was capital of a kingdom, Strathclyde. Long before this the Roman galleys, patrolling the western waters, creeping timidly out to Ultima Thule, made this their station and winter port, named Theodosia. Then a Roman fort crowned the summit, and bulwarked the end of Antonine's defensive wall. What it was earlier, and what

26

skin-robed tribe first held its summit, is and
shall be unknown, but certain we may be that
it has been a refuge and a strength in this
low land ever since human eyes first beheld it.

The Rock of Dumbarton is a basalt mass,
upthrust by primeval fires through the red
sandstone. Thus it resembles Ailsa Craig, the
Bass Rock, Stirling Castle Rock and Abbey
Craig, its neighbour, and other sharp-featured
cliffs throughout South Scotland. Five hundred and sixty feet in height, a mile about its
base, it precipitously overhangs the Clyde and
the Leven where they join. A deep and narrow cleft bifurcates the rock, giving it the
shape of a mitre, the western half, called
Wallace's Seat, being slightly higher. On it
still grows the Scotch thistle, a rare plant in
its native country, recalling Ossian's description of Balclutha, as he names the rock: " The
thistle shakes there its lovely head."

The castle of Dumbarton is to-day a fortification of little account. Since cannon have
been employed in warfare it has been com-
mandable by the rocky hill of Dumbuck, a
mile away; nevertheless it is still garrisoned
and will be while England remains a military
power, for it is one of the four fortresses of
Scotland appointed, at the Union, to be for-

ever held defensible. The buildings are small, and the ramparts weak; its frowning guns are ancient smoothbores; but it holds a phantasm of domination over the great commercial river, and offers to the eye a picturesque vision of old-time military strength.

Of its history much is lost. After the Roman era it was taken as a fortress by the Britons, and was their chief stronghold in the eighth century. In 756 it is said to have been reduced through famine by Egbert of Northumberland. In spite of this tradition, it has ever been esteemed so strong that it has never passed out of the possession of the Crown, but has been continuously a royal castle. The town of Dumbarton was the chief seat of the Earls of Lennox, but when Alexander II confirmed Earl Maldwyn in his estates early in the thirteenth century, the castle and some surrounding land were specially reserved, and erected into a free burgh royal, with extensive rights to levy dues on Clydeborne commerce.

At the commencement of the competition for the crown of Scotland between Bruce and Baliol, Dumbarton, with the other royal strongholds, was delivered over to Edward I, and in 1292 was given to Baliol as one of the appurtenances of his crown. In 1296 it was again occupied by the English under the governorship of Alexander de Ledes. In 1305 Sir William Wallace, loaded with chains, was sent from Dumbarton to London, and for the next four years the castle was governed by Sir John Menteith, his alleged betrayer. In 1309 Robert Bruce gained the castle by stratagem, but how is not recorded. We know only that the capture was planned and executed by " Oliver, a carpenter," who received for it a grant of lands.

Over and over again in the next two hundred years, the castle changed hands, sometimes peacefully, again by treachery or force. At whiles it was besieged in vain, as in 1481 by an English fleet. It was the naval headquarters of Scotland on the west coast, and here was fitted out the little squadron which was uselessly dispatched against England shortly before Flodden.

After the battle of Pinkie in 1547, the care of little Queen Mary was of the utmost importance and she was brought to Dumbarton from the island of Inchmahone in Lake Menteith in Perthshire. Nearly two years she remained here, and then, when not yet five years old, she was handed over to Monsieur de Breze, sent by Henri II to conduct her to

France. Fifteen years later she revisited the
castle on a royal progress, and even after her
dethronement Lord Fleming faithfully held
the castle for her. It had been her goal when
her little army was intercepted and defeated
by the Regent Moray at Langside, near Glasgow. The fortress held out until May, 1571,
when it was most gallantly captured by a
force sent by the Regent, the Earl of Lennox,
as is thus detailed by Tytler:

" Captain Crawford of Jordanhill, to whom
the attack was intrusted, had been long attached to the house of Lennox. He was the
same person whose evidence was so important
regarding the death of Darnley, and who afterwards accused Lethington of participation
in the murder, since which time he appears to
have followed the profession of arms. In the
enterprise he was assisted by Cunningham,
commonly called the Laird of Drumwhassel,
one of the bravest and most skilful officers of
his time, and he had been fortunate in securing the assistance of a man named Robertson,
who, having once been warden in the castle,
knew every step upon the rock familiarly, and
for a bribe consented to betray it. With this
man, Crawford and his company marched
from Glasgow after sunset. He had sent

before him a few light horse, who prevented
intelligence by stopping all passengers, and
arrived about midnight at Dumbuck, within
a mile of the castle, where he was joined by
Drumwhassel and Captain Hume, with a hundred men. Here he explained to the soldiers
the hazardous service on which they were to
be employed, provided them with ropes and
scaling ladders, and advancing with silence
and celerity, reached the rock, the summit of
which was fortunately involved in a heavy fog,
whilst the bottom was clear. But, on the first
attempt, all was likely to be lost. The ladders lost their hold while the soldiers were
upon them; and had the garrison been on the
alert, the noise must inevitably have betrayed
them. They listened, however, and all was still.
Again their ladders were fixed, and their steel
hooks this time catching firmly in the crevices,
they gained a small jutting-out ledge, where
an ash tree had struck its roots, which assisted
them as they fixed the ropes to its branches,
and thus speedily towed up both the ladders
and the rest of their companions. They were
still, however, far from their object. They
had reached but the middle of the rock, day
was breaking, and when, for the second time,
they placed their ladders, an extraordinary

impediment occurred. One of the soldiers in ascending was seized with a fit, in which he convulsively grasped the steps so firmly, that no one could either pass him, or unloose his hold. But Crawford's presence of mind suggested a ready expedient; he tied him to the ladder, turned it, and easily ascended with the rest of his men. They were now at the bottom of the wall, where the footing was narrow and precarious; but once more fixing their ladders in the copestone, Alexander Ramsay, Crawford's ensign, with two other soldiers, stole up, and though instantly discovered on the summit by the sentinel who gave the alarm, leapt down and slew him, sustaining the attack of three of the guard till he was joined by Crawford and his soldiers. Their weight and struggles to surmount it, now brought down the old wall and afforded an open breach, through which they rushed in, shouting 'a Darnley, a Darnley!' Crawford's watchword, given evidently from affection to his unfortunate master, the late king. The garrison were panic-struck, and did not attempt resistance."

Lord Fleming, from long knowledge of the place, was able to make his escape down an almost perpendicular cleft or ravine in the face of the rock, and reached Argyllshire in a fishing boat. Lady Fleming was very courteously treated and eventually allowed to depart with all her plate and furniture. Not so fortunate was Archibald Hamilton, Archbishop of St. Andrews, who was taken to Stirling and cruelly hanged on a tree.

Later the castle was used as a state prison. The most important prisoner was the ex-Regent Morton, sent here in December, 1580, and removed to Edinburgh a few months later, to be tried and condemned for his knowledge of the murder of Darnley.

During the civil war Dumbarton changed hands three times, and finally was garrisoned by Cromwell in 1652. At present it has a small garrison, and in the armoury are a few relics, among them a two-handed sword which belonged to Sir William Wallace.

Craignethan or Tillietudlem

Craignethan Castle, one of the stock show places of Scotland, lies about three-quarters of a mile from the town of Crossford, on the craggy banks of the Nethan, a mile above its junction with the Clyde. The banks of the river are bold and picturesque, and the castle, placed on a high promontory at a bend in the stream, occupies a situation which was both beautiful and defensible. The former qualification presumably did not appeal to the builders, though it now is an important factor in the pleasure of the numerous visitors to the spot.

The great attractiveness of the castle to visitors lies in the charm of romance added by the identification of the ruins with Scott's castle of Tillietudlem, described in " Old Mortality." For this we have Scott's partial authority, as follows:

" The Castle of Tillietudlem is imaginary; but the ruins of Craignethan situated on the Nethan about three [actually one] miles from its junction with the Clyde, have something of the character of the description in the text."

The Castle of Craignethan is usually visited by a round trip excursion from Glasgow which also takes in the Falls of the Clyde. A short walk from Crossford brings us to the foot of the hill on which the castle stands, which we climb by a zigzag path. At the top we find ourselves before the west front of the castle. This is a battlemented wall with an arched gateway in the centre and square towers at each corner. The front is well provided with embrasures for cannon, and impresses the average visitor as a most martial façade.

Passing through the gateway, we find ourselves in the outer courtyard, one hundred and ninety by one hundred and forty feet in dimension. This is surrounded by a continuous battlemented wall nearly four feet thick, and well provided with embrasures for guns. The courtyard contains some lean-to buildings of the same date as the walls, and a house erected by Andrew Hay, who bought the castle in 1665. The inner court is reached through a narrow gateway, formerly defended by a portcullis. This gave on to a drawbridge over the moat, which was thirty feet wide and twelve feet deep, and faced with stone. The west wall of the inner courtyard was sixteen feet thick, probably to furnish an adequate platform for heavy artillery. It is now very ruinous, but the south wall is fairly well preserved. This was defended by two towers with embrasures for guns.

The keep is the oldest part of the building. It is built on an unusual plan, being divided longitudinally into two compartments by an internal wall. The principal floor is on the ground level, instead of being raised one story, and there is a vaulted underground basement.

The entrance door is an arch, defended by double doors and a bar, but without a portcullis. Inside is a lobby with a staircase leading up and down, and beyond is the vaulted hall, forty feet by twenty. On the north side are the private hall and a guard-room, both with newel stairs to the apartments above, which are so ruined as to be inaccessible. In the vaulted basement is a well faced with cut stone. The keep has battlements supported by a double row of corbels, and open bartizans at the angles.

The southeast tower, reached by a narrow passage between the wall and the keep, is very large, and contains on the ground floor the kitchen. This has a large fireplace which was provided with machinery on which whole animals could be roasted. Below this is a vaulted basement, and above a gun room, provided with horizontal embrasures.

Probably most of the castle was built by Sir James Hamilton of Finnart, Superintendent of the Royal Palaces and Castles for James V in the first half of the sixteenth century, but the keep was undoubtedly built much earlier. The estate was originally known as Draffane, and was acquired by James, Lord

Hamilton, in the middle of the fifteenth century.

Bothwell Castle

Another castle of Lanarkshire, which by its easy accessibility and the majesty of its ruins and surroundings attracts many visitors, is Bothwell, on the Clyde. This may be visited on Tuesday and Friday from nine till five, except when the family are at home, in which case it can be seen on Tuesdays only.

This is the grandest thirteenth century ruin in Scotland. It stands on a high and rocky promontory overlooking the Clyde, and was defended on the landward side by a deep and wide moat. The castle consists of an enormous courtyard, with high walls of enceinte. At one end of this was the great donjon, dominating the whole, and surrounded by its own moat. The walls were strengthened by several round and square towers. The total length of the castle is three hundred and twenty-five feet, and it is nearly as wide, thus ranking with the largest castles of Scotland.

The keep is sixty-five feet in diameter and ninety feet high, with walls fifteen feet thick. It has several floors, the principal one of which was the hall. The upper floors com-

municate with the parapets of the curtain by
narrow passages, thus providing a way of escape if the entrance were stormed. The several towers, as usual in very early castles, were
made independently defensible, and one of
them has its own drawbridge, of a different
pattern from that of the keep.

At the eastern end of the courtyard is the
hall, built at a later period when the accommodations of the donjon proved too cramped.
This is built over a row of vaulted rooms, and
is sixty-five feet by thirty-two. At the same
time were built the chapel and private apartments along the south wall, only the windows
of which now remain.

Bothwell Castle has experienced vicissitudes
of ownership almost unprecedented in number.
In the time of Alexander II, it belonged to
Walter Olifard, justiciary of Lothian, who
died in 1242. Later it passed by marriage to
the family of De Moravia or Moray. It was
captured by Edward I, who gave it to Aymer
de Valance, Earl of Pembroke. It was captured by the Scotch by storm in 1337, and dismantled. Bruce gave it to Andrew Moray,
Lord Bothwell, husband of Christian, the
king's sister. His granddaughter married

Archibald the Grim, Earl of Douglas, and brought him the castle as a marriage portion. Archibald rebuilt the castle, and it remained in the family of Douglas until its forfeiture in 1455. James II gave most of the lordship of Bothwell to Lord Crichton, son of Chancellor Crichton, who forfeited it in 1485, for joining Alexander, Duke of Albany, against James III. The king gave the estate to Lord Monipenny, but afterwards took it back, on the ground that as a minor he had not been capable of alienating it. He then gave it to John Ramsay, who held it till 1488, when it was again bestowed by James IV on Adam Hepburn.

Hepburn's descendants held the castle until November, 1567, when James, Earl of Bothwell, lost it because of his connection with the murder of Darnley. The next possessor was Francis Stuart, a grandson of James V; when he fell into disfavour, the estate was gifted to the lairds of Buccleugh and Roxburgh, from whom it was acquired by the Marquis of Hamilton. Hepburn, Earl of Bothwell, exchanged Bothwell Castle and a third of the estate with the Earl of Angus for Hermitage Castle and Liddesdale. It remained in the family of Douglas until 1859, when it descended to the Countess of Home.

Rothesay Castle

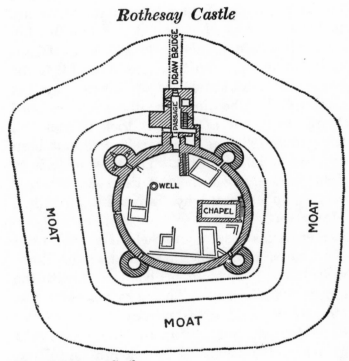

Plan of Rothesay Castle

Overlooking the sheltered bay and pleasant town of Rothesay in the isle of Bute stands the ancient castle of the same name, one of the most remarkable in Scotland. Its origin goes back to very remote times, so that its early history is obscure. Originally it was probably one of the fortalices built in 1098 by Magnus Barefoot, King of Norway, for the purpose of securing his conquests among the western islands. The Norsemen did not hold it permanently, and in 1228, during the reign of Alexander III, it was attacked by Olave, King of Man, and Husbac, a Norse chieftain, with eighty ships of Norway. After a siege, the walls were mined and breached, and the tower was taken by assault, at the expense of three hundred and ninety lives. After the battle of Largs in 1263 it was retaken by the Scotch. During the wars of Bruce and Baliol it was twice taken by the English and twice retaken by Bruce. Robert II and Robert III each spent much time in the castle, and the latter died of grief within its walls on hearing that his younger son, afterwards James I, had been captured by the English. The castle was seized in 1685 by Argyle, who burned it and converted it to an utter ruin.

Rothesay Castle furnished the title of the first dukedom which was created in the Scotch peerage, an honour which is still borne by the eldest son of the British sovereign as his principal Scotch title. The dukedom of Rothesay

was created in council at Scone in 1398, and
conferred on David, Earl of Carrick, Prince
and Steward of Scotland, eldest son of Robert
III. On his death in 1402 it passed to his
brother James. In 1409, by act of parliament,
it was declared that "the lordship of Bute,
with the castle of Rothesay, the lordship of
Cowal, with the castle of Dunoon, the earldom
of Carrick, the lands of Dundonald, with the
castle of the same, the barony of Renfrew,
with the lands and tenantries of the same, the
lordship of Stewarton, the lordship of Kilmarnock, with the castle of the same, the lordship of Dalry, the lands of Nodisdale, Kil-
bryde, Narristoun and Cairtoun, also the lands
of Frarynzan, Drumcall, Trebrauch, with the
fortalice of the same, ' principibus primogeni-
tis Regum Scotiæ successorum nostrorum, per-
petuis futuris temporibus, uniantur, incorpo-
rentur, et annexantur.'" Since then, the
eldest born son and heir-apparent of the sovereign has borne the titles of Duke of Rothesay, Prince and Steward of Scotland, Earl of
Carrick, Lord of the Isles and Baron Renfrew.

The castle stands on low ground and is surrounded by a wide and deep ditch. This has

been cleared out in recent years, and a new
bridge of approach built.   The castle is an
admirable specimen of the simple wall of enceinte of the thirteenth century, but is extraordinary in that the courtyard is circular instead
of four-sided.   It is very large, being about
one hundred and forty feet in diameter, with
walls eight to ten feet thick.   The wall is
strengthened and guarded by four round towers, projecting sufficiently to make the ground
plan almost square.   Only one of these still
stands, the battering bases of the others being
the only parts left.   Each has a doorway from
the courtyard on the ground level.

The entrance to the castle was originally
through a square gate-tower on the north
side, but later, probably in the fourteenth century, a quadrilateral keep was built in front
of this.   The entrance is now by a long passage through the keep.   Above is the hall,
formerly entered from the guard room on the
lower floor, but now by a stair from the courtyard.   From the hall, passages in the wall
lead to the two nearest towers, which were
probably utilized as sleeping apartments.   In
the courtyard is a well, as well as some walls
of the chapel.   The foundations of other build-

ings are scattered irregularly about the enclosure.

Crookston Castle

Three miles south of Paisley, on an ancient mound surrounded by ditches, stand the ruins of Crookston Castle, a venerable keep of unknown date. The barony of Crookston belonged in the twelfth century to Robert Croc, a Norman gentleman. In the thirteenth century it passed into the great family of Stuart, and thus descended to Henry, Lord Darnley. Tradition states that it was here, under a stately yew, long known as the " Crookston Tree," that he plighted his troth to Mary, Queen of Scots, and that under its branches she experienced, in the blissful days of young love, the only happy moments which he ever gave her. This tree died in 1782, and its remnants were removed in 1817 to preserve them from the devastating hand of the relic collector.

Another traditional report is that from the towers of Crookston Mary beheld the rout of her army at Langside. Though this is physically impossible, as Langside is four miles away and hidden by intervening hills, Scott

adopted it not only in " The Abbot," but also
in his " History of Scotland."

An anonymous poet has thus written of
Crookston:

"Thou proud memorial of a former age,
 Time - ruined Crookston; not in all our land
 Romantic with a noble heritage
 Of feudal halls, in ruin sternly grand,
 More beautiful doth tower or castle stand
 Than thou! as oft the lingering traveller tells.
 And none more varied sympathies command;
 Though where the warrior dwelt, the raven dwells,
 With tenderness thy tale the rudest bosom swells.
 Along the soul that pleasing sadness steals
 Which trembles from a wild harp's dying fall,
 When Fancy's recreative eye reveals
 To him, lone-musing by thy mouldering wall,
 What warriors thronged, what joy rung through thy
     hall,
 When Royal Mary — yet unstained by crime,
 And with love's golden sceptre ruling all —
 Made thee her bridal home.   There seems to shine
 Still o'er thee splendour shed at that high gorgeous
     time! "

CHAPTER III

THE CASTLES OF ARGYLLSHIRE

ONE of the most popular approaches from Glasgow to Oban, the principal town of Argyllshire, is by Loch Fyne. Leaving Greenock or Gourock by steamer, we pass Dunoon, with its scanty remains of a keep of the time of Bruce — the first castle captured by him when he rose against Baliol. The town is a thriving summer resort, much frequented by the citizens of Glasgow. Not much farther on, the steamer leaves the Clyde to enter the Kyles of Bute. Just within the entrance is Rothesay Castle, previously described, picturesquely situated in the town of the same name, also a summer resort. On the other side of the strait, on Toward Point, stands Toward Castle.

This consists of a fifteenth century keep, about forty by thirty feet, with a large courtyard of later date. The keep was four stories high, two of which were vaulted. The entrance door is a dozen feet from the ground, on the level of the first floor. The courtyard

46

buildings are of considerable extent, indicating a structure of some little importance in its day. The gateway is a beautifully carved arch.

Toward belonged to the family of Lamont. It has not been inhabited since 1646, when the Campbells attempted to exterminate the whole clan of the Lamonts. Two hundred of them defended the castle, but were starved into surrendering, when the most horrible cruelties were perpetrated on them, from their leader, Sir James Lamont, down. No less than thirty-six of them were hanged in the charred and bloody ruins of their devastated house, which has never since been occupied.

Leaving Rothesay, the steamer traverses the Kyles of Bute, a narrow strait between the island of Bute and the mainland, famed for its beautiful scenery.

Skipness Castle

As we pass out of the strait to round the point into Loch Fyne, there may be seen on a cape directly ahead of us the gray walls of Skipness Castle, one of the finest and best preserved castles of the first period to be found in Scotland. It consists of an oblong enceinte with walls six feet thick or more, and thirty-five feet high. This is one hundred and twenty-five feet long and one hundred wide. It was originally provided with two strong towers, to which has been added a keep of later date, still roofed and in good preservation. The gateway was defended by a portcullis and projecting overhead defences, which have all been removed. The castle was intended to be of great strength, and the outer walls have very few and very small openings. This castle, like Dunstaffnage, has a thirteenth century chapel some little distance outside. Skipness originally belonged to the Macdougalls, but, like most of Argyle, passed into the hands of the Campbells, who possessed it until about the end of the eighteenth century.

Tarbert Castle

Just within the entrance to Loch Fyne, the steamer stops at the little town of Tarbert, situated on a narrow isthmus which joins the district of Kintyre to the mainland. About sixty feet above the sea, overlooking the town, stands Tarbert Castle, a fortress of very early origin. It was one of the royal fortresses which Edward I caused to be handed over to Baliol. Bruce, in 1325, had the castle repaired and considerably extended, making it one of his chief strategic positions for the overawing of the western Highlands, an office which its commanding position enabled it to fulfil most satisfactorily.

The original castle was an enceinte nearly one hundred and twenty feet square, consisting of double walls about twenty feet apart. These exist now merely as mounds of grass, with a few fragments of masonry peeping through. To this structure Bruce added an outer courtyard three hundred feet long and two hundred and forty broad, with strong walls defended by circular towers, the whole enclosing a sloping hillside and affording excellent shelter for a numerous peasantry and their flocks and herds. He also built a hall and a dwelling in the original castle, as appears by exchequer records still existing. The small keep, the only conspicuous part now existent, was built about the beginning of the sixteenth century, and not by Bruce, as the inhabitants fondly assert. This was presumably erected by James IV in 1494, when he was engaged in suppressing the turbulent western clans, as the treasury accounts show that he expended considerable money in the rebuilding of the castle.

As we journey on to Inveraray the scenery of Loch Fyne is extremely picturesque, a combination of near and distant mountains most beautiful on a clear day. At Inveraray, the country town of Argyle, we leave the steamer, and after an excellent lunch take coaches for the trip to Dalmally. We pass Inveraray Castle, the seat of the Duke of Argyle, one of the greatest landed proprietors in Scotland. His castle was built in 1745, burned in 1877, and rebuilt on somewhat altered plans. Its lack of beauty was well expressed by the traveller who described it as " the ugliest castle in Europe," a description from which I am not inclined to dissent.

The coach road climbs up the valley of Glen Aray, through one of the most magnificent forests in the British isles. Century-old beeches throw out their gnarled and moss-grown branches over beautiful beds of bracken. The little stream brawls and leaps down its stony bed. Through the glades of the forest timid deer peep at the coach and flee in terror. The rabbits scamper across the road; the grouse and the pheasant whir away before the approaching horses. Little by little the trees grow smaller and thin out, until finally we leave the forest for the moor, blazing with yellow whins in June or glorious with the purple carpet of the heather in

August. Then up and up and up we go, over
the crest of the moor, until there bursts on our
vision the noble spectacle of lovely Loch Awe,
dotted with islets and overhung by the mighty
mass of Ben Cruachan, a lake view equal to
any in Scotland.

Kilchurn Castle

Backed by the noble height of Ben
Cruachan, the castle of Kilchurn, on its island
in the midst of Loch Awe, cannot be excelled
for picturesqueness of situation. It has long
been a favourite with artists and poets, because
of its magnificent situation and its picturesqueness of outline, which, however, is more im-
pressive from a distance than on close inspection. From the heights on either side of the
loch, its beauty is indeed deserving of the
poetic description:

> " It is paramount, and rules
> Over the pomp and beauty of a scene
> Where mountains, torrents, lakes and woods unite
> To pay it homage."

The castle stands on a rocky promontory
which is sometimes an island, sometimes connected with the mainland by a marshy peninsula, but was evidently entirely cut off when

the castle was built. The keep is five stories
high, and of fair size. It was erected by the
wife of Sir Colin Campbell of Glenorchy, the
Black Knight of Rhodes, founder of the noble
family of Breadalbane. Sir Colin was a
Knight Templar, and during his seven years
of absence on a crusade, the rents of his lands
were appropriated to the construction of this
fortress.

In 1693 the castle was greatly enlarged by
the addition of an extensive quadrangle by
John, first Earl of Breadalbane. This is defended by round towers at each corner, and,
while by no means strong enough to stand
a siege, would be sufficiently secure against
the attacks of Highland raiders. The castle
was defended for the king in 1745, and was
habitable long after, until a factor, merely to
obtain an easy supply of wood, unroofed it.
Since then it has rapidly decayed.

Ardchonnel Castle

Another castle of Loch Awe is Ardchonnel,
the original home of the family of Argyle, in
the island of Innischonnel, near the east side
of the lake. This was originally a simple enclosure of the thirteenth century, with walls

seven or eight feet thick, but has been extended and rebuilt in later times. It is now
an ivy-covered ruin, whose internal arrangements are scarcely distinguishable. Here originated the famous slogan of the Campbells,
" It's a far cry to Loch Awe! " With it the
clan derided their foes, indicating the impossibility of reaching their well-defended and distant home.

In the fifteenth century this castle was the
prison of the infant heir of the Lord of the
Isles. The child was named Donald Dubh,
and was the son of Angus, who had rebelled
against his father John, Lord of the Isles.
Father and son fought at " Bloody Bay," and
the child was carried off by Athole and confined by the Earl of Argyle in Ardchonnel.
He did not escape until he had grown to manhood, when he raised an army and invaded
Badenoch in 1503. He was defeated and carried off a prisoner to Edinburgh Castle, where
he remained for nearly forty years. Escaping in 1545, he became Lord of the Isles, concluded a treaty with Henry VIII and Lennox, and supplied the latter with troops.
Again misfortune was his lot, and he was
forced to flee to Ireland, where he soon died.

From Dalmally we take train to Oban, pass-

ing through the dark Pass of Brander, the
scene of celebrated conflicts of both Wallace
and Bruce, both of the most sanguinary description. The scenery is most majestic; the
furious river leaps and roars in its narrow
channel under the flanks of the great mountain which has striven in vain to hold it back.

Oban has been called the Newport of Scotland, and is thronged with people from all
parts of the world in the summer. It possesses a most beautiful situation on the Sound
of Kerrera, and is a most attractive place for
a stay of some length, being the natural starting point for all excursions in the western
Highlands.

Dunolly Castle

Only a mile from Oban, and easily reached
by a good carriage road, lies Dunolly Castle,
in such a situation as to form one of the
town's great scenic attractions. " Nothing
can be more wildly beautiful," says Sir Walter Scott, " than the situation of Dunolly.
The ruins are situated upon a bold and precipitous promontory, overhanging Loch Etive,
and distant about a mile from the village and
port of Oban. The principal part which remains is the donjon, or keep; but fragments

of other buildings, overgrown with ivy, attest
that it had once been a place of importance,
as large apparently as Artornish or Dunstaffnage. These fragments enclose a courtyard,
of which the keep probably formed one side;
the entrance being by a steep ascent from the
neck of the isthmus, formerly cut across by a
moat, and defended doubtless by outworks
and a drawbridge. Beneath the castle stands
the present mansion of the family, having on
the one hand Loch Etive, with its islands and
mountains; on the other two romantic emi-
nences tufted with copsewood. There are
other accompaniments suited to the scene; in
particular, a huge upright pillar, or detached
fragment of that sort of rock called plum-
pudding stone, upon the shore, about a quarter of a mile from the castle. It is called
Clach-na-cau, or the Dog's Pillar, because
Fingal is said to have used it as a stake to
which he bound his celebrated dog Bran.
Others say, that when the Lord of the Isles
came on a visit to the Lord of Lorn, the dogs
brought for his sport were kept beside this
pillar. Upon the whole, a more delightful and
romantic spot can scarce be conceived; and it
receives a moral interest from the considerations attached to the residence of a family once

powerful enough to confront and defeat
Bruce, and now sunk into the shade of private
life."

As mentioned in the account of Dunstaffnage, the Macdougalls of that ilk are descended from Alexander of Argyle, adversary
of the Bruce. "The islands," says Pennant,
"remained governed by powerful chieftains,
the descendants of Somerled, Thane of Here-
gaidel, or Argyle, who, marrying the daughter of Olave, King of Man, left a divided dominion to his sons Dugal and Reginald.
From the first were descended the Macdougalls of Lorn; from the last the powerful clan
of the Macdonalds. The lordship of Argyle,
with Mull, and the islands north of it, fell to
the share of the first; Islay, Kintyre, and the
southern isles, were the portion of the last."
Nisbet says: "There was a great and old
family of this name in Argyleshire, called
M'Oul, M'Dowall, or M'Dugall, Lords of
Lorn, whose title and lands went, by an heiress, to Stuart, Lord of Lorn, and are now
in the family of Argyle; Colin Campbell, the
first Earl of Argyle, having married Isabel,
heiress of Stuart of Lorn."

The name Dunolly comes from Olave, and
signifies "the fortified hill of Olave." This

was a very common Norwegian name, and was borne not only by the King of Man mentioned above, but by at least two Norse kings of Dublin. From which of these it received its name remains open to conjecture, but it was a considerable place as early as the seventh century, and is mentioned several times in the Annals of Ulster.

The present castle was erected not earlier than the beginning of the fifteenth century, and consists of a keep with walls of enceinte. The keep is set diagonally on the corner of the north and east walls, the only ones which remain. The others, abutting on a precipitous rock, were probably weak, serving only as a minor defence. The keep is about forty-five feet high and contained one vaulted story and several with timber floors. The stairs are straight and in the thickness of the walls. In spite of Scott's statement, the castle was never more than half as large as Dunstaffnage in either dimension, and possessed very inadequate living accommodations.

Gylen Castle

Facing Oban lies the island of Kerrera, and on its southern end, about four miles from

Oban, stands the little castle of Gylen, an L-keep of the sixteenth century. Though unroofed it is in a good state of preservation, and is architecturally very interesting. The keep is four stories high, and occupies a narrow projecting neck of rock, thus having a very defensible situation. The destruction of the castle dates from 1647, when it was besieged by General Leslie. During this siege the " Brooch of Lorn " was stolen, not to be restored to its hereditary owners until during the last century.

Dunstaffnage Castle

As we leave the harbour of Oban on one of the numerous steamers which ply the beautiful waters of Loch Etive, our attention is soon attracted by the picturesque ruins of Dunstaffnage Castle, four miles north of the town. Its site is a rocky peninsula jutting into the sea. The walls of the castle rise sheer from the edge of the crags, their bases some thirty feet above the water, so that there is no possibility of an enemy getting a foothold between them and the sea.

The ground plan of the castle is an irregular quadrangle, and the structure is an interesting example of the castles of the first period, built as simple walls of enceinte. In this case the north front is guarded at either end by a round tower. The curtain walls are extremely massive, being on the average ten feet thick and sixty feet high on the outside. The castle is one of the largest of the first period, being nearly one hundred and forty feet long and over one hundred feet wide. The towers at the corners are round; besides these, there is a square tower to guard the entrance, which is at the southeastern corner. This was formerly reached by a drawbridge and an arched doorway, which in later times has been built up, so that only a narrow passage remains. The original accommodations of this castle were very limited, as the keep, in the northwestern tower, contains only three low stories. The other tower probably contained rooms also, but is so utterly ruinous inside that this cannot now be determined with certainty. Beside the tower accommodations, there were a number of buildings within the courtyard, one of which was a kitchen, while the others served for other domestic uses. There are also small chambers in the south and west walls. The present buildings in the courtyard are of the seventeenth and eighteenth centu-

ries.   The battlements have been altered for
guns, and lying on them are three beautiful
Spanish cannon, relics of the Great Armada.
About five hundred feet southwest of the castle
stands the chapel, a beautiful Gothic building
of Early Pointed style.   This may almost certainly be assigned to within a few years of
1250, and as the castle was probably built by
the same builders, its date is approximately the
same.

Both tradition and legend carry the foundation of Dunstaffnage back to a much earlier
date than that just assigned for its origin, and
from the strong nature of the site they are
probably   correct.   But   little   fortification
would be required to render it secure against
the early forms of attack.   The castle was
for several centuries after 300 A. D. the capital
of the Pictish princes, and here for centuries
was preserved " the stone of power," the palla-
dium of Scotland.   This is best known as the
" stone of Scone," and is now preserved in the
coronation chair at Westminster Abbey.   It is
one of the most famous pieces of mineral matter in the world, and the legend asserts that this
is the identical rock on which Jacob pillowed
his head at Bethel.   From the Holy Land it
was transported to Spain, and thence made

its way into Ireland. Fergus, the son of Erc, brought it with him to Icolmkill, better known to us as Iona, where it pillowed the head of the dying St. Columba. Thence its holiness caused it to be carried to Dunstaffnage and used as a seat for the Scottish princes to be crowned upon. Long it rested in Dunstaffnage, until Kenneth Macalpine took it to Scone. Edward I seized it here, and carried it off to London, and there it is likely to rest for many centuries longer.

The stone gave rise to the following proverb: —

"Ni fallat fatum, Scoti quocunque locatum
Invenient lapidem, regnare tenentur ibidem."

This has been translated by Scott: —

"Unless the fates be faithless grown,
And prophet's voice be vain,
Where'er is found this sacred stone,
The Scottish race shall reign."

This prophecy was easily declared verified when James VI of Scotland ascended the English throne as James I.

Dunstaffnage Castle was also for centuries the safe place where were kept the ancient

regalia of Scotland, and some of them were
here as late as the eighteenth century, when
they were purloined by servants.

When Kenneth Macalpine removed the seat
of government from Dunstaffnage to Perthshire, in 843, the castle dropped out of historical importance. The Norwegians had begun
to make inroads into this region, and it became
one of their strongholds. Not until the time
of Robert Bruce is it again mentioned in Scottish history. It was then possessed by Alexander of Argyle, father of John Macdougall,
Lord of Lorn, nephew of the Red Comyn.
The Macdougalls were adherents of Baliol,
and made themselves especially obnoxious to
Bruce by being factors in his defeat at the
battle of Dalry, near Tyndrum, when the
famous " Brooch of Lorn " was wrenched from
his person. In 1308 Bruce obtained his revenge by defeating the army of John of Lorn,
and besieging his father in Dunstaffnage Castle. Unable to hold out, he surrendered the
castle to the king; but, his pride refusing to
allow him to do homage for it, he took safe-
conduct from the monarch for himself and his
followers, and retired to England, where he
died. The son continued his rebellion, and a
large part of the family lands was alienated.

The family still owns the lands of Dunolly, and their descent from this Alexander seems indisputable.

Dunstaffnage passed from the Macdougalls to the Argyles, who claimed it as their share of the spoil. Scott says: " When the wars between the Bruce and Baliol factions again broke out in the reign of David II, the Lords of Lorn were again found on the losing side, owing to their hereditary enmity to the house of Bruce. Accordingly, upon the issue of that contest, they were deprived by David II and his successor of by far the greater part of their extensive territories, which were conferred upon Stuart, called the Knight of Lorn. The house of Macdougall continued to survive the loss of power, and affords a very rare, if not an unique, instance of a family of such unlimited power, and so distinguished during the Middle Ages, surviving the decay of their grandeur, and flourishing in a private station."

A charter of Robert I is still in existence, which grants to Arthur Campbell, fourth son of the Sir Colin Campbell of Lochow, " the constabulary of Dunstaffnage, and the maines thereof, whilk Alexander Argyle had in his hands." The fortress is

still in the hands of this family, which seems
to dispose of Pennant's assertion that in 1455
it was a residence of the Lords of the Isles.
The other historians agree that James, Earl
of Douglas, after his defeats in Angus, here
met Donald, Earl of Ross, and Lord of the
Isles, and induced him to make war on
James II.

In 1490 James IV twice visited Dunstaffnage in order to win to his allegiance
the wild western chiefs, and after this the
castle seems to have been held in the interest
of the reigning monarchs. Much of it was
destroyed by fire in 1695, but it was restored
sufficiently to be garrisoned both in 1715 and
1745. In 1746 it formed for a while a place
of refuge for Flora Macdonald. It was
partly occupied until 1810, but now serves
only as a refuge for a few fishermen.

Duart Castle

As we enter the Sound of Mull, we see on
our right the massive ruin of Duart Castle,
one of the most imposing and powerful castellated structures in the western islands. It
stands on a high rock, and presents a most
martial appearance, due principally to the

great keep, with walls fifteen feet thick and
sixty in height. The oldest part of the building is the great wall of enceinte enclosing a
large courtyard. This is about thirty feet
high, and from six to ten feet thick. The keep
is of the second period. The architectural
features are similar to other more accessible
castles.

The castle was probably built by Lauclan
McLean, called Lubanach, who married, in
1366, Margaret, daughter of the first Lord of
the Isles, and founded the House of Duart.
He rapidly gained power, and became owner
of a number of other castles. When the
Highlanders were forced to resign themselves
to peace by the naval forces of James VI,
Hector McLean submitted and was allowed to
keep his castle. He was a person of great
importance, as evidenced by the fact that he
was allowed by the Privy Council to entertain
in his house eight gentlemen retainers, and to
consume four tuns of wine in a year, both
being the largest number permitted to any
chieftain. He was also allowed to maintain
a galley of eighteen oars, and required to present himself annually to the Privy Council
with four kinsmen, as security for his good

behaviour.   His son was created a Nova
Scotia baronet in 1631.

Ardtornish Castle

Opposite Duart, on the Morven side of the
Sound of Mull, stand the ruins of Ardtornish
Castle.   This was the stronghold of the first
Lord of the Isles, who died there in 1380, and
was interred with elaborate rites at Iona.
Although Scott depicts it as a castle of great
extent, there are no indications at present to
show that it was ever more than a simple keep.
The walls are about ten feet thick, and are
now about fifteen feet high.   No signs of any
courtyard can be found.   This seems a very
unsatisfactory place to hold any such festivities as Scott describes, when —

> " the noble and the bold
> Of Island chivalry,"
> " met from mainland and from isle,
> Ross, Arran, Islay and Argyle,"

to celebrate the nuptials of the hapless Maid
of Lorn.   Still, it was at this castle that John
de Yle, Earl of Ross and Lord of the Isles,
in 1461 called a council of his chiefs, and, like
an independent sovereign, appointed two of

his kinsmen ambassadors to sign with Edward IV a treaty of offensive alliance against Scotland.

Kinlochaline Castle

Just beyond Ardtornish Castle, there opens into the sound of Mull the beautiful bay known as Loch Aline. It is about two and a half miles long, and at its head, in surroundings of the utmost beauty, stands the Castle of Kinlochaline. It occupies the high summit of a pointed rock, and adds greatly to the beauty of the wild and rugged mountain scenery. The castle is a simple keep of great strength, built probably in the fifteenth century, and somewhat altered in the next. The walls are about ten feet thick, and carry at the top a beautiful corbel course to support the parapets. All that tradition or history have to say of the fortalice is that it was built by a MacInnes, and that Colkitto captured it in the seventeenth century.

Aros Castle

Aros Castle, the fragmentary ruin of a once powerful stronghold of the Lords of the Isles, stands on a high basaltic promontory on

the south shore of the Sound of Mull. Placed
at a bend of the channel, its position would
enable its sentries to observe the approach of
an enemy from either direction. The walls
at present standing are but portions of a keep,
but the place was anciently of considerable
importance. Its chief historic interest lies in
the fact that it was here that, in 1608, Lord
Ochiltree called together the chieftains of the
isles. When they arrived, he entertained
them at dinner on his vessel, and after the
feast informed them that they were prisoners
by order of the King, James VI. The unfortunate gentlemen were then carried off as
prisoners to the various royal castles in the
Lowlands, thus ensuring a term of peace to
the west of Scotland.

Mingarry Castle

At the extreme western end of the Sound
of Mull, near to the stormy point of Ardna-
murchan, the division between the Norderies
and the Suderies, stands Mingarry Castle,
commanding this end of the sound as completely as Duart does the other. Like Duart,
it is a castle of enceinte of the earliest period,
dating back certainly to the thirteenth century.

It occupies a lofty and isolated rock which commands the entrances of the Sound of Mull and Loch Sunart, and enjoys a view of almost the entire length of the sound. The castle is an irregular hexagon, about two hundred feet in circumference, and its walls, in spite of their great age, are tolerably entire, showing some of the original crenellations. Like all the early castles, it is almost without external openings, being furnished only with a few narrow pointed loopholes. The gateway is on the south, accessible to ships, the principal means of communication in this region. It is defended by an iron gate, still in place. The present buildings which stand within the enclosure are of no great antiquity.

The castle was anciently the seat of the MacIans, a Macdonald clan, descended from Ian or John, a grandson of Angus Og, Lord of the Isles. In 1493 and 1495 it was occupied by James IV when he was engaged in asserting his authority in the west. In 1644 it was besieged and taken by Allaster Macdonald of Colkitto, the famous partisan of the Marquis of Montrose. Colkitto used it as a prison for his captured Covenanters. John of Moidart, captain of Clanranald, was sent by the Marquis of Argyle to recapture it; but he sent it relief instead, and wasted Argyle's district of Stuart.

If, when leaving Oban, instead of turning into the Sound of Mull, we keep on to the northward, we find both islands and mainland beset with castles and towers. The little island of Lismore contains three, Auchindown, Tirafour and Rachel. Opposite them is Barcaldine on the mainland, and Stalker and Shuna, each on its own island. Most of them are simple keeps of early date, similar to a thousand others strewn over these isles and capes. Barcaldine is a little more pretentious, having been built at the end of the sixteenth century by Sir Duncan Campbell of Glenorchy. Achanduin or Auchindown is a thirteenth century enceinte, about seventy feet square, situated on a steep conical hill. This castle was the residence of the Bishop of Argyle, whose see was transferred to this island in 1236, soon after which the castle was probably erected.

Castle Stalcaire or Stalker is a well-preserved keep, built by Duncan Stuart of Appin in the reign of James IV, who is said to have used the castle as a hunting lodge. It stands on a small island in full sight of the steamers which ply north from Oban, and is a well-known scenic object. The keep is not peculiar in its architecture in any degree, and would poorly repay the trouble of a visit.

CHAPTER IV

STRETCHING northeast from Oban in almost a straight line, the great depression now known as the Caledonian Canal cuts Scotland into two islands. While the scenery on both sides is wild and mountainous, the western region is much less accessible and settled. Towns of any size are few, agriculture is little practised, and most of the great region is given over to sheep pastures and deer forests. Consequently, castles are not numerous in this region. The Caledonian Canal is guarded by two or three, and a few more may be found on the coasts of Sutherland and Caithness, and in the outlying isles. Most of these latter are relics of Norwegian domination in the islands. The mainland of Caithness and the islands of the Shetland and Orkney groups are noted for the rude erections discussed in the first chapter under the name of brochs, rude circular towers built by the Celts and serving the same purposes as the later castles of other parts of Scotland. The best known and best preserved of these is Mousa, on the island of Mainland in Shetland, which will be described in its proper place.

Inverlochy Castle

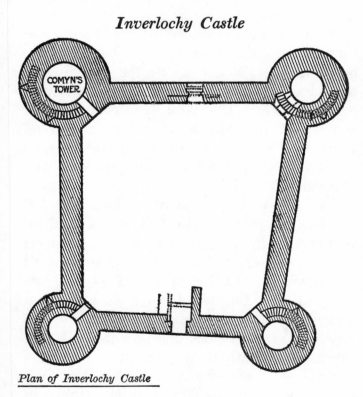

COMYN'S TOWER

Plan of Inverlochy Castle

Setting out from Oban as the usual method of entering the Caledonian Canal, we reach at

Fort William, on the southern edge of the great county of Inverness, the first of the well-known castles which lend so much to the picturesqueness of the scenery of the Canal. The origin of Inverlochy Castle is shrouded in mystery, tradition ascribing it to the Comyns. Some authorities have given the fifteenth century as the date of its erection, but MacGibbon and Ross place it among the structures of the thirteenth century on purely architectural grounds. The main reason for this attribution is the fact that the walls of enceinte stand alone, with no trace of courtyard buildings, or windows and shot-holes to indicate that any ever existed.

The courtyard is about a hundred feet square. Its walls are nine feet thick and about twenty-five in height. It stands on level ground, and about thirty feet from the wall was a moat forty feet wide. This was formerly filled by the river Lochy, which has long pursued another course. The entrance was through two gateways, one on the north and one on the south side, each protected by a portcullis. Each corner is provided with a round tower, mounted by a winding stair in the thickness of the wall. Three of these are about fourteen feet in internal diameter, while the fourth, Comyn's Tower, at the northwest corner, was used as a keep, and is about twenty feet in diameter inside.

According to a fabulous tradition, here was the site of an ancient Pictish city, one of whose rulers, King Achaius, in 790, signed a treaty with Charlemagne, and which was a great place of resort for French and Spanish merchants and mercenaries. This town, being destroyed by the Danes, was never rebuilt. The castle was probably built in the thirteenth century, as stated, and occupied by the thanes of Lochaber, including Banquo, the founder of the royal family of Stuart. In the time of Edward I, the castle belonged to the Comyns, then at the height of their power.

Because of its retired situation in the heart of the Highlands, the castle never was required to resist a foreign invader, and served simply as a stronghold in the interminable tribal disputes which were the chronic state of the Highland clans. In 1645, the castle saw a bloody battle between a Jacobite army under the Marquis of Montrose, and Argyle's troops, partly Highlanders and partly Lowlanders. Montrose, after devastating Argyllshire, had started through the Great Glen to capture Inverness, when his scouts brought

him intelligence that the Marquis of Argyle,
with an army twice as large as his, was close
on his heels. Montrose doubled on his tracks,
and made a forced march over the mountains
and through the glens to surprise his enemy.
Argyle turned over the command of his troops
to his cousin, Campbell of Auchinbreck, and
retired to a boat in the loch. Montrose attacked at dawn on the 2d of February. Although Argyle had a favourable position,
flanked by the castle, in which he had posted
a body of his troops, his right wing crumpled
at the first charge. Disheartened, his whole
army took to precipitate flight, save about two
hundred men, who held the castle. Montrose's
troops pursued the fleeing Campbells for eight
miles, slaughtering without mercy, in spite of
the efforts of Montrose to stop the carnage.
About fifteen hundred of Argyle's men fell,
while Montrose had only three privates killed.
The castle surrendered, and its Lowland officers were paroled. Montrose sent an exult-
ing letter to Charles, in which he said, " Give
me leave, after I have reduced this country,
and conquered from Dan to Beersheba, to say
to your Majesty, as David's general to his
master, Come thou thyself, lest this country be
called by my name." The King received this

letter while the royal and parliamentary commissioners were negotiating peace at Uxbridge, and immediately broke off the negotiations, a circumstance which led to his ruin.

Invergarry Castle

Near the centre of the Caledonian Canal, on a thickly wooded and precipitous bank, and forming one of the most picturesque objects on the route, stands the majestic but ruinous Castle of Invergarry. This was the stronghold of the Macdonalds of Glengarry, and owes its present dilapidated condition to the fact that it was sacked and burned in 1746 by the Duke of Cumberland, because of the attitude of its proprietors in the rebellion of the previous year. It is said that Prince Charlie was twice sheltered within its walls.

The castle was an L-shaped structure of the seventeenth century, with an oblong staircase tower in the re-entering angle, and a round tower at the northeast corner. The building was five stories high, and had a noble hall forty-five by twenty-two feet. It was very commodious, but not adapted for serious defence.

Urquhart Castle

The ancient and extensive fortification known as Urquhart Castle stands on the southern side of Urquhart Bay, overlooking Loch Ness from the west. It occupies two hills of sandstone and encloses an area of about five hundred by one hundred and fifty feet. The southern court is much larger and higher than the northern one, and the two combined form an irregular figure eight. The castle was defended on the east by the loch, and on the west by a ditch sixteen feet wide and twenty-five feet deep. This was crossed by a drawbridge at the lowest point between the two hills. This naturally weak spot was defended by a gatehouse consisting of two towers with rounding fronts, between which was the entrance. The bridge did not lead directly to the gateway, which was defended by a portcullis, but abutted on the base of the northern tower. Opposite this gateway was another on the water side, giving access to a sloping beach where boats might land.

The most imposing part of the remaining structures is the keep at the extreme northern end of the site. This is an oblong tower forty-one by thirty-six feet, and four stories high.

The entrance was on the first floor, and was reached by a drawbridge from a pier in the courtyard. The castle was originally an enceinte of the earliest period, and the western walls date from its first construction. The keep, at least in its upper portions, was built by Grant of Freuchie in the first years of the sixteenth century.

Urquhart Castle was built as early as the twelfth century, for the purpose of repressing the Highland tribes, and extending the royal domains into the uncivilized northwest. It was a royal castle of William the Lion, and afterwards was held by the Durwards and the Comyns. In 1297 it was besieged and taken by Edward I. Six years later he again laid siege to it, but the works which he had constructed while previously in possession enabled the garrison to make a most determined and protracted resistance. As a result, when it was finally taken by storm, the garrison, from the governor, Alexander Bois, down, was put to the sword. Bruce again made Urquhart a royal castle. In 1359 it was given to William, Earl of Sutherland, and in 1371 Robert II granted the castle and barony of Urquhart to his son, David Senechalus, Earl of Strathearn, failing whom, to Alexander Senechalus. In

1450 it was given to the Earl of Ross, but reverted to the Crown when his estates were forfeited. The last change of possession took place in 1509, when the estate was acquired by the Grants in reward for eminent services against the Lords of the Isles. James IV in this year granted a charter to John Grant of Freuchie, requiring him to repair, build up and construct in the capital messuage of Urquhart a tower, with a counterscarp or rampart of stone and lime, and also within the castle a hall, chamber and kitchen and all other needful houses and offices. Having fulfilled these conditions, the Grants have maintained possession to the present day, although the castle has been abandoned for two centuries.

Inverness Castle

The last of the great castles of the Caledonian Canal stood at Inverness, and had a most stirring history. No traces of it now remain, as it has been replaced by a jail and other county buildings. This castle was the home of Macbeth, but not the scene of the murder of Duncan. Malcolm Canmore razed Macbeth's castle after avenging the murder of his father, and built another on the summit of the Castlehill, which for centuries was the most important royal stronghold in the north of Scotland. The Comyns of Badenoch wrested it from the Crown in the thirteenth century and held it for fifty years. From them it passed to Edward I, and then to the Bruce. James I held a parliament in the castle in 1427, and imprisoned Alexander, Lord of the Isles, for a year. When released, he speedily came back with an army and burned the town, though unable to take the castle. John, his successor, in 1455, was more successful, and took the castle by surprise. James III, James IV, and the Regent Mary of Guise, all occupied the castle at various times. In 1562, Queen Mary entered the town with the Earl of Moray, and was refused admittance to the castle by the governor, a subordinate of the Earl of Huntly. She took up her residence in a private house, but was speedily joined by so many of the Mackintoshes, Frasers and Monroes, that she was able to reduce the castle and put the governor to death. In 1645 the parliamentary forces successfully withstood a regular siege, but four years later the fortress was taken and half destroyed by the royalists. It was finally blown up and entirely ruined by Prince Charles Edward in 1746.

Muckrach Castle

Muckrach Castle stands about four miles southwest of Grantown. It was built in 1598 by the second son of John Grant of Freuchie, and was the original home of the well-known family of Grant of Rothiemurchus. It is a square keep with a round turret at the north-west corner, and was formerly connected with an extensive courtyard, a corner tower of which alone stands. The keep offers rather scanty accommodation, being only about twenty feet square inside, but more room is given on the upper floors by corbelling out the staircase turret to form a square room.

Ruthven Castle

Ruthven Castle has a very imposing effect from a distance, but on close examination presents nothing of interest. The present structure is the ruinous remnant of an eighteenth century barrack. The castle stands on a mound about a mile from Kingussie, which has been fortified for ages. Here stood a fortress of the Comyns, and this was the chief

stronghold of the Wolf of Badenoch in the
fourteenth century. Another castle was built
on the site in the sixteenth century, but demolished by Claverhouse in 1689. Again rebuilt, it played a part in the Rebellion of
1715. This castle was built in 1718, and was
burned after Culloden in 1746.

Castle Roy

Castle Roy or Redcastle, in the Abernethy
district of Inverness-shire, stands about a mile
northeast of Broomhill on the Highland Rail-
way. The enclosing wall crowns a rocky
hillock, ten or fifteen feet higher than the surrounding fields, on a position considerably
higher than the valley of the Spey. The castle
is a simple quadrangular enceinte of the
thirteenth century, about eighty feet long, and
two-thirds as wide. The walls are seven feet
thick, and still remain standing to a height of
twenty-five feet. At one corner is a square
tower and another corner seems to have been
pulled down to add a tower, which was never
erected. The only means of defence seems
to have been from the parapet, as there is no
trace of a ditch. The castle seems to have
been originally built on the simplest possible

plan, a square wall to enclose the neighbouring population and their property. The only
buildings were wooden sheds resting against
the curtain, of which naturally no trace now
remains. Nothing is known of the history of
the tower, except that it is said to have been
a stronghold of the Comyns.

Loch-an-Eilan Castle

The Castle of Loch-an-Eilan covers an
island in a loch, surrounded by lofty mountains, three miles from Aviemore Station.
Like Lochindorb Castle, which it much resembles in situation, it is a thirteenth century erection, and was a stronghold of the Wolf of
Badenoch. As the castle is occupied by os-
preys, no boat is allowed on the loch, and no
description of the character of the castle exists. It forms a most picturesque feature in
the landscape.

Castles of the Far North

In the divisions of Ross and Cromarty castles are widely separated. The only one of
great antiquity seems to be Ellendonan, which
occupies a strong position at the junction of

three lochs, Alsh, Duich and Long. The scanty ruins are very picturesquely situated. This site was originally occupied by a vitrified fort, which was replaced in the thirteenth century by a castle of enceinte. It was conferred on Colin Fitzgerald, son of the Earl of Desmond, by Alexander III, in 1266, after the battle of Largs. In 1331, Randolph, Earl of Moray, Warden of Scotland, as a warning to the turbulent inhabitants of the district, executed fifty delinquents, and adorned the walls with their heads. In the fifteenth and sixteenth centuries it was the manor house of the Mackenzies of Kintail. It was destroyed in 1719 by three English men-of-war because of the attitude of its owners in the Rebellion of 1715.

Among the other castles of Ross, all simple structures of the fourth period, may be mentioned Ballone Castle, Castle Craig and Kilcoy Castle, on the seacoast, and Fairburn Tower, all ruined, and Castle Leod, Kinkell Castle and Redcastle, which are still inhabited.

The county of Sutherland is even poorer in castles than its southern neighbour. Dunrobin, now the palatial seat of the Duke of Sutherland, overlooking the German Ocean,

contains fragments of an early keep, later
extended to form a courtyard castle, but these
are so surrounded by structures of the last
century as almost to lose their individuality.
The castles of Ardvreck, Balnakiel and Edder-
chalder are structures of late origin, and
Helmsdale Castle is the fragmentary ruin of
a simple keep.

In Caithness we are able to enumerate Braal
Castle and the Old Man of Wick, keeps of the
second period, Ackergill, Bucholie and Dirlot,
ruins of the third period, and a number of
structures of later date. The most important
of these is Girnigoe, a tremendous courtyard
castle situated on a narrow promontory reaching out into the German Ocean. This equals
in extent many of the more southern castles,
but by reason of its inaccessible situation and
lack of historic interest, is little visited. The
other castles of the fourth period which may be
enumerated are Berriedale, Brins, Downreay,
Dunibeath, Forse, Keiss and Knockinnan.

Kirkwall Palace

Crossing the stormy Pentland Firth to the
Orkney Islands, and from there to the bleak
Shetlands, we shall find in both groups castel-

lated structures which are well worthy of our attention. One of the most important buildings in Kirkwall is the Palace of Earl Patrick, one of the finest specimens of Scotch domestic architecture. This was built in 1607 by Earl Patrick Stuart, who was ruler of Orkney and Shetland from 1600 to 1614. In order to build the palace, he taxed the inhabitants most unmercifully, and otherwise ruled in such a cruel and despotic manner that he came to death on the scaffold. The last inhabitant of the place was Bishop McKenzie, who died in 1688. A few years ago, a plan was broached for restoring these buildings for use as a Sheriff's Court, but was abandoned. As the structures are practically complete except the roof, and of great architectural interest, it would be eminently desirable if they could be thus preserved. The palace fronts toward the west and forms three sides of a square. The principal doorway in the courtyard is a remarkable rendering of the Doric order, unique in Scotland at such an early date. The exterior of the palace is adorned with a number of oriel windows, the architectural details of which are well designed and carried out. Our illustration will give an excellent idea of these.

The ground floor of the palace is vaulted, but the other stories had timber floors which have disappeared. The first floor is reached by a wide and handsome stair. The principal apartment is the great hall, a noble room fifty-four feet long and twenty wide. It is lighted by several oriels and other windows, and contains two fireplaces, one of which is finely carved. There are several private apartments, and one called the chapel. On the ground floor is a kitchen with a fireplace almost as large as the room.

Near the Earl's Palace and attached to the cathedral is another palace of somewhat similar architecture, built about sixty years earlier, and long used as an episcopal residence. A portion is still used as a domicile, but the greater part stands roofless and floorless. At one end is a large round tower, with several square rooms within. The upper story of this is raised on the original parapets.

Birsay Palace

Twenty miles from Kirkwall, at the northwest corner of the island of Mainland, quite isolated from towns or habitations, the traveller will find the imposing ruins of the ancient palace of the Earls of Orkney. This was considerably enlarged by Robert Stuart, natural brother of Mary, Queen of Scots, and his son Patrick, builder of the palace at Kirkwall. Earl Robert established in Orkney a kind of independent regality, hardly amenable to the rule of the monarch, and Patrick kept up this policy until it brought him to the block for treason. Among the principal counts in the indictment against him was the maintenance of the famous inscription which was placed on Birsay Palace: " Dominus Robertus Stuartus, filius Jacobi quinti *Rex* Scotorum, hoc opus instruxit." While he perhaps only intended to state that his father, James V, was King of Scots, his use of the nominative instead of the genitive case caused him to appear as assuming the title for himself. The bad Latin in this case cost his son his life.

Birsay Palace is a two story building constructed about a courtyard. It is one hundred and seventy feet long and one hundred and seventeen wide, with towers at three corners. Except the kitchen and the hall above it at the north end, the apartments are so dilapidated as to make their uses obscure. The palace, however, had large accommodations, and it is certainly remarkable to find such an

extensive structure in so remote a corner of
Scotland.

Notland Castle

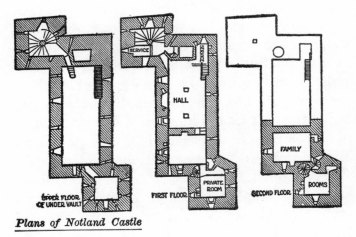

Plans of Notland Castle

Notland Castle, on the island of Westray,
in the Shetland group, is a remarkable castle
of the fourth period, built on the Z-plan, to
which has been added a large courtyard of
later date. Externally the castle is remarkable by the extraordinary number of large
shot-holes which are spotted all over it. At
least sixty may be counted at present, and
numerous others formerly existed, so that, if
all were used, the castle must have bristled
with guns.

Internally the most surprising feature in

this out-of-the-world castle is the great stair-case in the southwestern tower. This is one of the finest in all of Scotland, and is excelled only by those at Fyvie and Glamis. The steps are made of single slabs of red sandstone seven feet long. The newel is over three feet in diameter, and is capped with an elaborately carved ball-shaped head.

The castle probably dates from the sixteenth century and the architect was undoubtedly familiar with Fyvie, which it closely resembles in style. In 1560 Gilbert Balfour of Westray obtained possession of the castle from Adam Bothwell, Bishop of Orkney, and it is said that he prepared it for the reception of Queen Mary and Bothwell, who made plans to flee hither. After the defeat of Montrose, his officers fled here, and the castle was conse-quently captured and destroyed by the forces of Cromwell.

Scalloway Castle

Shetland possesses the ruins of two castles of some importance. One of these is Scallo-way, on the Mainland, situated in the centre of a landlocked harbour on a bold peninsula. It consists of an oblong building about sixty feet long and thirty feet wide, to one corner of which is joined a square tower. All the corners are furnished with round turrets, which must have given it a most picturesque appearance when the roof was in place. The general style of the architecture is the same as that of the palace at Kirkwall, and Muness, and it is of the same date, and probably designed by the same builder. Scalloway was erected in 1600 for Earl Patrick, and was occasionally used for holding the law-courts. It was built by forced labour, the despotic earl compelling the inhabitants of the island to furnish men for its building and provisions for its victualling. He personally, at the head of an ample force of solders, superintended the carrying out of his orders. It was last occupied by the forces of Cromwell, who, in accordance with their usual custom, burned it on departing.

Muness Castle

The most northern castle in Scotland is Muness, on the island of Unst, the northernmost of the Shetland group. The inscription over the doorway places its origin, as follows:

" List ye to know this building quha began?
Laurance the Bruce, he was that worthy man,

Quha earnestlie his airis and affspring prayis,
To help and not to hurt this wark alwayis.
The zeir of God 1598."

In spite of the wish, not only the castle walls, but the very stone on which this inscription is written, threatened to fall. Laurance Bruce was the son of a laird of Perthshire. His mother was mother of Robert Stuart, Abbot of Holyrood and Earl of Orkney, natural son of James V. He took up residence in this remote spot because of a murder he committed in Perthshire, from punishment for which his brother's power in this quarter was able to save him.

Muness Castle is a long oblong structure, with round towers at diagonally opposite corners. It is of architecture similar to the Earl's Palace at Kirkwall and Scalloway Castle, and probably was planned by the same architect.

The Broch of Mousa

A constant feature of the landscape in Unst, as in many of the other northern islands, is the presence of brochs. Most of these are in a ruinous state, which is not to be wondered at, considering their great age, and simple mode of construction. The best example of these towers stands on Mousa, the southeasterly island of the Shetland group. It occupies a small rocky promontory facing the mainland, about twenty feet above high water mark and the same distance from the edge of the plateau. It is built of slate rocks, laid flat without lime. The tower is fifty feet in external diameter at the base and thirty-eight feet at the top, and is forty-five feet high inside. The walls are more than fifteen feet thick at the bottom. They are full of galleries and small rooms, extending entirely around the building on six different levels, and reached by a continuous staircase from bottom to top within the wall. The only external opening is the entrance door, about five feet by three. Inside there are numerous windows opening on the court. Probably the court was surrounded by wooden sheds, as a set-off course about eight feet from the ground seems to have been intended as a support for the rafters.

Mousa is first referred to in Egill's Saga, which states that about A. D. 900 Bjorn Brynulfson fled from Norway to Shetland with Thora Ronaldsdatter because her father would

not consent to their marriage. He was ship-
wrecked on the rocky coast, and found in the
empty broch a refuge for the winter and a
storehouse for his cargo while the ship was
being repaired. Again, about 1156, as told
in the Orkneyinga Saga, the Jarl Erlend
Yunga became enamoured of the mother of
Jarl Harold and carried her off from Orkney
to Shetland. They took possession of Mosey-
arborg, and Jarl Harold, arriving in pursuit,
was obliged to sit down for a blockade, as the
place could not be captured except by starv-
ing out the occupants. This process took so
long, however, that the two earls finally made
peace, and the siege was abandoned.

CHAPTER V

Cawdor Castle

As in the northwestern Highlands, so in the northern parts of the great territory east of the Caledonian Canal, castles of historical interest are few and far between. Far removed from the southern and debatable parts of the kingdom, and protected by mountain and flood, the waves of foreign invasion rarely reached the northern castles, and their chief sieges were those of tribal battle. Consequently, the mansions in general are hardly worthy of mention on grounds of historic interest, and a great number of them show no noteworthy architectural beauties or peculiarities. We shall, however, find a certain number worthy of mention and illustration, and preëminent among these is Cawdor Castle.

This imposing structure stands on the edge of the shire of Nairn, in the town of Cawdor, and on the banks of the burn of the same

name. The appearance of the castle is that
of a magnificent ancient fortalice, battlemented, turreted and gabled in a most picturesque manner; most of the buildings, however,
are of comparatively recent date, though built
in harmony with the older keep, which occupies the centre, and towers above all the surrounding buildings.

The Calders of Calder are said to have descended from a brother of Macbeth, to whom
he resigned his thanedom of Calder when he
ascended the throne. Their original castle was
at Nairn, and they received a license to build
the tower of Calder in 1393, and another in
1454. It was at this latter date, in all proba-
bility, that the present keep was built. The
last of the line was Muriella Calder, born
about the beginning of the sixteenth century.
As heiress to the estates she was a personage
of some consequence, and John of Lorn, head
of Clan Campbell, decided that her person was
a valuable possession. So, one day in the year
1510, while the child was walking with her
nurse in the grounds of Calder Castle, a band
of Campbells swooped down and abducted her.
The nurse fled shrieking and warned the girl's
uncles, who gathered their forces hastily and
set out in pursuit. They soon came up with

the group which had the child in charge, and would have rescued her but for a stratagem of Campbell of Inverliver. This resourceful soldier inverted a large camp-kettle as if to conceal the heiress, and charged his seven sons to defend it to the death, while he rode on with the prize. The seven young men made a most heroic defence of the kettle, and all of them were killed before the uncles could overturn it — to find no Muriella. Meanwhile the rest of the band had made good their escape. The nurse, before her charge had been taken from her, had bitten off a joint of her little finger as a mark for future identification. That this precaution was not unnecessary is shown by the remark of Campbell of Auchinbreck. While congratulations were being showered on the raiders over their safe arrival in Argyle with their prize, some marsport asked what would happen if the child died before reaching marriageable age. " She can never die," said he, " as long as a red-haired lassie can be found on either side of Loch Awe." She did not die, but was married to John of Lorn, and thus the Campbells acquired the lands of Calder, the name of which they changed to Cawdor. By them the castle was much enlarged, and thus assumed its present aspect,

It is famous as having been the hiding place of Lord Lovat after the rebellion. The following description is quoted from Tytler:

" The whole of Cawdor Castle is peculiarly calculated to impress the mind with a retrospect of past ages, feudal customs, and deeds of darkness. Its iron-grated doors, its ancient tapestry, hanging loosely over secret doors and hidden passages, its winding staircases, its rattling drawbridge, all conspired to excite the most gloomy imagery in the mind. It was indeed a fertile spot for the writers of our modern romances. The mysteries of Udolpho would vanish in contemplation of the less perspicuous intricacies in the castle of Cawdor. Among these must be mentioned the secret apartment which so effectually concealed Lord Lovat from the sight of his pursuers. Never was anything so artfully contrived. It is impossible for the most discerning eye, without previous information, to discover the place of his retreat. And even after being told that a place of this nature existed in the castle, I doubt whether it could be discovered. It is placed immediately beneath the rafters in one part of the roof of the castle. By means of a ladder you are conducted by the side of one part of a sloping roof into a kind of channel between two, such as frequently serves to convey rainwater into pipes for a reservoir. By proceeding along this channel, you arrive at the foot of a stone staircase, which leads up one side of the roof to the right, and is so artfully contrived as to appear a part of the ornaments of the building when beheld at a distance. At the end of this staircase is a room with a single window near the floor. It is said Lord Lovat used to be conducted to this place when his pursuers approached, the ladder being removed as soon as he ascended. When the search was over, and the inquirers gone, the ladder was replaced, by which means he lived comfortably with the family, and might long have remained secure, if he had not quitted the place of his retreat. A remarkable tradition respecting the foundation of this castle is worth notice because circumstances still remain which plead strongly for its truth. It is said the original proprietor was directed by a dream to load an ass with gold, turn it loose, and, following its footsteps, build a castle wherever the ass rested. In an age when dreams were considered as the immediate oracles of heaven, and their suggestions implicitly attended to, it is natural to suppose the ass — as tradition relates — received its burden and its liberty. After strolling about from one thistle to another, it arrived at last beneath the branches of a hawthorn tree, where, fatigued with the weight on its back, it knelt down to rest. The space round the tree was immediately cleared for building, the foundation laid, and a tower erected: but the tree was preserved, and remains at this moment a singular memorial of superstition attended by advantage. The situation of the castle accidentally proved the most favourable that could be chosen; the country round it is fertile, productive of trees, in a wholesome spot; and a river, with a clear and rapid current, flows beneath its walls. The trunk of the tree, with the knotty protuberances of its branches, is still shown in a vaulted apartment at the bottom of the principal tower. Its roots branch out beneath the floor and its top penetrates through the vaulted arch of stone above, in such a manner as to make it appear, beyond dispute, that the tree stood, as it now does, before the tower was erected. For ages it has been a custom for guests in the family to assemble round it, and drink, ' Success to the hawthorn; ' that is to say in other words, ' Prosperity to the house of Cawdor! ' "

Spynie Palace

Spynie Palace, about three miles north of Elgin, was at once the castle and palace of the bishops of Moray. While the cathedral was removed from here to Elgin in 1224, the palace remained. The ruins comprise a large and strong keep, and portions of other buildings surrounding an extensive courtyard. The keep, which is at the southwest corner, is sixty-two feet long and forty-four feet wide. The walls are more than ten feet thick, and still more than seventy feet high. The tower was six stories high, two being vaulted, and the rest of wood. In the basement is a large dungeon, lighted and ventilated only by a single narrow slit. The cellar also has gun-holes, with enormous splays to the outside. The enceinte formerly had towers at the other three corners, one wall of the southeastern still remaining. The gateway in the eastern wall, though ruinous, is a very fine piece of architecture, and was probably designed by the builders of the cathedral, showing finer work than is usual in fifteenth century castles.

The keep is said to have been built by Bishop David Stuart, who died in 1475. The Earl of Huntly had made a threat to

" pull him out of his pigeon-holes," and the bishop retorted that he would build a tower from which the nobleman and his whole tribe could not pull him. He did.

The buildings of the enceinte are now wholly ruinous and show little of the interior arrangements.

Lochindorb Castle

Lochindorb Castle, seven miles from Grantown, occupies the whole of an island in the middle of the loch, supposed to be wholly artificial. It is on the usual quadrilateral plan of the castles of the thirteenth century, with round towers at the four corners. The walls are seven feet thick, and about twenty high. The most remarkable thing about this castle is what remains of an outer court extending around the south and part of the east sides. This has a gateway facing the lake, but no communication with the castle itself.

The castle belonged to the Comyns of Badenoch in the thirteenth century. Edward I led an expedition into their territories in 1303 for the purpose of reducing them to submission, and, after capturing Lochindorb Castle, resided there for a month. The English remained in possession for a number of years,

probably adding the outer court before spoken
of, to enclose the whole island and prevent an
enemy landing on it. It passed into royal
possession when the English left Scotland. In
1335 the Regent, Sir Andrew Moray, besieged in it the Duke of Athole, who was holding it for Edward Baliol. In 1372 it became
the stronghold of the fierce son of Robert II,
" the Wolf of Badenoch." In the fifteenth
century it was a Douglas stronghold, and was
destroyed by the Thane of Cawdor in 1458 by
order of James II. The iron gate of Cawdor
came from here.

Fyvie Castle

Fyvie Castle, on the banks of the river
Ythan, in northern Aberdeenshire, is the finest
example extant of Scottish castellated architecture. The castle occupies a mound in the
midst of an extensive marshy valley, and because of the security of the position, the spot
has been fortified since very early times. The
castle forms two sides of a quadrangle, the
south face measuring one hundred and forty-
seven feet and the western front one hundred
and thirty-seven feet. " At the three corners
are massive square towers finished with angle
turrets and high crow-stepped gables, and in

the centre of the south front are two projecting drum towers with the main entrance to the

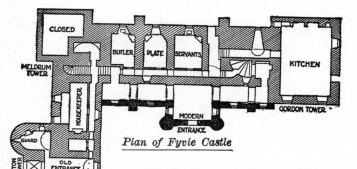

Plan of Fyvie Castle

castle between them.   These
two towers, at the height of
about forty-two feet from the
ground, are united by a bold
arch eleven feet wide, into
one grand central mass or
pavilion called the Seton
Tower.   Just beneath the
springing of the arch the
drums are corbelled out to the square, and
on either side they terminate in turrets, with
a fine gable in the centre, and dormers between the gable and turrets, the whole forming a magnificent centre to what is perhaps
the most imposing front of any ancient domestic edifice in Scotland."

The earliest part of the building is the south-

eastern tower, twenty-four feet square, built
about 1400 by Sir Henry Preston. The Mel-
drum Tower, at the other end of the front, and
the curtain between, with the exception of the
front of the Seton Tower, were built by the
next proprietors, who held the estate until
1596.

The present form of the front is due to
Alexander Seton, Lord Fyvie and Earl of
Dunfermline, who built the Seton Tower and
placed the ornamental turreted upper stories
on the corner towers.

The great staircase of Fyvie Castle is the
finest wheel-stair to be found in Scotland.
The steps are nearly nine feet long, resting on
a newel post twenty-one inches in diameter.
They are supported by arches every ninety
degrees.

Billings thinks that Fyvie was built by a
French architect, but MacGibbon and Ross,
who trace the distinctive Scotch style rather to
the Low Countries than to France, dispute
this assertion, as follows:

" If a French architect designed this building, he must have changed his style very much
to suit his Scottish patron, as the architectural
style of Fyvie has almost no resemblance to
French work. All the details are most de-

cidedly Scottish in their character, and bear
a close resemblance to those of nearly all the
castles and mansions erected about the same
time in Scotland. No one will surely maintain
that all the Scottish castles were designed by
Frenchmen, although the assertions in Mr.
Billings' work amount to almost this assump-
tion. Yet if Fyvie was the work of a French
architect, we do not see how any other Scottish building of the period can be claimed as
of native design. . . .

" If an example were to be selected of any
building in which the work is more peculiarly
characteristic of the Scottish style than another, we do not think a better instance could
be adduced than Fyvie Castle. In the south
front we have all the distinguishing features
of the style — plain walls below the parapet
and exuberance of enrichment above; corbelling freely used where the central round towers
change to the square as well as to support the
angle turrets; sharp-roofed turrets perched on
every corner; dormer windows raised on the
top of the parapet; gables finished with crow-
steps, and plain chimney heads; minor details
all equally Scottish, including the small corbel
ornaments under the turrets, the cable and

billet patterns, and the whole form and application of the mouldings."

Kildrummie Castle

Kildrummie Castle is situated on the north bank of the river Don, a few miles from Alford. It is one of the largest castles in Scotland, two hundred feet by one hundred and seventy-five, and was built by Gilbert de Moravia, Bishop of Caithness, in the thirteenth century. The position is very strong. The castle stands on a high and steep bank, protected by a rivulet on two sides, and by a ditch on the other two. The plan is nearly quadrangular. The original enceinte was strengthened by six towers, four at the corners, and two on each side of the gateway on the south side. The largest was called the Snow Tower, and was over fifty feet in diameter. This is now a mere stump. The gate towers have entirely vanished. The hall on the north side is seventy-three feet by forty-one feet, and the chapel also is very large. The walls of these buildings are almost level with the ground.

The castle has had a varied history. It was early a royal domain, belonging to the family of Bruce, and from them it passed to the house of Mar. It was besieged by Edward I in 1306, and made a strong resistance, but was finally captured through being set on fire. Its destruction took place in Cromwell's wars.

Drum Castle

Drum Castle is situated a short distance north of the river Dee, three or four miles below Crathes. It consists of a massive and ancient keep, to which has been added a seventeenth century mansion. The castle was probably built by William de Irvine, on whom the estate of Drum was conferred by Robert I. The charter, dated 1323, is in the possession of the family, who still own the estate. The keep is fifty-three feet by thirty-nine, with walls twelve feet thick, and rounded corners. The tower contains three vaulted stories, one of which was formerly divided into two, and is seventy feet high. The battlements are rounded at the corners, following the curve of the lower portion of the walls. The house was considerably extended in 1619, and again in the last century, but the additions have no special interest.

CHAPTER VI

THE SOUTHEASTERN HIGHLANDS

Dunnottar Castle

DUNNOTTAR CASTLE stands on a plateau of rock projecting into the German Ocean, two miles south of Stonehaven. This plateau is at the average level of this part of the coast, about one hundred and sixty feet above the flow of the tide, and is isolated from the mainland by a deep and wide cleft. As its precipitous walls are washed by the sea on all sides except the west, and inaccessible except at one place on this side, the natural position is the strongest imaginable site for a fortress. The resources of art have been added to those of nature to form one of the most extensive and important castles of Scotland. The area occupied by the structure is more than three acres.

At the end of the thirteenth century the rock was occupied by a parish church. Sir William Keith, perceiving the possibilities of the spot for defence, built a tower here, and was excommunicated by the Bishop of St. Andrews for building on sacred ground. The case was referred to Rome, and on July 13th, 1394, Pope Benedict issued a bull, ordering the bishop to remove the excommunication. The property was abandoned to secular use, and Sir William was obliged to build a new church in a more convenient location. He obtained the estate of Dunnottar from Lord Lindsay of the Byres in exchange for Struthers in Fifeshire, about 1390, and these two events serve to fix the date of the first building at Dunnottar.

The path to the castle descends the steep cliffs of the mainland, and passes under defensive outworks on an outlying spur called the Fiddlehead. A flight of steps leads up to the base of a thirty-five-foot wall which fills a cleft in the rock, and is pierced by a narrow gateway, the only entrance to the castle. Behind the arch is a portcullis and a further flight of steps with five embrasures for guns at the top. At the top of the steps the roadway turns to the left and ascends twenty-nine feet. It then turns again at right angles to the right. Twenty-nine feet further on is a strong door, then a tunnel twenty-six feet long with another door at the further end, and more open roadway. Another tunnel of the same length is also defended by doors at each end, beyond which the top of the rock is reached. All the open passages are commanded by buildings on both sides and high rock slopes, so that the passage is as impregnable as could be imagined.

The oldest part of the buildings on the platform is the keep, of the first part of the fifteenth century, at the southwest corner. It is L-shaped, and four stories high. The internal arrangements are similar to other keeps of the period. The parapet is carried on corbels and machicolated. To the east of the keep are storerooms and stables, built at a later date, when the keep became too small. Near these buildings is a sixteenth century structure containing a hall and private apartments, and called the Priest's House. The increasing wealth of the family caused the erection late in the sixteenth and early in the seventeenth century, of the very extensive quadrangle at the northeastern corner of the rock. This contained all the apartments necessary for a very large establishment conducted on the most sumptuous lines.

In 1297 four thousand Englishmen retired

into Dunnottar Castle to escape from Sir
William Wallace. He scaled the crag and
entered by a window, opened the gates, and
let in his troops, who slaughtered the garrison
to the last man. In 1336 Edward III refor-
tified Dunnottar during his progress through
Scotland, but it was retaken by Sir Andrew
Moray as soon as he left the kingdom. It
later came into the possession of the Keiths,
Earls Marischal, and had an uneventful
history until the civil war. It was then besieged by the Marquis of Montrose, the Earl
Marischal being a Covenanter, and having
given refuge to sixteen covenanting clergy-
men. The Earl rejected Montrose's terms of
surrender, and in consequence saw all his prop-
erties on the mainland burnt and wasted. As
the smoke rolled up in clouds, he deeply regretted his resolution, " but the famous Andrew Cant, who was among the number of
his ghostly company, edified his resolution at
once to its original pitch of firmness, by assuring him that that reek would be a sweet-smell-
ing incense in the nostrils of the Lord, rising
as it did from property which had been sacri-
ficed to the holy cause of the Covenant."

During the Commonwealth, Dunnottar Castle was selected, as the strongest fortress in the

kingdom, as a place of deposit for the Regalia
of Scotland. They were deposited here by
order of the privy council, and the Earl
Marischal was furnished with a garrison, am-
munition and provisions. As the English
were extremely anxious to get possession of
the insignia, General Lambert blockaded the
fortress in 1652. When it became evident that
the castle must finally surrender, the Dowager
Countess Marischal devised a stratagem by
which the jewels were saved. Mrs. Granger,
wife of the minister of Kinneff, with her maid,
had been permitted to visit Mrs. Ogilvy, wife
of the lieutenant-governor of the castle.
When she left, she carried the crown packed
among some clothes which she carried in her
lap, and her maid took the sword and sceptre
in a bag of flax on her back. The English
general was so far from suspecting the ruse
that he assisted the lady to mount her horse.
So the precious insignia came safely through
the English lines, and were buried under the
pulpit of the church of Kinneff until the
Restoration in 1660. The governor's son, the
minister and his wife were all tortured after
the surrender of the castle, but the secret was
not betrayed. All parties asserted that the
jewels had been conveyed to Paris by Sir John

Keith, and the English were completely baffled. Though the garrison was permitted to march out with drums beating and colours flying, Ogilvy was long imprisoned in England for saving the regalia. He was eventually made a baronet by Charles II.

In 1685 Dunnottar was used as a prison for one hundred and sixty-seven Covenanters, who were crowded for a whole summer into two cellars, so closely that there was not room for them all to sit down at once. They were treated with the most atrocious cruelty, and many of them died of their sufferings. Twenty-five finally managed to escape, but most of them were recaptured, and tortured by inserting burning slowmatches between their fingers, and in other diabolical ways. After being confined here from May until September, they were sold as slaves to Scott of Pitlochy and embarked for New Jersey. Most of them died of fever on the voyage, as well as their owner and his wife.

Crathes Castle

Crathes Castle, a picturesque and well-preserved L-keep of the fourth period, stands in fine woods on high ground on the north side

of the river Dee, in the town of Banchory. It
is owned and occupied by the Burnetts of

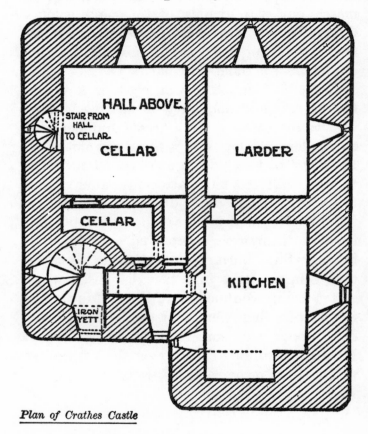

Plan of Crathes Castle

Lys, proprietors of the estate since the days
of Robert Bruce. It is a large and ample
keep, and the staircase tower almost fills the

angle of the L. The basement is vaulted and contains the kitchen and offices. The upper floors contain a hall and a large number of bedrooms. On the top floor is a large gallery with a finely panelled oak roof.

The great beauty of the house is the remarkable assemblage of corbelled and gargoyled turrets, dormer windows, and gables into which the upper stories burgeon out. The lower part has the characteristic plain walls of Scotch castles, with rounded corners.

Edzell Castle

About a mile to the westward of the pleasant town of Edzell, where the plains of Forfarshire end at the base of the lower range of the Grampians, stands in solemn if ruinous majesty the imposing bulk of Edzell Castle. This was the most magnificent baronial residence in the shires of Angus and Mearns, and is rivalled only by Dunnottar in extent. For luxury it has no peer in this region. The castle consists of an original fifteenth century keep which was extended in the following century into a castle built around a quadrangle. At the same time it was adorned with a large and elegant garden surrounded by a remarkable wall, to which were attached a summer house and a bath house.

The keep is called the Stirling Tower, after the family from which the estate descended to the Lindsays by marriage in the fourteenth century. It is built on the usual plan, with two vaulted stories. The upper floors are gone, and the battlements can no longer be reached. Externally this tower is remarkable for a double row of corbels arranged in checkerboard fashion below the parapets. The upper ones alone support the projecting parts above, the lower row being merely ornamental. This form of decoration came into vogue in the latter half of the fifteenth century, at which time the keep was constructed.

About the end of the sixteenth century the ninth Earl of Crawford built to the north of the keep a very extensive quadrangle. The buildings on the west and north sides still stand, though the northern ones are very ruinous; those on the east and south are entirely removed, leaving only the outer wall. The only feature worthy of remark in the quadrangle is the kitchen fireplace, which attains the enormous dimensions of twenty-three feet by ten. The great hall was of fair size, fifty feet by twenty-four feet.

On the south of the quadrangle is the garden. While of course the flowers and fruit are long vanished, the fine architecture is well preserved. The space is covered with smooth and even turf, and the walls are overhung by noble trees which stand without, so that the scene is one of peaceful beauty. The walls enclose a space one hundred and seventy-three feet long and one hundred and twenty-four feet wide, and are elaborately decorated on three sides. They are divided into panels, which contain recesses for flowers cut out checkerwise. Above these are stars pierced with loopholes for musketry. Above them are recesses for busts. Alternately with these groups are single large openings above which are carved bas-reliefs. These represent the Celestial Deities, the Sciences and the Virtues, and are well preserved, though somewhat debased in style. The summer house, which is very picturesque, contains several volumes of autographs of visitors, but they apparently became so numerous that the supply of books was exhausted some years since.

Edzell Castle, like many others in Scotland, boasts of a visit from Mary, Queen of Scots, in August, 1562, while on her northern expedition to quell the Huntly Rebellion. On her return, accompanied by Lords Moray, Maitland and Lindsay (the last of whom afterwards compelled her to abdicate at Lochleven Castle), she held a Council at Edzell and there passed the night. Most unaccountably, tradition has failed to immortalize the room in which she slept.

History the castle most signally fails to have. The Lindsays were a warlike race, but their castle was far removed from danger of foreign invasion, and not until the civil wars were hostile forces seen without its walls. Strength indeed it needed, for the Caterans were wont to issue forth from the Grampians, and the lairds were ever alert to protect the plains of Forfarshire from the raiding bands. For this purpose they kept up to the last of their prosperity a feudal militia. " They were remarkable," says a traveller, " for being chief over a numerous set of small tenants, and kept up to the last the parade of being attended to church by a band of armed men, who served without pay or maintenance, such duties being then esteemed honourable."

They were most liberal lords to the poor, and from the magnificent style in which hospitality was dispensed at the castle, it was called " The Kitchen of Angus." Oxen were roasted whole, a feat easily accomplished in the enormous fireplace already mentioned, and all other foods were prepared in correspondingly liberal quantities. Each day, after the family dinner was over, the parish poor gathered in the courtyard, sitting on the stone benches which still remain outside the entrance door. Here they were served with their allowance of meat from the hands of the lady or daughters of " the proud house of Edzell."

The lairds of Edzell were sheriffs in their own domain, and had the power of pit and gallows. Consequently they possessed a hereditary doomster, the head of the family of Durie, who held Duriehill on this tenure. Besides the estate, the executioner was vested with the privilege " of fishing in the almost waterless burn of Wishop, and of hunting on the hill of Wirren with a hawk blind of an eye and a hound crippled of a leg ! " Besides, he received four pennies Scots for ringing the bell of St. Lawrence at the birth or funeral of a lord or lady of Edzell.

The ruin of the family came with the fall of the Stuarts, and the castle was deserted by them in 1715. Its destruction was accomplished in 1746, when three hundred Argyle Highlanders were stationed in the castle to hunt down the Jacobites, and pillaged and despoiled their quarters.

The end of the family is pathetically told by Lord Lindsay, in his "Lives of the Lindsays:" —

"The Laird, like his father, had been a wild and wasteful man, and had been long awa'; being engaged with the unsuccessful party of the Stuarts. One afternoon the poor Baron, with a heavy heart, followed by one of a' his company, came to the Castle, almost unnoticed by any. Everything was silent — he gaed into his great big house, a solitary man — there was no wife and no child to gie him welcome, for he had never been married. The Castle was almost deserted; a few old servants had been the only inhabitants for many months. The broken-hearted ruined man sat all night in the large hall, sadly occupied — destroying papers sometimes, sometimes writing, sometimes sitting mournfully silent — unable to fix his thoughts on the present or to contemplate the future. In the course of the following day he left the Castle in the same manner in which he had come; and, turning round to take a last look of the old towers, he drew a last long sigh, and wept. He was never seen here again."

He had two sisters. One, Janet, who had always been followed about the castle by a pet lamb, fell victim to the seductive words of a dashing cavalier and followed him to England, where she died in ignominy. The other, Margaret, married Watson of Aitherny, in Fife. Her last visit to the ancestral home is thus touchingly described: —

" Year after year passed away, and the Castle fell to ruin — the pleasance became a wilderness, and the name of the old proprietors was seldom mentioned, when a lady arrived one day at Edzell, in her own coach, and drove to the Castle. She was tall and beautiful, and dressed in deep mourning. 'When she came near the ancient buryingplace,' says the same faint voice of the past (tradition), 'she alighted and went into the chapel. The doors had been driven down, the stone figures and carved work was all broken, and bones lay scattered about.

" 'The poor lady went in and sat down among it a', and wept sore at the ruin of her house and the fate of her family, for no one doubted of her being one of them, though no one knew who she was or where she came from. After a while she came out, and was driven in a coach up to the Castle; she went

through as much of it as she could, for stairs
had fallen down and roofs had fallen in, —
and in one room in particular she staid a
long while, weeping sadly. She said the place
was dear to her, though she had now no right
to it, and she carried some of the earth away
with her.'

" It was Margaret of Edzell, the lady of
Aitherny, so ascertained by an independent
tradition, derived from a venerable lady of the
House of Aitherny, who lived to a great age,
and always spoke of her with bitterness as the
proud bird out of the eagle's nest who had
ruined her family. ' She came once to my
father's house,' said she to my informant,
' with two of her children. She was on her
way to Edzell Castle. My father did all he
could to persuade her from so waefu' a journey, but go she would; and one morning she
set off alone, leaving her children with us to
await her return. She was a sair changed
woman when she came back. She had found
everything changed. For the noise and mer-
riment of those days, she found silence and
sadness — for the many going to and fro,
solitude and mouldering walls — for the plen-
tiful board of her father, his house only, roofless and deserted. When she looked out from

the windows, it was the same gay and smiling
landscape, but all within was ruin and deso-
lation. She found her way to what in former
days had been her own room, and there, over-
come with sorrow she sat down and wept.'
And such was the end of the ' proud house of
Edzell.' "

Auchmull and Invermark Castles

The Lindsays possessed two other castles,
Auchmull in Edzell, and Invermark in Loch-
lee, a few miles up Glenesk. In Auchmull
young Lindsay of Edzell took refuge in 1607,
when he was being hunted down after the
murder of Lord Spynie in the High Street of
Edinburgh. This castle was pulled down in
1772 to build a farmhouse, and only a few
fragments now remain. Hunted out of here,
he retired up the glen, spending part of his
time in Invermark Castle, and part in the
heather. On one occasion he was surprised in
the glen by a band commanded by his uncle,
the Earl of Crawford, and was forced to flee
for his life. The pursuers were between him
and the hills, and his only choice seemed to be
between capture and death by drowning in
the torrent of the Mark. Nerved to desperation, he made a mighty leap and cleared the

terrible chasm at a place still known as the "Eagle's Loup," thus gaining refuge and safety in his castle.

The Castle of Invermark, a simple keep commanding the entrances of several glens, was an outpost against the Caterans. A fortress was here from the fourteenth century, but this tower was built at the beginning of the sixteenth. It is now a roofless, but fairly well-preserved ruin, standing in beautiful scenery, and itself adding greatly to the landscape. Here died in 1558 the ninth Earl of Crawford, bequeathing his soul "to the Omnipotent God, and the whole Court of Heaven," and his body to be buried "in my own aisle within the Church of Edzell."

The castle was formerly entered by a huge drawbridge which rested on a pier of masonry built at some little distance from the castle, and approached by stairs on either side. It is defended by a massive iron grate, erected by royal permission, and made of iron found in the neighbourhood.

Glamis Castle

Glamis Castle, known to all the world by the connection of the thane of that name with

Shakespeare's tragedy of Macbeth, is situated in the town of the same name. It is needless to say that no part of the existing structure goes back to the shadowy times of King Duncan, nor indeed farther than the fifteenth century. The central portion of Glamis Castle is an L-shaped keep, with walls more than ten feet thick. With its multitude of turrets and pinnacles, it makes a most attractive spectacle, but the beauty of the castle is much diminished by the miserable horizontal Gothic battlements affixed to the roofs of the lower portions. The central tower, together with the views of Crathes and Fyvie, will give an excellent idea of Scotch castellated architecture at the height of its development. It is hardly worth while to describe the internal arrangements, as the castle is not accessible to visitors. It has been often described by the older writers, who are enthusiastic about its beauties. It is said that the son of James VII, when he returned to Scotland in 1715, lodged for a night at Glamis, and said that there was no castle on the continent to compare with it.

Glamis was the residence of Malcolm II, and here he was slain in the year 1031. His murderers fled across an unfamiliar country by night, and everything being covered with a layer of snow, they happened upon the thin ice of the frozen Loch of Forfar, broke through, and perished.

The Bonnie House o' Airlie

Airlie Castle, the ancient seat of the Ogilvies, Earls of Airlie, is five miles northeast of Alyth, on a rocky promontory at the confluence of the Melgum and the Isla. The grounds are open to visitors on Tuesdays and Saturdays. "It possessed great strength of both position and masonry, and ranked as one of the proudest and most massive fortresses in Central Scotland; and previous to the introduction of artillery, it must have been almost if not entirely impregnable. It had the form of an oblong quadrangle; and occupied the whole summit of the promontory, with the exception of a small space at the extremity, which is traditionally said to have been used for exercising the horses. The wall which protected it on the eastern and most accessible side — high and massive, together with the portcullis entry — still remains in connection with the modern mansion of Airlie; and the fosse also continues distinct, but has been partially filled up, in order to render the place accessible to carriages. In July, 1640, the Earl of Argyle, acting secretly upon the personal resentment which he had all his life entertained against the Ogilvies, but overtly upon an express commission given him for the public service by the Committee of Estates, raised a body of five thousand men of his own clan, and led them across the Grampians and down Strathtay to devastate the territories of the Earl of Airlie. He is said by an old tradition to have halted them for the night on the haughs at the village of Rattray; and, in accordance with this, though most diminishingly out of reckoning with regard to the numbers, the old ballad says: —

> " 'Argyle has raised a hunder men,
>   A hunder men and mairly,
>   And he's awa doun by the back o' Dunkeld,
>   To plunder the bonnie house o' Airlie.'

The Earl of Airlie at the time was absent in England, whither he had gone as much to avoid the necessity of subscribing to the Covenant, as to render immediate service to the king's cause. Lord Ogilvie, the Earl's eldest son, held the charge of Airlie Castle, and had recently maintained it against the assault of a party under the Earl of Montrose; but, on the approach of Argyle's army, he regarded all idea of resisting them as hopeless, and hastily abandoned the castle and fled. Argyle's men plundered the place of everything which they coveted and could carry away, and then proceeded to damage the castle to the utmost of their power by dilapidation and fire; and Argyle himself acted so earnest a part in the demolition, that, according to the report of the historian Gordon, ' he was seen taking a hammer in his hand, and knocking down the hewed work of the doors and windows till he did sweat for heat at his work.' " The modern house of Airlie incorporates only a single wall of the ancient castle.

CHAPTER VII

Stirling Castle

THE Castle of Stirling stands upon one of those isolated outpourings of trappean rock which have made so much history for Scotland by their excellence as sites for fortifications. Like Dumbarton and Edinburgh Castles, it has in all ages commanded the low country at its base, and been one of the great fortresses on which the safety of the kingdom depended. Even more than either of the others, Stirling has been the key of Scotland. It stands athwart the natural road from the Highlands to the Lowlands, and under its walls has ever passed all the traffic between north and south. It commands the windings of the Forth, and under it stood for centuries the only bridge across the river. Below Stirling, until within recent times, there were no ferries across the river; above, though fords may be found, they are in a mountainous and difficult country, impracticable for ordinary travel, and also far out of the usual road of those who would fare between north and south Scotland. Consequently Stirling was, during the greater portion of Scotland's history, the key to the Highlands, and its possession, carrying with it the control of the passages of the river, was indispensable to him who would have the mastery of the kingdom. It was naturally a strong place, rising precipitously two hundred and twenty feet from the level plain of the Forth, and its natural defences were augmented on every side by artificial strengths of ditch and wall.

The Castlehill of Stirling is strikingly similar in external aspect to the Acropolis of Athens, and the Castlehill of Edinburgh, to the latter of which it is in every respect geologically similar. It rises in a moderate slope from southeast to northwest, ending in a tremendous and abrupt precipice. The ancient town clustered along the two or three streets which follow the backbone of the hill, and open into the esplanade which lies before the castle. From the upper end of this we enter the structure by the drawbridge, passing through a double gate, formerly defended by portcullis and double ditch. This portion of the defences is comparatively modern, dating only from Queen Anne's time. The eastern battery, commanding the Forth Bridge, was erected by Mary of Lorraine and is called the French Battery, because built by French engineers. The only similar one in Scotland is at Berwick-on-Tweed.

Before us is now the earlier entrance gateway, flanked by two round towers, which dates from the time of James III. Passing this we find ourselves in the outer courtyard. To the right is the palace, curiously adorned on the outside with rude statues and gargoyles. These are the earliest Renaissance sculptures in Scotland, done by French sculptors brought over by James V after his residence and marriage in France. The architecture is a curious medley of Gothic and Renaissance. The figures on the east side represent deities and mythological personages, those on the south side are soldiers, while the northern ones are perhaps the most interesting, including statues of James V and his daughter Mary, and Cleopatra with the asp. This palace was begun by James V and completed by his daughter, though it was never made as large as was planned, by reason of the western tier of rooms not having been added, though a corridor exists from which they were to have been entered. Within the block is a courtyard called the Lions' Den, because James IV is said to have kept his lions here. The square tower on the southwest is much older than the palace, being a guard tower of the original wall. The palace is now occupied for military purposes, and inaccessible to visitors.

Passing under an arch at the north end, we enter the inner court. On the east is the Parliament Hall, pure late Gothic, and older than the palace or any of the buildings of the inner court. This was probably built by James III. It contains what was originally a noble hall with timbered roof, one hundred and twenty-five feet long. It has now been cut up into numerous floors and apartments, to serve the purpose of a barracks. On the north side is the Chapel Royal, built on the site of an earlier collegiate church by James VI for the baptism of his son, Prince Henry. It is now sadly mutilated by internal changes. Part of it is used as an armoury. The buildings on the west are modern, but occupy the site of the earliest royal residence, that of James II, and perhaps contain some of the original walls. One of the rooms, the principal one in the castle which may be seen by visitors, is called the Douglas Room, and is popularly supposed to be the identical chamber where James II assassinated the Earl of Douglas. This haughty nobleman, then in league with the Earls of Ross and Crawford, was induced in 1452, by promises of safe-conduct, to enter the castle and take supper with the king. After the meal the king took him aside and urged him to withdraw from the league. His uncompromising refusal so angered the king that he immediately drew his dagger and plunged it into the Earl's heart. The poet thus pictures the Douglas's refusal:

> " 'No, by the cross it may not be;
>   I've pledged my knightly word,'
> And like a thunder-cloud he scowled,
>   And half unsheathed his sword.
> Then drew the king that jewelled glaive,
>   Which gore so oft had spilt
> And in the haughty Douglas' heart
>   He sheathed it to the hilt."

The Douglas Room contains a miscellaneous assortment of relics, of more curiosity than value. The visit is apt to be disappointing, as the room was devastated by fire a few years ago, and the panelling is mostly modern.

What will well repay the most hardened

sightseer, however, is to climb to the battlements at the eastern side of the Douglas garden, and slowly survey the view from their whole length. There is no fairer prospect in the whole of Scotland, and I know of but three or four in Europe which in my opinion can equal it, — the Bosphorus from the Galata Tower at Constantinople, the plain of Attica from Lycabettos, the east coast of Sicily from Taormina.

The foreground of the view from Stirling Castle is everywhere formed by the rich alluvial plain, abundantly fertile, and sprinkled with village, wood and farm. Its monotony is broken at short distances by half a dozen bold masses of trap rock, well disposed to adorn the landscape. Not too far away for good scenic effect, on the north and south respectively, rise the green and softly rounded slopes of the Lennox and Ochil hills. To the east curve interminably the famous windings of the Forth, leading the eye gradually to the blue firth and the distant Lothians, dominated by Arthur's Seat. On the northwest and the west our eye ranges over the valleys of the Allan, the Teith and the Forth, above which rise the distant peaks of the southern Highlands. The eye never tires of gazing at this diversified loveliness, and it has called forth the admiration of more than one author. "Who," says Macculloch, "does not know Stirling's noble rock, rising the monarch of the landscape, its majestic and picturesque towers, its amphitheatre of mountain, and the windings of its marvellous river; and who that has once seen the sun descending here in all the blaze of its beauty beyond the purple hills of the west, can ever forget the plain of Stirling, the endless charm of this wonderful scene, the wealth, the splendour, the variety, the majesty, of all which here lies between earth and heaven?"

For a while withdrawing our gaze from the distant landscape, we shall find in nearer objects much to interest us. To the east lies a rocky mass, called Gowlan Hill, now partly occupied by cemeteries. Here were formerly to be seen the ramparts thrown up by Prince Charles Edward in 1746, when he besieged the castle. This low ridge stretches away to the north, where it ends near the bridge in the Moat Hill, the feudal place of justice, where executions formerly took place. On this hill, in sight of the towers of their own castle of Doune, and their own fair hills and farms, died by the axe in 1425 Duncan, the old Earl of

Lennox, his son-in-law, the Regent Murdoch, Duke of Albany, and Walter and Alexander Stuart, the latter's sons. At an earlier date Sir Robert Graham and his associates were executed here for the murder of James I. The popular name of this mount is Hurley-Haaky (*haaky* being an old Scotch word for cow, and *hurley* the amusement of coasting), because James V used to coast down the steep slope on a cow's skull.

Between these hills and the ramparts of the castle a steep road or pass comes up from the houses below, and leads to a point where formerly was a large gateway in the castle wall. Opposite this in the inner wall is a low-arched sallyport, known as the "Laird of Ballangleich's entry," and said to have once been the main entrance of the castle. This path was anciently of much importance and was known as the road of Ballangleich, meaning the windy pass, a name which is still abundantly justified. This name furnished an incognito to James V who, as the Laird of Ballangleich, was wont to make many a surreptitious excursion on errands of gallantry or curiosity which frequently led him to adventures similar to those of Haroun al Raschid.

Passing to the other side of the ramparts,

we may note, carved in the stone, the initials
M. R., Mary Regina. The place is known as
Queen Mary's Lookout, and verily she could
have found no better spot from which to survey the beauties of her kingdom.

In the valley below lies what was formerly
known as the King's Park, and long stretches
of its enclosing wall still exist. It was formerly wooded and full of deer kept for the
royal hunts. At the east end were the royal
gardens. Though the flower beds and fruit
trees have long since disappeared, the terraces
and mounds on which they stood are clearly
visible. In the centre of these paths and
mounds rises an octagonal mound of some
size, flat on top, known as the King's Knot.
This is of great antiquity, and is said to have
been the scene of court festivities of various
kinds. Presumably it was a place for knightly
reunions, for it was called the Round Table
as early as the time of Bannockburn, when
Edward of England was told by Moubray,
the governor, not to expect safety by being
admitted to the castle, and so " took the way
beneath the castle by the Round table."

Like Edinburgh and Dumbarton, Stirling
Castle Rock has been a fortress since times so
ancient that its founders are forgotten. The

Romans recognized its strength, and Agricola placed a garrison here, while his successors found it very useful in overawing the northern tribes. The Roman military road from south to north passed through here, and persisted much longer than their dominion. After Roman times, Stirling was a prize to be contended for by belligerent tribes. In the ninth century, the Northumbrians added much of the territory of Scotland to their own, either by conquest or treaty, and Stirling was included. They rebuilt the castle, and under protection of its garrison, bridged the Forth with a stone structure which was adorned with a cross and the motto, part of which is borne on the ancient seal of the burgh, —

"Anglos a Scotis separat crux ista remotis.
   Hic armis Bruti: Scoti stant hic cruce tuti."

The castle at this remote period, however, was probably nothing but a rude and small tower, and as such it appears in the seal of the burgh. Even if the Scots did temporarily lose possession of the hill, they soon regained it again, and made common cause with the Saxons against the Danes.

In the tenth century, learning of a Danish invasion, Kenneth III appointed Stirling

Castle as a place of rendezvous for his barons, and marched from it to the victorious field of Luncarty. Two centuries later William the Lion was captured by the English during an unsuccessful expedition across the border, and to secure the ransom which was promised for his deliverance, the four principal fortresses of the kingdom, Stirling, Edinburgh, Roxburgh and Berwick, were impignorated to the English. This was the first time English troops held any important part of Scotch territory, and occurred during the reign of Henry II. His son, the generous Richard Cœur de Lion, freely forgave, at his accession, the unpaid instalments of the ransom, withdrew his troops from Scotch soil, and renounced all claims he had upon the kingdom. William the Lion afterwards held some of his parliaments here, and here occurred his death in 1212. Alexander II here had enacted several important statutes, notably that establishing trial by jury. John Baliol also convoked parliament in Stirling Castle, and from here in 1295 wrote to the King of France, asking for a French princess to marry to his son.

In 1296, when Edward I overran Scotland, the garrison of Stirling deserted it without offering resistance. The next year the English were repulsed on the field of Stirling; the garrison which they left in the castle speedily surrendered to Sir William Wallace, who dismantled and destroyed it after the battle of Falkirk. Edward II repaired it and held it for a year, when the Scots again captured it. In 1300 Sir William Oliphant defended it for three months, but was finally obliged to capitulate to the English, who held it three years. Then it was retaken, and Oliphant again assumed the governorship. He maintained the castle against Edward when all of Scotland was at his feet, and all the resources of the king, who besieged the castle in person for three months, seemed inadequate to force its surrender. The king called a council at St. Andrews and obliged the assembled barons of England and Scotland to pronounce sentence of outlawry on Sir William Wallace, Sir Simon Frazer, and the garrison of Stirling Castle. When at last necessity forced the garrison to offer to capitulate, the king was so incensed that he refused the offer, and finally took the place by storm. The garrison was distributed among various English jails, and the governor sent to the Tower of London.

For a long time the castle was now held by the English, who were masters of most of Scotland. Though besieged several times by Bruce, it was not taken until 1339.

When the Stuart kings succeeded to the throne, Stirling Castle became one of their favourite places of residence, and to them it owes its present form, as we have seen. James II was born and brought up here, and here he perpetrated the abominable treachery of the murder of the Earl of Douglas. James III, a mild-mannered monarch wholly out of sympathy with the turbulent manners of his age, here secluded himself from his nobles, and surrounded himself with favourites. After his death on the field of Sauchie, his son ascended the throne, and often resided here during Lent that he might do penance in the Franciscan church for his share in the death of his father. James V was born and crowned in Stirling, and popular tradition has made it the scene of many gallant or amusing adventures of the "Laird of Ballangleich."

In 1543, Queen Mary was crowned here when scarcely nine months old, and the fortress was her residence for many years. Her son James was brought hither soon after his birth in Edinburgh Castle and baptized in the

Chapel Royal on December 15, 1566. When Mary was forced to sign her resignation of the crown, in the following year, he was crowned here, and spent his boyhood in the castle. He convoked his first parliament in the great hall, which so incensed his friends that it nearly provoked a civil war. In spite of all opposition, he continued to live here much of the time.

The castle was besieged and taken by General Monk in 1651, and Scotland suffered severe and irreparable loss, for he removed the national archives, which were here for safe keeping, to the Tower of London. There they remained for years, and when they were shipped back by sea, a storm overwhelmed the vessel which was carrying them, and they were for ever lost. The castle played a part in 1689, and 1715, and was besieged in 1746 by Charles Edward, who might have taken it if he had not been forced to retreat by the arrival of the Duke of Cumberland.

Doune in Menteith

The Castle of Doune, one of the best preserved ruins of a feudal fortress at present existing in Scotland, stands on a mound, prob-

ably partly artificial, on a tongue of land
between the rivers Teith and Ardoch, near the
town of Doune. It was formerly defended by

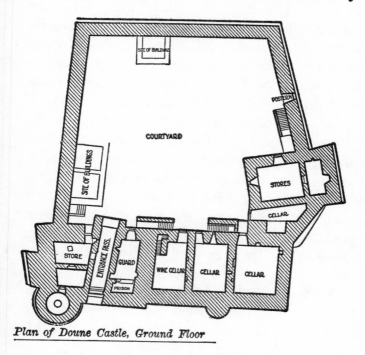

Plan of Doune Castle, Ground Floor

ditches, which can still be traced, and by an
outer wall at the top of the sloping bank, the
foundations of which still exist.

The castle has been recently restored with
much good taste and moderation, and gives at
present an excellent idea of its appearance at

its time of greatest strength. The single blemish on the work is the atrocious zinc structure erected as a ventilator in the middle of the roof of the banqueting hall. While we may safely assume that in so well-built a castle as this, some means of allowing smoke to escape would be provided, a much less conspicuous and modern-appearing structure should have been placed in this prominent position.

The date of erection of the castle is usually placed at the beginning of the fifteenth century. Its present appearance is exceptionally homogeneous, and there seems to be little doubt that it assumed its present form at that time, and that it was designed and built on a predetermined plan. As its builder, Murdoch, Duke of Albany, erected it during the years he was Regent of Scotland, the date seems well fixed. This nobleman's viceroyalty was terminated in 1424, when James I returned to Scotland and ascended the throne after his long imprisonment in England. The new monarch at once took vengeance on the unfaithful guardians of his kingdom. He quickly took possession of all the great fortresses of the kingdom, including Doune. Isabella, Duchess of Albany, was locked in her own dungeon and later confined at Tan-

tallon, while the Duke was taken to Stirling.
Here, on the Heading Hill, in sight of his
own proud towers, he and two sons were executed in the following year.

While most of the present structure thus
dates from this period, there is no doubt that
there was a castle at Doune long before Murdoch's time. The Earls of Menteith probably
had a seat here at least a century earlier, and
Robert, Murdoch's father, dated several char-
ters from "the Castell of Downe in Men-
teyth," during the latter half of the fourteenth
century.

The character of the masonry on the inner
side of the southwest gable seems quite different from that of the rest of the courtyard in
the lower part of its structure, and it seems
from this, and a study of the plan, that this
is probably what remains of an earlier square
keep. This keep was rebuilt and perhaps extended to the west, during Murdoch's operations.

The castle is built on the courtyard plan,
and contains three blocks of buildings, the
keep, the portion containing the banqueting
hall, and the kitchen block, which I have assumed to be the original keep. It is evident
that the plan was not completely carried out,

for pointed windows in the southern wall were evidently pierced for a chapel or other building, and projecting tusks in the southwest tower show that this side was to have been continued.

The keep is a large castle in itself, and was without internal communication with the rest of the structure. The castle entrance is under it by means of an arched passage running through into the courtyard. This had an oaken door, and an iron grate which still remains. It was defended also by a portcullis, worked from a window embrasure above, and flanked by the great round tower of the northeast angle. On the right of the gate passage are the guard room and prison, and on the left storerooms and a well room in the round tower.

On the first floor is the great hall, forty-four by twenty-seven feet and twenty-four feet to the crown of the vault. It has been repanelled and floored and is very satisfactorily restored. This hall was entered only by an outside stair. Its only internal communication with the basement is by a hatch in the floor beside the fireplace, and another in the adjoining tower room, through which water was obtained from the well. Over the gate

passage at the courtyard end is a retiring
room, with a window overlooking the hall,
which afforded a view of all that went on

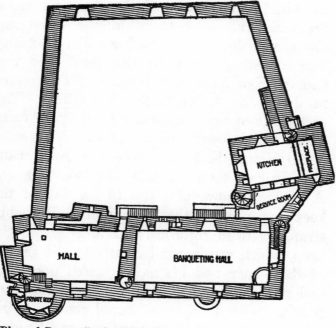

Plan of Doune Castle, First Floor

there. Over the entrance is a wide window
recess, from which the portcullis was worked.
The fireplace is remarkable; it is a double
arch, with crudely carved shafts and lintels,
and is divided into two parts by a partition in

the centre on the line of the supporting column.

From the hall two spiral stairs lead to the upper chambers and the roof. Over the hall is the withdrawing room, which contains a single fireplace and an oratory in the courtyard tower, with locker and piscina still remaining. The top story had a wooden floor, and this and the roof have been restored. The rooms in the round tower were all vaulted. The east gable of the keep was carried up to form a high watch tower with a beacon.

Adjoining the keep on the west is the banqueting hall, sixty-eight feet by twenty-seven. A doorway now joins this to the hall of the keep, but was not there originally. Probably strangers were rigorously excluded from the keep, which was accessible only to the family of the owner and his most trusted domestics and retainers. The banqueting hall has been restored with an open timbered roof. In the floor are indicated the positions of the dais and the central fireplace, the smoke from which found its way out of the unglazed windows and perhaps an opening in the roof. This hall was the centre of domestic life. Here nobles, soldiers and domestics lived and ate, and the majority of them slept. Here were brought the trophies of war and of the chase, and here, after a day of drenching rain or snow, wet clothes steamed around a six-foot pile of blazing logs, while rusted weapons were cleaned and sharpened. In an earlier age, this same fire would have served for roasting hunted deer or stolen cattle, but when Doune was built kitchens had come into use, and this contribution to the mingled odours of the hall was lacking. This hall was entered by an outside stair, and had an inside staircase to the wine cellar. At the west end was the minstrel's gallery, over the screens.

The banqueting hall communicates with the kitchen through a serving room, which has two arched openings for passing in food. The kitchen has an enormous fireplace. Over it are numerous guest-rooms and apartments.

The courtyard is surrounded by a wall forty feet high with six-foot parapets. It has open bartizans at the corners and midway of the sides, but no machicolations except over the postern gate in the west side. The parapets are continued entirely around the castle, over all the roofs and gables, both externally and on the courtyard side.

On the whole it was a castle of great strength, when artillery was unknown. The courtyard wall is the weakest point, but this was formerly covered by an outer wall. The courtyard gained, the buildings were accessible only by steep outside stairs, with gates at the bottom. The keep, the final stronghold, was entirely isolated, and even if entered, was defensible floor by floor, with means of escape either by a newel stair to the top of the wall, or by a secret passage underground which opened in the bed of the Ardoch.

Doune has been described at length, as perhaps the best preserved and most accessible feudal fortress of great strength to be seen in Scotland. For picturesqueness of situation and for completeness of arrangement, it is well worthy of a visit.

Its history is not as stirring as that of some other strengths. As related before, it was long the seat of the Earls of Menteith. It came into the royal family by the marriage of Robert, Duke of Albany, son of Robert II, with Margaret, Countess of Menteith, in the fourteenth century. Their son was Murdoch, Regent of Scotland, executed by his cousin, James I, as told previously. His duchess, Isabella, after a long imprisonment in Tantallon, was allowed to retire to Inchmurran Castle in Loch Lomond, where she died about

1460. Their youngest son, James Stuart,
after a futile attempt to resist the king, fled
to Ireland, and there founded an eminent
family. The castle was confiscated, and became the dower house of the queens consort.
It was granted in 1451 by James II to his
queen, Mary of Gueldres, in 1491 by James
III to Margaret of Denmark and in 1503
by James IV to Margaret of England. In
1528, James V, with his mother's approbation,
granted the castle to James Stuart, great-
grandson of Duke Murdoch. By direct descent it is now property of the Earl of Moray.
This grant occasioned the death of the gran-
tee, for the custody of the castle had been
hereditary with the family of Edmonstone of
Duntreath, and the head of that family finally
assassinated James Stuart.

Another unfortunate owner of the castle
was the first Earl of Moray, James Stuart's
grandson, to whom the Mains of Doune were
ratified by the Scots Parliament in 1592. He
was murdered at Donibristle by his hereditary
enemy, the Earl of Huntly, as related in the
melancholy ballad, "The Bonnie Earl of
Moray." His widow Elizabeth, daughter of
the Regent Moray, is thus referred to: —

> "O lang, lang will his lady
>   Look ower the Castle Downe
> Ere the bonnie Earle of Moray
>   Comes sounding thro' the town."

Queen Mary had, long before this, frequently resided in the castle, with her young son, James VI, whose nursery is still shown in the round tower. It was here that he is supposed to have formed, in 1580, a project, under the guise of a hunting party, for freeing himself from the guardianship of the Earl of Mar.

Doune Castle was frequently used as a political prison. James VI often attempted to usurp the power of the burghs to nominate their own rulers, and tried in 1599 to force the council of Montrose to elect the Earl of Mar as their provost. They refused, and he summoned before the Privy Council the whole of the town's officers. Having been found guilty, they were all condemned to be incarcerated in Blackness Castle and in Doune in Menteith.

In 1745, despite the presence of the royal garrison at Stirling, it was successfully held for Prince Charles Edward by Gregor Macgregor of Glengyle, with two hundred men. After the battle of Falkirk, Charles sent his

prisoners here. Among these was the poet
John Home, author of "Douglas," who un-
dertook and succeeded in a plan of escape for
himself and his fellows. They twisted their
bedclothes into ropes, and five of them had
descended safely when the rope broke. The
sixth, Thomas Barrow, an Englishman, risked
the attempt, nevertheless, but fell, breaking his
ankle and several ribs. In spite of this, his
friends carried him off and made their escape,
as Home relates in his "History of the Rebellion."

Finlarig Castle

Finlarig Castle, a mile from Killin, at the
head of Loch Tay, was apparently built in
1609, as appears from a dated coat of arms
over the entrance door. It was probably built
on the Z-plan, but the northeastern tower is
now entirely gone. Though this castle is comparatively modern, there is no doubt that a
castle has existed on the site from very ancient
times. The spot, situated between two rivers,
and protected on the third side by the loch, is
well adapted for a fortification, and the ancient
trees about the place, together with the justice
mount hard by, confirm this supposition. The

castle has a small chapel, which has been the burial place of the Breadalbanes since the sixteenth century.

Kinclaven Castle

The scanty remains of Kinclaven Castle stand on the high right bank of the Tay, opposite the infall of the Isla, eight miles from Perth. The castle, which was a royal residence in the thirteenth century, consists of a large wall of enceinte, and is about one hundred and thirty feet square. The walls are about eight feet thick, and the remains are from fifteen to twenty-five feet high. The gateway is on the west side, away from the river, and there is a postern on the south side. This was once guarded by a tower, and others stood at all four corners, the narrow entrances being still visible. These openings were only about two feet wide, defended by barred doors. Two sides of the castle were defended by the steep bank sloping down to the Tay, and on the other sides were ditches, some traces of which still remain.

The castle was a royal residence of Alexander III, and is mentioned in the Exchequer Rolls of Scotland in the year 1264. In 1297, according to Blind Harry the Minstrel, Wallace took Kinclaven, which had been visited by King Edward I in the previous June. Wallace and his folk stayed in the castle for seven days, wrecking and pillaging it, and leaving it a desolate ruin. The English soon rebuilt it, and it is enumerated in 1335 among the castles in the possession of Edward III. It was again taken by the Scots in the following year. As it was never anything but a place of strength, it seems to have gone to ruin many centuries since.

Huntingtower or Ruthven Castle

Huntingtower, formerly known as Ruthven Castle, stands above the river Almond, about three miles west of Perth. It consists of a square three-story keep of the fifteenth century, to which other buildings have later been added. The first addition consisted of an independent tower on the L-plan, which was built alongside the first building, but nine feet away from it. The two towers had no communication except by a movable drawbridge between the ramparts. This seems to be a reminiscence of the ancient method of building castles as a series of detached and independent posts. Huntingtower also shows well the transition from open battlements to gables springing from the top of the parapets. In the sixteenth century the two houses were connected by building up the gap, in which a staircase was placed. The first Lord Ruthven was invested with the estate in 1488, and the second tower was probably built by him. Patrick, third Lord Ruthven, was one of the principal conspirators who assisted at the murder of Rizzio. His son, created Earl of Gowrie in 1581, was the author of the famous " Raid of Ruthven," the enticement to Huntingtower, and imprisonment there, of the boy-king James VI, with the object of removing him from the influence of his two early favourites, the Earl of Arran and the Duke of Lennox. For this offence he was beheaded. The castle was forfeited, and was bestowed by James VI on the family of Tullibardine, from which it passed by marriage to the Dukes of Athole.

The tower is also famous for the legendary " Maiden's Leap," the exploit of a daughter of the first Earl of Gowrie, who, in a fit of terror, leaped across the chasm between the two buildings, a distance of over nine feet, sixty feet in the air.

Elcho Castle

Elcho Castle, belonging to the Earl of Wemyss, in whose family the estate has been for centuries, is situated on the Tay, a few miles below Perth. It is a sixteenth century castle, curiously modified from the keep plan. The main oblong building is provided with no less than five towers, four of which are on the northern face. It has a number of corbelled turrets and gables, but can scarcely be said to be picturesque from any point of view. The south-west tower, which is mostly occupied by the stairway, alone has battlements, so that the castle can hardly be said to be defensible. The castle has no history worth mentioning, but in the time of Wallace there was a tower called " Elchoch " by Blind Harry, which often served him as a refuge. This may have been the predecessor of this one, as the site is a good one for a fortification.

CHAPTER VIII

FIFE AND VICINITY

St. Andrews Castle

THE first Castle of St. Andrews was built about 1200 by Bishop Roger, son of Robert, third Earl of Leicester. It was seized by Edward I, and he held here the parliament at which the Scottish barons gave him their allegiance. It was again garrisoned by Edward III, but shortly after he retired to England, Sir Andrew Moray, the Regent, captured it after a siege of three weeks, and entirely demolished it. It was reconstructed by Bishop Trail about the end of the fourteenth century. At his death in 1401 the governor, Albany, took possession, and confined here the Duke of Rothesay, heir to the Crown, before his death by starvation at Falkland. The strength of the castle at this time is shown by the fact that the revenues of the kingdom, by act of parliament, were kept in "a kist of four keys," in the "Castle of St.

Andrews, under the care of the bishop and prior of the monastery." James III was born in the castle.

In the days of Archbishop Beaton (1523-1539), the castle was kept with great splendour. The English ambassador wrote, " I understand there hath not been such a house kept in Scotland many days before, as of late the said archbishop hath kept, and yet keepeth; insomuch as at the being with him of these lords (Angus, Lennox, Argyle, etc.), both horses and men, *he gave livery nightly to twenty-one score horses."*

On the 28th of March, 1545, George Wishart of Pitarrow, the famous divine, was burned alive before the castle by order of Cardinal Beaton. The tower was hung with tapestry as for a festival, and the cardinal and his friends reclined on cushions of velvet in the windows to enjoy the spectacle. Before his death Wishart foretold the cardinal's impending death with much exactness. At this very time, Henry VIII had entered into a conspiracy with several Scottish noblemen, including Norman Lesley, Master of Rothes, his uncle John Lesley, and Kirkcaldy of Grange, for the murder of the prelate.

On the 29th of May of the same year, the

conspirators, about a dozen in number, gained admittance to the castle early in the morning when the drawbridge was lowered to admit workmen who were strengthening the fortifications. They stabbed the porter, sent off the workmen, and gradually turned out all the servants as they appeared from their beds. Eventually, having thus quietly disposed of more than one hundred and fifty of his defenders, they were left alone in the castle with the cardinal. They forced open his door, and stabbed him repeatedly with daggers. "A few angry words, a bright gleam of steel as the weapons flashed in the morning light, and the cardinal fell covered with wounds, crying 'Fy! fy! I am a priest; all is gone!' and vengeance was satisfied. The citizens having been aroused, assembled at the gate, clamouring for 'a word with my lord cardinal,' but were, instead, presented with his mangled body, suspended from the balcony of the tower 'by the tane arm and the tane fut,' and requested to look at their god." Sir David Lindsay of the Mount thus expresses the feeling of most of the reformers: —

> "As for the cardinal, I grant,
>   He was the man we well might want;
>   God will forgive it soon.

> But of a truth, the sooth to say,
> Although the loun be well away,
> The deed was foully done."

The conspirators were soon joined in the castle by one hundred and twenty of their friends and held the place for more than a year. The French finally sent twenty-one galleys under the command of Leo Strozzi, Prior of Capua, a knight of Rhodes, to finish the siege. Lindsay of Pitscottie relates that " when the news came that these vessels were seen off St. Abb's Head, steering for St. Andrews, the governor well content hereof, hasted him to St. Andrews, with the gentlemen of Fife, Angus, and Strathearn, and welcomed the French captain. . . . They clapt about the house so hastily and unexpectedly, that many were closed out, and divers were closed in, against their will. Then they mounted their ordnance both upon the college steeple, and also upon the walls of the abbey kirk, wherewith they commanded the castle close; so that no man durst walk therein, or go up to the wall head. The captain told the governor, that they had been unexpert warriors who had not mounted their ordnance on the steeple heads in that manner, and that he

wondered at the keepers of the castle; that
they had not first broken down the heads of
the steeples. He caused also the great battery
to be laid to the castle, the two Scottish cannons and six French; and to prevent slaughter, he devised that the cannons should pass
down the streets by engines, without any man
with them; which thing when the Italian engineer (which had been sent from England
for the support of those within the castle) perceived, he said that they had now to do with
men of war, and therefore had need to take
heed to themselves. They answered that they
should defend their castle against Scotland,
France, and Ireland, all three. But the battery within a few hours made such breaches
in the wall that, despairing of their strength,
after consultation, they yielded the castle and
themselves to the King of France. The
French captain entered and spoiled the castle
very rigorously; wherein they found great
store of vivers, clothes, armour, silver, and
plate, which, with the captives, they carried
away in their galleys. The governor, by the
advice of the council, demolished the castle,
least it should be a receptacle of rebels."

The castle was rebuilt by Archbishop Hamilton, and what stands to-day is mostly his

work, though portions are represented by the guides as being much older. " A genial keeper was one day conducting a party of tourists over the ruins, and was describing their various parts and explaining the uses to which they were put in the heyday of the castle. ' This, gentlemen,' he said, ' is the room used by Cardinal Beaton, and that,' pointing to the opening, ' is the window from which he witnessed the burning of George Wishart the martyr.' ' But,' interrupted one of the party, ' this is not Beaton's castle; what remains is the work of Archbishop Hamilton.' ' I ken that,' replied the keeper, ' but if I were to pay off Cardinal Beaton and George Wishart I might just as well close the gate.' "

The ruins of St. Andrews Castle, standing on a bold headland washed by the North Sea, offer a conspicuous landmark to mariners. The castle was very extensive, but is now reduced to a very ruinous condition. It was originally a courtyard about one hundred and fifty feet square, partly surrounded by a moat, with towers at each corner. The entrance was once through the central tower of the south side, the highest portion of the ruins. A new gate, reached by a drawbridge, was later cut through the north curtain on this side. Little of the internal arrangements remains.   The chief items of interest to visitors are the bottle dungeon in the northwest dungeon, and a subterranean passage under the moat, recently discovered.

Macduff's Castle

A little to the east of the village of East Wemyss stand the remains of a fifteenth century castle, popularly called Macduff's Castle, because supposed to have been built by Macduff, Maormor of Fife in the reign of Malcolm Canmore.   While this castle was not his, he had seats in the vicinity, and his direct descendants in the thirty-first and thirty-second generation, of the name of Wemyss, are still living in the village.   The ruins of the castle consist of remains of two rectangular buildings at the top of a steep sandstone cliff a hundred feet above the sea.   They have not been occupied since the middle of the seventeenth century.

Newark Castle

Newark Castle, in the little town of St. Monance, consists of a few fragments of an early thick wall of enceinte, and a round tower and domestic apartments built at a much later

date. It stands on a rocky cliff overlooking
the Firth of Forth. It once belonged to the
famous soldier, David Leslie, renowned in the
civil wars of the seventeenth century, who
built much of what now stands.

Falkland Palace

The domain of Falkland belonged originally
to the Crown and was gifted by Malcolm IV
to Duncan, sixth Earl of Fife, who married
Ada, the king's niece. It remained in this
family until 1371, when Isabel, last countess
of the line, transferred the estates to Robert
Stuart, Earl of Menteith, second son of Robert II, who became sixteenth Earl of Fife, and
was afterwards created Duke of Albany.
This nobleman was for thirty-four years Regent of Scotland, and resided in the Castle of
Falkland. Of this building no trace now remains. In his days the castle received its first
historic notoriety, from the tragic fate of
David, Duke of Rothesay, eldest son of
Robert III.

The Duke of Albany early perceived the
brilliant promise of the young heir to the
throne, and feared lest he should menace his
power. Playing on the credulity of the imbe-

cile king, he persuaded him to issue an order
for the arrest and confinement of the prince,
representing that this was necessary to teach
him self-restraint. He was inveigled to the
castle of Falkland, and imprisoned to die of
starvation. His life was prolonged for some
time by the compassion of the daughter of the
governor, who fed him with small cakes
through a crevice of the wall. When she was
discovered and murdered by her own father
for her merciful kindness, her task was taken
up by another tender-hearted woman, a wet-
nurse in the governor's family, who supplied
the prince with milk from her breasts by
means of a long reed, until she too was discovered and put to death.

When James I returned from captivity in
1424, Murdoch, son and successor in the Regency of Robert, was executed for treason, and
Falkland was forfeited to the Crown. As the
estate is well situated in a pleasant valley, at
a convenient distance from Edinburgh and
Stirling, and was surrounded by forests filled
with game, it became a favourite resort of
the Stuart kings. The palace was begun by
either James III or James IV, and completed
by James V. This latter monarch was particularly attached to Falkland, and died of grief

here after the rout of Solway Moss. Mary of
Guise often lived here, and it was a favourite
resort of her daughter, Mary Stuart. Between
1561 and 1566 the latter visited it many times,
and found much pleasure here in hunting and
other outdoor sports. James VI was also partial to living here, and two attempts on his
person, one of them the famous Gowrie conspiracy, were made here. The last monarchs
here were Charles I and Charles II, both of
whom made short visits. Its last visitor of
fame was Rob Roy Macgregor, who took possession and plundered it after the battle of
Sheriffmuir in 1715.

All that is now left of the original quadrangle is the south side, and a ruinous wall on
the east. The building is partly inhabited,
and architecturally resembles Stirling and
Linlithgow Palaces.

Lochleven Castle

Lochleven Castle is one of the best and least
changed examples of a fourteenth century keep
remaining in Scotland. It stands on an island
in the loch of the same name, which is under
the control of an association of anglers. This
association controls all the boats which are

allowed to ply upon the loch, and only from their pier in the town of Kinross can the castle be visited. The charge for a boat with two oarsmen for an excursion to the island is five shillings, irrespective of the number of the party, to the limit of capacity of the boat. The lake is the home of a peculiar species of trout, of which an average of twenty-five thousand per year are taken by the anglers, who are required to keep an exact record of their baskets.

The loch was lowered by drainage works in the beginning of the last century, so that the water, which once lapped the castle walls, has left a considerable space of greensward on all sides at present. The island seems to have been connected in very ancient times with the mainland by a causeway, which has now sunk well under the surface. Still, in very dry seasons, it is possible for a man to wade all the way to the island.

The castle consists of a small keep, only about thirty-eight feet by thirty, with walls seven or eight feet thick, and five stories high. This has a vaulted basement below the level of the court, with no access to the floor above save by a hatch. The entrance is two floors above this, leaving the first floor without external communication. The upper floors are gone, and there is no access to the battlements, which have corbelled bartizans at the three external corners.

This keep is provided with an extensive courtyard, which has a continuous rampart walk. At the corner opposite the keep is a ruinous round tower, in which Queen Mary was confined. This is of the sixteenth century, as were the other buildings in the courtyard, of which only the foundations now remain.

The earliest castle in the island is said to have been built by Congal, son of Dongart, King of the Picts. The first authentic history of the castle is given in the following quotation: " In the wars which harassed Scotland during the minority of David II, the castle of Lochleven was held in the patriotic interest by Allen de Vipont, against the troops of Edward III, who acted in behalf of Edward Baliol. John de Strivilin blockaded it, and erected a fortress in the churchyard of Kinross, which occupies the point of a neighbouring promontory; and, at the lower end of the lake, where the water of Leven issues out of it, it is said that he raised a strong and lofty bulwark, by means of which he hoped to lay

the castle under water, and constrain Vipont
to surrender. The water continued to rise
daily, and the besiegers thought themselves
certain of success, when, the English general
and most of his troops having left the camp
to celebrate the festival of St. Margaret at
Dunfermline, the besieged, seizing the favourable opportunity (June 19, 1335), after much
labour and perseverance broke through the
barrier, when the water rushed out with such
impetuosity as to overwhelm the English en-
camped on that side."

The most famous association of Lochleven
Castle is undoubtedly the imprisonment here
of Mary, Queen of Scots. The Douglases had
held the castle and lands on the mainland since
the time of Robert III. Sir Robert Douglas,
the laird of Mary's time, was a kinsman of
James, Earl of Morton, and stepfather to the
queen's natural brother, James, Earl of
Moray, so that he was entirely in sympathy
with her captors. She was delivered into his
keeping on June 16th, 1567, immediately after
her surrender at Carberry Hill. On the 4th
of July she was visited by Lord Ruthven,
Lord Lindsay of the Byres, and Sir Robert
Melville, who wrung from her her signature
to an instrument purporting to resign the

crown to her infant son James. This scene
has been graphically depicted by Scott, in
" The Abbot," as well as the other events of
her stay here, and is portrayed with great
pathos.

Mary was not content with her unhappy
lot, and succeeded in gaining the affections
of George Douglas, younger son of her
jailer, and in persuading him to help her to
escape. The first attempt, on the 25th of
April, was unsuccessful, and George was ex-
pelled from the castle. He remained in the
neighbourhood and kept up correspondence
with her. With the assistance of William
Douglas, a young relative of the family, the
second attempt, on May 2d, 1568, was entirely
successful. The young lad stole the keys of
the castle from the place where they were
kept, while his lord was at supper. " He let
the queen and a waiting-woman out of the
apartment where they were secured, and out
of the door itself, embarked with them in a
small skiff, and rowed them to the shore.
To prevent instant pursuit, he, for precaution's sake, locked the iron grated door of
the tower, and threw the keys into the lake.
They found George Douglas and the queen's
servant, Beaton, waiting for them, and Lord

Seton and James Hamilton of Orbieston in attendance, at the head of a party of faithful followers, with whom they fled to Niddrie Castle, and from thence to Hamilton." The freedom of the unfortunate queen was of short duration, however, ending with her defeat at Langside. The keys of the castle were recovered when the loch was lowered, and are now in the Armoury at Abbotsford. The castle later served as a prison for the Earl of Northumberland after his rebellion in England and capture in Scotland. He was confined here from 1569 to 1572, and then delivered to Elizabeth, by whose orders he was executed.

Burleigh Castle

This ancient seat of the Balfours, built in the fifteenth century, stands near the village of Milnathort, just north of Loch Leven. While it was formerly a quadrangular enclosure, all is now gone except the keep and the gate and gatehouse of the courtyard. These are loopholed for both guns and musketry in a curious manner, and are exceedingly picturesque.

History tells us little about the castle. The most famous owner was Lord Balfour of

Burleigh, ambassador of James VI to the
Duke of Tuscany and the Duke of Lorraine.
He was general of the Scottish forces in 1644
and was defeated by the Marquis of Montrose near Aberdeen. He was also one of the
commanders of the parliamentary army which
lost the bloody battle of Kilsyth because of
the dissensions of its leaders.

"About a mile north of Lochleven, in this
neighbourhood, are several remarkable hollows, which, from their shape, have been de-
nominated the Ships of Burleigh. One of
these is distinguished by the designation of
Lady Burleigh's Jointure, and tradition thus
relates its story. A Lord Burleigh, it seems,
had obtained in marriage a lady less enamoured than provident. Her applications for
an ample settlement becoming somewhat teas-
ing, his lordship, in rather an angry mood,
desired her to attend him early next day, when
he would take her to a field not half a mile
distant from the castle, and there settle upon
her all the lands within her view. Avarice is
often credulous, and it was so in this instance.
The lady walked forth with elated expecta-
tions; but when, from a level road, descending
a gentle slope, she was told to look round her,
she beheld, with disappointed emotion, only

a verdant circle of about fifty yards in diameter, finely horizoned with a lofty cope of
azure."

Dunfermline Palace

A few miles west of Edinburgh the Firth of
Forth contracts to a narrow channel, and here
since the earliest times has existed a ferry
which enabled easy communication between
the capital and the eastern border, and the
peninsula of Fife. Not far from the northern
end of this ferry route, within easy reach of
Edinburgh, yet not exposed to sudden raids
from the southland, sprang up the town of
Dunfermline, which has played a prominent
part in Scottish history. The region was much
affected by Malcolm Canmore, and here he
built him a tower, some small remains of which
may still be seen on a rocky promontory projecting into a small glen near the palace and
abbey. This was a keep apparently about fifty
feet square, now but a grass-grown stump.
" The site of Malcolm's tower," says Mercer,
" was strikingly adapted for a stronghold, and
could not fail of attracting a rude engineer of
the eleventh century. Fordun says it was a
place extremely strong by natural situation,

and fortified by steep rocks; in the middle of
which there was a pleasant level, likewise defended by rock and water, so that it might be
imagined that the following words were descriptive of this place: — *Non homini facilis,
vix adeunda feris.* ' It is difficult to men,
scarcely accessible to wild beasts.' The *venusta
planities,* — or ' pleasant level ' on which the
tower was built, — forms the summit of a very
steep eminence that rises abruptly out of the
glen, and causes the rivulet to wind round its
base, forming a peninsula. The whole sub-
structure of the glen on both sides is formed
of freestone, which projects in many places
from the surface; and these rugged declivities
must have been clothed with thick impervious
woods, rendering the summits extremely difficult of access on three sides."

In this tower lived Malcolm Canmore, King
of Scotland, and here he married the Saxon
princess Margaret, granddaughter of Edmund
Ironsides, King of England. When William
the Conqueror overthrew the Saxon dynasty,
Edgar, heir to the throne, with his mother
Agatha and his two sisters Margaret and
Christian, took ship to flee to Hungary. Being blown north by contrary winds, they
landed in a bay called St. Margaret's Hope,

near North Queensferry, and sought the hospitality of Malcolm.

Malcolm's Tower was but a poor residence for kings, and it was eventually replaced by a palace adjoining the abbey founded by Malcolm. It is said that Robert Bruce was the builder of the palace, but it was added to by later kings. It was frequently visited by the Scottish monarchs, as is evident from state papers dated there. James IV was very partial to the palace, and practically rebuilt it. James V visited it with his bride, Mary of Lorraine, and James VI resided here often. Here were born Charles I in 1600, and Elizabeth, Queen of Bohemia, in 1596. The last royal visitor was Charles II, in 1650, after which time it appears to have gone to ruin. The roof fell in in 1708, and all that is now left is the south wall, two hundred and five feet long, and the kitchen.

A curious anecdote is told of the infancy of Charles I: "Charles was, it is said, a very peevish child, and used to annoy his parents by his cries during the night. One night he was puling in his cradle, which lay in an apartment opening from the bedroom of the king and queen, when the nurse employed to tend him suddenly alarmed the royal pair by a loud scream, followed up by the exclamation, 'Eh! my bairn!'

"The king started out of bed at hearing the noise, and ran into the room where the child lay, crying: 'Hout, tout, what's the matter wi' ye, nursie?'

"'Oh!' exclaimed the woman, 'there was like an auld man came into the room, and threw his cloak ower the prince's cradle; and syne drew it till him again, as if he had ta'en cradle, bairn, and a' awa' wi' him. I'm feared it was the thing that's no canny.'

"'Fiend, nor he had ta'en the girnin' brat *clean* awa'!' said King James, whose demonological learning made him at once see the truth of the nurse's observations; 'gin he ever be king, there'll be nae gude a' his reign; the de'il has cusen (cast) his cloak ower him already.'

"This story is generally told," adds the writer, "and in the same manner, by the aged and more primitive portion of the inhabitants of Dunfermline, and the latter part of the king's observation is proverbial in the town, it being common to say to a mislearned or ill-conditioned person, 'I daresay the de'il has cusen his cloak ower you!'"

Castle Campbell

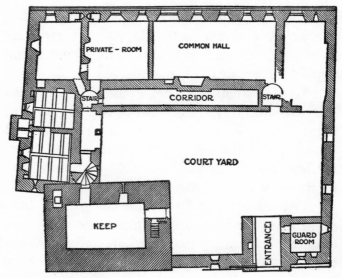

Plan of Castle Campbell

A couple of miles from the town of Dollar, on a high spur of the Ochil Hills, in one of the grandest situations enjoyed by any castle in Scotland, stands Castle Campbell. The only approach to it is up the bed of the burn, through a narrow cañon of tremendous depth, across dizzy chasms on narrow bridges, and finally up a stiff climb by the side of tumbling waterfalls. The ascent is difficult and arduous even now, after the way is smoothed as well as may be for the tourist. What must have been the prospect for the enemy who tried to compass the attack of the castle against a determined defence!

The castle stands on a green promontory between the two streams, known as the Burn of Sorrow and the Burn of Care, and its original name was the Castle of Gloom. The mound on which it stands is partly natural and partly artificial, and at least three hundred feet high. On the side toward the hills was formerly a deep chasm, spanned by a draw-bridge; but this is now partly filled up, so that the ascent on this side is not more than fifty feet. In such a situation, before the advent of artillery, an attack on this castle would have been perfectly useless. No engines could have been brought to bear on it, and a handful of men on the parapets could have resisted an army as long as their provisions held out.

The castle comprises a keep and enceinte of the fourteenth century, to which have been added buildings about the walls of the enclosure. The keep is a simple rectangle, twenty-eight by sixteen feet inside, with walls about eight feet thick. The original entrance is on the ground floor, and the hall floor is reached by a wheel-stair. The upper rooms are reached by another stair in the opposite corner, a most unusual arrangement. The keep has three vaults, the upper one cut in two by a wooden floor midway of its height. The dungeon in the ground floor is six and a half by three feet, and reached only by a trapdoor from the hall; truly, a desirable place to be imprisoned in!

Elevation Plan of Castle Campbell

The later buildings comprise ranges on both east and south sides. Those on the south were lighted by numerous windows cut in the south wall, and are therefore of comparatively late date. They comprised a row of vaults in the basement, and a large hall and private rooms above. The east wing contained private apartments. A new staircase here gave access to both the east wing and the keep, and two more angle turrets on the south side also carried staircases. The porch on the east side is an excellent piece of work. The gateway and gatehouse are late work, as is proved by the gun-holes for defence.

The name of the castle was changed to its present designation by act of parliament in 1489, at the request of its proprietor, the first Earl of Argyle. It was destroyed in 1645, when the MacLeans and Ogilvies, the fierce allies of the Marquis of Montrose, carried fire and sword through all the Argyle territories. It is now partly inhabited, and kept in good repair.

Clackmannan Tower

Clackmannan Tower is situated in the town of the same name, six or seven miles from Stirling, and two from Alloa. The tower belonged to David II, who gifted it in 1359 to his cousin Robert Bruce, in the possession of whose descendants it remained until 1791. King Robert Bruce is also said to have resided

here, and his sword and helmet were preserved
in the tower until the Bruce family died out,
when they were transferred to the Earl of
Elgin, as the nearest of kin. The old Jacobite lady, Mrs. Bruce, who knighted Robert
Burns with the sword of Bruce, resided here.

The tower is of peculiar construction. The
original keep, which has a gabled roof, eventually became too small, and another wing was
built on to the south, which is higher than the
original structure. This addition has an em-
brasured parapet with open machicolations
and rounded corners, which gives the structure
a very martial air.

Niddrie Castle

Niddrie Castle is easily to be seen by every
visitor to Scotland who passes by rail from
Glasgow to Edinburgh, as it stands within
fifty yards of the railroad track about three
miles east of Linlithgow. It is visible only
for a minute on the north side of the track,
as the train passes the only break in a long
deep cutting, but this glimpse shows practically all that could be seen by a visit to the
castle. It is an empty and ruinous L-keep
of the fifteenth century, of very massive con-

struction. When more room was needed, for security's sake it was gained by adding to the top. The castle was the ancient seat of the

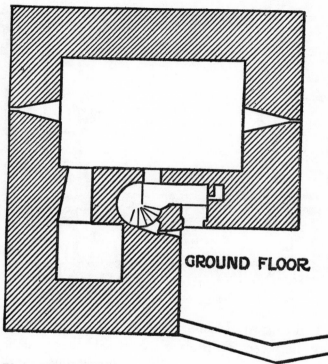

Plan of Niddrie Castle

Earls of Winton, and its sole historical interest lies in the fact that Queen Mary passed a night there while fleeing from Lochleven Castle to join her friends at Hamilton.

Linlithgow Palace

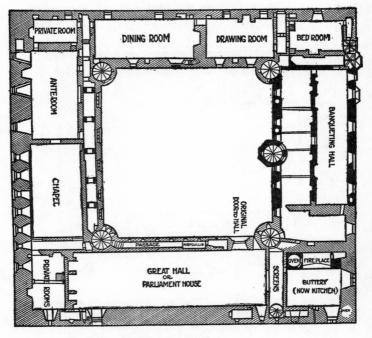

Plan of Linlithgow Palace, First Floor

Linlithgow Palace is situated about half-way between Edinburgh and Stirling, on a promontory projecting into a small lake, and was of such magnificence when complete as to fully justify the statement of Mary of Guise, who said, " She had never seen a more princely palace," and Scott's description in " The Lay of the Last Minstrel: " —

" Of all the palaces so fair
    Built for the royal dwelling,
In Scotland, far beyond compare
    Linlithgow is excelling:
And in its park in jovial June
How sweet the merry linnet's tune,
    How blithe the blackbird's lay !
The wild buck bells from ferny brake,
The coot dives merry on the lake, —
The saddest heart might pleasure take
    To see a scene so gay."

The palace is approached through a gate-house erected by James V and ornamented by shields on which are carved his four orders of knighthood, St. Michael, the Golden Fleece, the Garter and the Thistle. The palace is now entered by a gate passage on the south side. On the right of this is the guard-room, in which the Regent Moray expired after being shot in the main street of the town by Hamilton of Bothwellhaugh. The passage leads into a large court, about ninety feet square, around which the palace forms a complete quadrangle, with towers at each internal corner. On the east side is another passage which was the original main entrance of the palace. This has also a guard room, and was defended by three doors and a portcullis. It opens on the outside at a level considerably above that of the park, and was reached by a drawbridge from the outer wall, which was strengthened by towers, the bases of three of which still remain to the north of the entrance. The original gate is elaborately ornamented outside with carved niches and armorial bearings.

The ground floor of the palace is occupied with cellars, stables, kitchens, bakeries, and other domestic offices. The main public rooms were on the first floor. They include chapel, anteroom, dining room, drawing room, banqueting hall, kitchen, and the great hall called the parliament house, as well as a number of private rooms. The great hall is one hundred feet long and thirty wide, and had an open timbered roof. The fireplace is very fine, being divided into three parts, and extending across the whole end of the room. The columns and lintels are beautifully carved.

The private apartments of the king are on the west side, and in the one called the drawing room it is said that Queen Mary was born. The north side contains a fine hall called the banqueting hall, and numerous bedrooms. The angle turrets all carry stairs to the roof, which has continuous battlements for defence. The northwest tower is highest, and contains a room at the top known as "Queen Margaret's Bower," said to be her boudoir, where she watched vainly for the return of her husband, James IV, after Flodden.

The site of Linlithgow Palace was occupied by a Roman station, being connected by a road with the Wall of Antoninus at a point in the parish of Falkirk. In the time of David I there was a royal residence here. Edward I built " a Pele mekill and stark " here about 1300, and spent three months there during the winter of the next year. It remained in his hands until 1313, when it was taken by Bruce, with the aid of the stratagem devised by the peasant William Bunnock, or Binny. " Binny, who was known to the garrison, and had been employed in leading hay into the fort, communicated his design to a party of Scottish soldiers, whom he stationed in ambush near the gate. In his large wain he contrived to conceal eight armed men, covered with a load of hay; a servant drove the oxen, and Binny himself walked carelessly at his side. When the portcullis was raised, and the wain stood in the middle of the gateway, interposing a complete barrier to its descent, the driver cut the ropes which harnessed the oxen; upon which signal the armed men suddenly leapt from the cart, the soldiers in ambush rushed in, and so complete was the surprise, that with little resistance the garrison were put to the sword, and the place taken." The castle was destroyed by Bruce, in accordance with his usual policy. It was restored by David II, and became a favourite residence of the Scotch monarchs. It was destroyed by fire in 1424, and rebuilding operations were begun at once by James I. Between then and 1451, the west side and possibly the north side, afterwards rebuilt by James VI, were probably erected. The south side was completed before 1496. James III and James IV were very fond of the palace, and the latter built the east side. James V erected the gatehouse and changed the entrance to correspond. He presented the palace to his queen, Mary of Guise, whose comment has been already quoted. It was finally completed by James VI.

After the removal of James VI to England, the palace was little used, though it continued to be habitable. It was fortified by Cromwell, and afterward occupied by Prince Charlie. In 1746, when the royal army passed through here in pursuit of the Pretender, Hawley's Dragoons occupied the hall on the north side. When they departed, they neglected to extinguish their fires, and the building was soon in flames. By the time this was discovered the roof had ignited, and the lead with which it was covered melted and flowed down in streams, making it impossible to fight the conflagration. Since then the palace has remained in ruins, but is now kept in good repair by the royal authorities.

CHAPTER IX

EDINBURGH CASTLE

Of all the castles of Scotland, that which is most familiar both to the traveller and the reader is that of Edinburgh. Frowning down from its precipitous rock, the most conspicuous mass in the landscape for miles around, it is the first object which seizes the attention of the approaching traveller to-day, as it has in all ages. The time when men first used this rock as a fortress dates back to the age of hazy fable and tradition. When the Roman brought his legions hither, its history began, but long ere this the Picts had built a rude wall upon its summit. They were the Ottadini, the first whom we know to have lived upon this beetling rock. From them, the Romans wrested it, but their hold was transitory; their rule was soon forgotten in Valentia, as they named their northernmost province, in which the rock was, and with their rule vanished the name they must have given the Castlehill.

To the Romans succeeded the Britons, but most of what they did about here has dropped back into forgetfulness. Here, however, warred that hero of Romance, Arthur of the Table Round, and his deeds have riveted his name to several places in the neighbourhood. Best known of these is Arthur's Seat, the mighty mass of trap overlooking all Edinburgh from the southeast. There is little doubt that the northern Cymry, separated from their southern brethren in Wales by the relentless onsweep of the Saxons, sullenly retreated to the borders of Scotland under their great leader Arthur, and there waged their last desperate battles, which, however, were not able to prevent the submerging of their nationality in the peoples of the Scotch Highlands and Lowlands. As they did fight fiercely, and for long held back the Northumbrian princes, let us believe that tradition is right in telling us that Arthur, wearied with long war, sat on the brow of Arthur's Seat, and saw his victorious forces drive back the hated Saxons for a time at least.

From this fabulous time dates the earliest name recorded for the Castle Rock of Edinburgh, " Castelh-Mynyd-Agned," the Fortress of the Hill above the Plain. Later the monks mistranslated this, and called it " Castrum Puellarum," the Castle of the Maidens, fabricating the legend that the rock was the home of the daughters of the Pictish kings. In the year 617, when Northumbrian rule in the Lothians was well established, Edwin of Deira overthrew Ethelfrith of Northumbria, and fortified the rock to hold the Britons in check. He named the town which grew about the fort " Edwin's-burgh." The Celts modified this to Dun-Edin, which, besides meaning " the hill of Edwin," may be translated " the face of a hill," and may be regarded as a descriptive name.

Edwin's Castle protected his town, which gradually crept down the eastern slope of the hill. But the Picts did not relish this Saxon village in their territory, and in the middle of the century swept down upon the town while the castle garrison was away on a foray, and almost entirely destroyed it. Unhappily they stayed a little too long to burn and plunder, and the garrison caught them at their task, to take a bloody revenge. So for a generation it remained a Saxon thorn in the Pictish side. In 685 Brudi, Pictish king, in the great battle of Nectansmere, destroyed the forces of Northumbria with their King Egfrith, and

made Edinburgh his own. From that time on
Picts and Scots made common cause against
Angles, Saxons, and Britons, and held their
own against them. In 844 Kenneth Mac-
Alpine united the two peoples, and Scotch his-
tory begins.

Again a century later we find Northumbria
powerful in the Lothians, but Malcolm II, the
first Scotch king whose reign may be said to
belong in the realm of authentic history, determined to break its power. At first he was
unsuccessful, but in 1018, aided by King Owen
of Cumbria, he destroyed the Northumbrian
army at Carham on the Tweed, and settled
the frontier of Scotland for all time. King
Canute accepted the Tweed as the northern
boundary of England, and Edinburgh became
for ever Scotch.

The establishment of the frontier by no
means kept the English out of Scotland, and
Malcolm Canmore, the next king, decided to
build such a fortress that it would completely
dominate the roads from south to north. He
rebuilt Edinburgh Castle, and there made his
royal residence. It was the favourite home
of his beautiful and religious wife, Margaret,
sister of Edgar Atheling, and niece of Edward the Confessor. This pious queen tried

her best to introduce among the rude Scots some of the culture of more refined England, but without much success. The king preferred the clash of spear and shield, the chase or the foray, to mass and litany. But he idolized his beautiful wife, had her books of devotion bound in sumptuous gold and jewels, and kissed piously what he could not read.

For her he built the Chapel of Saint Margaret, the oldest and smallest ecclesiastical building in Scotland, standing to-day in the castle yard almost as it did in her time. He also endowed and built for her the Abbey of Dunfermline, on the other side of the Forth, and as she passed from one to the other for her devotions, she gave her name to what is still known as the " Queen's Ferry."

Margaret's chamber was where the Argyle Battery now stands, and here in November, 1093, the queen lay dying of a decline, brought on by her ascetic life. The king and his eldest son were off to the wars, and on the 13th of the month both were slain while besieging Alnwick Castle. On the fourth day thereafter, the queen heard mass and partook of the sacrament. Then, returning to her bed, she asked for her precious relic, the Black Rood of Scotland, which contained a fragment of the true cross. While she was holding this in ecstasy, there came to her her second son with the sad news that his father and brother were no more. The saintly queen spoke no word, but raised her relic to heaven and passed away.

Donalbain, the brother of the king, claimed the throne by the ancient Scotch law of tanistry, which excluded a chieftain's sons from the succession in favour of his brother or nephew, and stormed up against the castle walls with his wild Highlanders, bent on assuring his throne by the slaughter of his nephews. The firm walls held him out, but escape was necessary, as the castle was not prepared for a siege. Close beleaguerment seemed to make this impossible, but Turgot, the queen's confessor, having prepared the body for burial in her own Abbey of Dunfermline, caused the sally-port on the west side to be opened, and carried forth the corpse in solemn procession. A miraculous mist settled about the cortège, and dead queen and living princes passed unseen through the lines of blinded foes, across the Queen's Ferry, and on to the stately church of the Culdees, where the body was laid with those of her loved ones. Having seen the funeral rites performed, the sons returned and put their uncle to flight. Edgar took the crown, but soon died in the castle, and his brother became king as David I.

David lived his life in Edinburgh Castle, and changed the appearance of the surroundings. Until then the foot of the rock was surrounded by a deep and dangerous wilderness, a tangled forest seamed with dark pools and treacherous morasses. Much of this he cleared away and turned into a garden, being on the whole a man of peace, with some refined tastes. The town at this time was very small in extent, and composed of thatched mud huts. How small it was is shown by a famous passage in Boece, telling of a notable event in the king's life. He states that in the fourth year of his reign the king was resident at Edinburgh Castle, which was surrounded by " ane gret forest full of Hartis, hyndis, toddis (foxes) and sic lyk maner of Beistis." On the day of the Holy Rood, he determined to go forth into this wilderness to hunt, being pressed thereto by his thoughtless young nobles. In vain Alcuin, his confessor, entreated him to desist. He departed with a great multitude: " At last quhen he wes cumyn thorow the vail that lyis ti the eist fra the said Castell, quhare nou lyis the Canongaitt, the staill (train) passed thorow the wode with sic noyis and dyn of bugillis, that all the beistis wer raisit fra their dennis." In the ardour of the chase the king became separated from his companions, and suddenly found himself thrown from his horse, and about to be gored by a great stag. As he gave himself up for lost, a marvellous mist rolled about him, and a hand reached out of it a cross. He grasped it, and the stag took to flight. That night he dreamed that his adventure was a heavenly command to build an Augustinian monastery on the spot where his life was miraculously saved. Thus he came to endow the Abbey of Holyrood. He became thereafter so devout and expended so much money on religious foundations, that James VI, being told that his ancestor was a saint, testily replied, " Humph, he was a sair saunct to the Croon." Among his secular works, he greatly strengthened the castle, building the great Norman keep, whose fragments still serve as the foundations of the Argyle Tower, as well as several other of the outworks. He made the town one of the four burghs royal in 1128.

From this time on, Edinburgh always ranks as one of the most important places in Scotland. The kings were always crowned at

Scone, and the parliaments were held in various towns, but Edinburgh Castle was a favourite place of residence of all the kings from David I down. William the Lion was wont to reside there until he made an unfortunate expedition across the border and was taken prisoner by the English in 1174. He surrendered the castle to the English and did not regain it for twelve years. He then married Ermengarde, an English princess, and she brought it as a dower.

In 1215 the first parliament of Alexander II was held in Edinburgh. In 1235 there was held here a provincial synod of the Catholic Church, presided over by Cardinal L'Aleran, legate of Pope Gregory IX. Alexander III and his girl wife Margaret, daughter of Edward III, resided in the castle, and he made it the depository of his regalia and archives; but the queen was much dissatisfied with her habitation, and complained of it as " a sad and solitary place without verdure and by reason of its vicinity to the sea unwholesome." Alexander was surprised in the castle by a band of nobles headed by the Earl of Dunbar, who were favourable to the English, and laid down terms to the king, after driving out his loyal nobles.

Alexander died a tragic death in 1286, having been thrown from his horse near Kinghorn in Fife. His death was a sore blow to the kingdom of Scotland, and well justified the doleful words of Thomas the Rhymer which are reproduced elsewhere. The death of his granddaughter, the Maid of Norway, while on the way to claim her crown, opened the way to rival claimants for the throne, and the Wars of the Succession involved Edinburgh in dire disaster. Edward I, seizing the opportunity, asserted his feudal superiority over Scotland, and besieged Edinburgh in 1291. He captured the castle after a siege of fifteen days, but it was later withdrawn from his control, and he captured it again in 1294, after the battle of Dunbar. Thereafter, the magistrates and inhabitants of the burgh gave their fealty to him, and the castle remained in his hands for nearly twenty years. In 1313, Bruce had nearly recovered Scotland, and Edinburgh was one of the few strongholds which remained to Edward II.

The castle was defended by Sir John Wilton, whose loyalty was intensified by the fact that his promised bride had made their marriage conditional on his holding the castle a year and a day. Randolph, Earl of Moray, invested the rock, but the garrison was strong and well furnished, and it seemed impossible even to hope that it could be starved out before the return of the English king. Bruce informed Randolph that the castle must be taken at all hazards. The earl tried his best, but every approach to the walls called forth such a storm of arrows, bolts and rocks from the engines as made an assault hopeless.

At this juncture, on a cold March afternoon, William Francis, a trusted under-officer, informed the earl that he would undertake to lead a party up the crag by night and surprise the fortress. It seems that a number of years before his father had been keeper of the castle under Baliol. He was a soldier of the garrison, which was kept strictly within the walls, and forbidden to go out under any pretext. Being enamoured of a maiden who lived in the West Bow, and having as a boy clambered all over the castle rock, he had sought to make his way out to meet his lady love. By means of a ladder and a path which he had discovered, he had made his way up and down the cliffs by night until he was perfectly familiar with the way. He now offered to use this knowledge to lead a band of thirty men up to the base of the walls.

Volunteers were quickly found, though the way was, as Sir Walter Scott says, " fitter for a cat than for a man to traverse." The night was moonless and starless, windy, and bitter cold, — a night to make the sentinels cower under the shelter of the battlements, while the whistling of the blast would drown any noise made by the climbers. Fortunately, their path lay on the sheltered face of the crag.

Francis went first, and hooked the ladders into place for the more heavily armed men behind. Sometimes they had to traverse a horizontal ledge. The ladders were then carried on the outside, serving as a kind of balustrade to prevent an unlucky slip from hurling a man to death far below. Finally they reached a broad flat ledge near the top, where they paused to rest and await the changing of the watch. Some sentinel, presumably as a joke, or perhaps to prove to the approaching patrol that he was awake, suddenly called out, " Aha! I see you well! " and cast over a great rock, which passed close to the cowering band, and thundered from ledge to ledge until it reached the bottom. Not knowing whether they were discovered or not, they crouched in their cramped position, gnawed by the bitter cold, until the patrol had long passed, and all was quiet above.

Then they nerved themselves for the last portion of their tremendous climb. A few more feet over the sloping rocks brought them to the base of the walls, more than two hundred feet above the plain. The towering bulwarks were far too high for their ladders. Thrice the length was necessary. Finally they found a spot where two bound together enabled a man to grasp the top of the parapet. Strong and willing hands supported the unsteady ladders; dark forms stealthily clambered to the top. Claymore in hand, and dirk between his teeth, Francis was first on the parapet, with Sir Andrew Gray and Earl Randolph close behind. In a moment a dozen men had swarmed over the battlements. The bewildered sentinel barely could scream " Treason! " before a claymore stilled his cries. The alarm was given, however, and the Scotch battle cry, " A Randolph! A Moray! Claymore, claymore, ho! " warned Blantyre without the gates to be ready.

As the Scots clambered from the walls and rushed across the court toward the guard room and the gates, the constable and his guard opposed them. The struggle was fierce, but

short. Wilton fell at the head of his men, who
were bewildered and stupefied by the attack
by a band whose strength they did not know.
They broke and allowed Sir Andrew Gray to
reach and open the gates, and Blantyre entered with a force so large as to speedily quell
all opposition. Thus was successfully carried
out one of the bravest and most difficult sur-
prises in all the history of sieges.

Bruce adopted toward Edinburgh his historical policy, and stripped it of all defences,
that it might not shelter the English if they
came that way again. In fact nine years later
Edward II returned to Edinburgh, and sacked
Holyrood Abbey; but was compelled to retreat, as there was no castle left to protect him
from the harassing bands of the Scotch. In
1326 Robert Bruce held parliament in Edinburgh, and two years later another parliament
was called, famous for first seating the representatives of the burghs, and for ratifying the
treaty with Edward III which confirmed the
independence of Scotland.

In 1334 Edward Baliol, usurper and vassal
of Edward, convoked a parliament in Holyrood, which agreed to surrender to the English all of Edinburghshire. Guy, Count of
Namur, was sent with an army to take posses-

sion for Edward, but the Earl of Moray defeated him on the Borough Moor, chased his army headlong into Edinburgh, slaughtered great part of it in the narrow lanes and wynds, and drove the remnant to precarious shelter on the bare castle rock.

In 1337 Edward III penetrated as far north as Perth, and on his return rebuilt Edinburgh Castle, and placed in it a strong garrison. Four years later Sir William the Douglas, the Black Knight of Liddesdale, captured the castle by as ingenious a stratagem as ever brave soldier invented or put into execution. The plan was made by an ex-priest, William Bullock, who disguised himself as a French sea-captain, and sailed into the Forth with a cargo of wines and biscuits. He presented himself to the castellan, Richard de Limoisne, and offered his lading for sale. The governor purchased the whole cargo, and as the pretended captain seemed to be very much afraid that the Scots would injure him, allowed him to deliver it early the next morning.

At dawn appeared the carts, escorted by twelve sturdy mariners. The portcullis was lifted, and the train entered the gateway. As the first wagon was under the portcullis, the escort upset it so that the grating could not be lowered, and attacked the guard. A bugle call brought the band of Douglas from their ambush hard by, and a bloody struggle ensued in the castle yard. The garrison was annihilated, and the Scotch banner was raised, never to be lowered again from Edinburgh Castle until the union of the crowns.

David II was captured by the English and ransomed by his burghs, with Edinburgh for the first time as chief town, for one hundred thousand marks annually. The town was thus becoming prosperous, yet some years later, in 1384, Froissart, who was there with a party of French knights, said that its four thousand houses could not afford the knights due accommodation. On his return from England, David II resided in the castle, and completed the restoration begun at the orders of Edward III. His architect and military engineer was John Stuart, Earl of Carrick, afterwards Robert III, who was familiar with the modes of fortification then current in France. He built the lofty tower long known as " David's Tower," on the north side of the castle and in which David II, the last king of Bruce's line, died in 1370. Carrick's work made the castle so impregnable that neither

Richard II nor Henry IV was able to reduce it by siege.

Robert II, David's nephew, the first of the Stuart kings, made Edinburgh the capital of his kingdom. It was yet a mean town, built of cheap materials. It was open to assault from Border raiders, and often the bale-fire's gleam warned the citizens that their safety lay in flight. Then, packing up their goods, they retreated with their families and cattle to a more secure place, often removing even the straw thatch of their houses to save them from conflagration. When the enemy retired in disgust from the shell of a town which was left, they had repaired damages almost before he was across the Tweed.

On account of such invasions, in 1383 all respectable burghers were granted permission to build themselves houses within the castle walls, but this was so inconvenient that few took advantage of it. Two years later the burghers regretted it, for Lancaster invaded Scotland and laid the city, including Holyrood and St. Giles, in ashes. For five days his troops raged through the town and thundered at the gates of the castle, but the Duke of Rothesay, heir-apparent, successfully defended it. In 1383 the castle had seen the ambassador of France entertained by the first Stuart king, and the league of perpetual amity, entered into a century before, formally renewed.

Seven years later, when Robert III succeeded his father, the ambassadors of Charles VI once more came to Scotland and renewed the treaty of 1383. Henry IV, at whom this league was aimed, answered by reviving his claim to suzerainty over Scotland, and formed an army to enforce it. In 1400 he laid siege to the castle. The Scots laid the country waste about him, and privation and the approach of winter forced him to raise the siege ingloriously, and retreat, pursued far into his own dominions by a harassing but invisible foe.

Robert III loved Edinburgh, and resided almost wholly either in its castle or its abbey. The mysterious death of his heir, the Duke of Rothesay, and the capture of his second son James by the English, while travelling to France, broke his heart, and he died in faraway Bute, leaving Scotland to a regency, with its monarch a prisoner in the hands of his hereditary enemies.

During the regency of Albany, and the reign of James I, Edinburgh and its castle were little regarded by those in power. James I lived mostly at Perth. With the

accession of James II, however, the city
became the chief place of Scotland, its claims
as capital never again to be disputed. He had
been brought up in the castle, and had a deep
affection for it. From the castle he was led
solemnly by the Lords of Parliament to the
altar of Holyrood to be crowned. When he
went back there, guarded by the Earl of
Douglas, Duke of Touraine in France, and
Lieutenant-Governor of Scotland, on one side,
and by the Lord Chancellor Crichton and the
Regent Livingstone on the other, it was vir-
tually as a prisoner. Whichever lord could
control the person of the seven-year-old boy
could practically rule Scotland.

For two years Crichton held the control.
But when he refused to allow either the queen-
mother, guardian of the king, or the Regent
Livingstone to see the boy, and began to rule
despotically in his name, a change occurred.
The wily queen pretended to quarrel with
Livingstone, and sought the protection of
Crichton in the castle. There she lived for
several weeks. Then she bade the chancellor
farewell, saying that she was going to White-
kirk to redeem a vow, and tenderly commit-
ting the young king to his care. But when she
left the castle early the next morning, the little

king was safely packed in a chest on one of her baggage horses, and was shipped from Leith to Stirling, where Livingstone was waiting.

Regent, king and queen soon returned to Edinburgh and besieged the castle. Crichton saw that he was no match for the three and surrendered, on condition of keeping his offices of chancellor and governor of the castle. Livingstone carried off his king to Stirling and proceeded to act much as Crichton had; so that the queen soon stole her son again while he was hunting and fled to Crichton. Livingstone, infuriated, followed with his forces. Civil war was imminent, but some of the bishops succeeded in reconciling the two in the Church of St. Giles, on the basis of making common war against the Douglases.

The great earl, Lieutenant-Governor of Scotland, and more powerful in wealth and vassals than the king himself, had just died, leaving two sons. William, the elder, chose to markedly resent the fact that he had not been raised to his father's office. He displayed the most superb arrogance, never riding to Edinburgh save with a retinue of fifteen hundred mail-clad warriors, and sending two ambassadors to France to secure for him his title

to the Duchy of Touraine. As the privilege
of sending embassies was strictly a royal pre-
rogative, the chancellor and the regent saw
in this presumptuous youngling an enemy to
the throne, and laid plans for his undoing.

They invited him to come to Edinburgh to
join in counsel for the realm with them. At
Crichton Castle he received lordly entertainment, but also warnings from his friends not
to put all the Douglas eggs in one basket, by
taking his brother David to Edinburgh. He
resented the suggestion, and the two youths
marched into Edinburgh.

They were conducted to the castle, but their
train was excluded for lack of room to entertain it. They were well received in the fortress,
and the king was charmed with his young
guests. The feast was set forth, and every-
body was happy until it was time for the principal course to be served. Then, to the horror
and consternation of both the king and his
guests, there was set upon the table the head
of a black bull. This, an ancient Scottish
custom, doomed to death the principal guest.
The unfortunate boys, seeing that they were
betrayed, drew their swords, but were speedily overpowered by Crichton's vassals, who
swarmed in. They were hurried to the " back

court of the castle which lyeth to the wast,"
and pronounced traitors by a mock court which
was hastily made up. When they were sentenced to be beheaded, the king protested most
vehemently, and drew his sword to defend
them, but Crichton told him coldly that either
he or they must die, as there was not room
in Scotland for both a Stuart and a Douglas.
Then the headsman's axe was stained with
youthful blood, and the most horrible tragedy
of the castle was perpetrated. The effect on
the popular mind may be read in the words
of the ballad:—

> "Edinburgh Castle, town, and tower,
>   God grant thou sink for sin,
>   And that even for the black dinner
>   Earl Douglas gat therein."

No attempt was ever made to avenge this
fearful outrage, and there is no doubt that
James the Gross, great-uncle of the earl, and
his heir, was privy to the crime. He was soon
succeeded by his son, who formed an alliance
with Livingstone to destroy Crichton and steal
the king. But Crichton, safe behind the castle's walls, not only laughed at their siege, but
sallied forth and inflicted great losses on them.
When he did finally surrender to the king

himself, the terms involved his restoration to his office and the royal favour.

When the king attained his majority, he was married with great pomp, in which all factions joined, to Mary of Gueldres. After his marriage, he defended his city and castle by the first city wall, of which only the Wellhouse Tower, at the northern foot of the Castle Rock, now remains. As a further protection to the castle, he destroyed King David's gardens, and made the Nor' or North Loch, an artificial lake extending along the whole northern base of the rock, both wide and deep.

The next unusual event in the history of the castle occurred in the reign of James III. The king allowed himself to be deluded by an astrologer into believing that his two brothers, the Duke of Albany and the Earl of Mar, were about to compass his death. The one was imprisoned in Edinburgh Castle, the other in Craigmillar. Mar was soon brought to a house in the Canongate, as he was ill of a fever, and being bled by the king's own physician, he was thereafter found dead in a warm bath, his wound having burst open and left him too weak to call for help.

Albany was more fortunate. He was committed to King David's Tower, and his ward-ers were informed that his escape would mean their death. Nevertheless, his friends managed to inform him that a French vessel was waiting for him at Leith. From this they sent him as presents two casks of Gascon wine, in one of which was a rope, and a waxen roll containing a letter. This informed him that "the king's minions had resolved he should die ere to-morrow's sun set." Albany invited the officers of the guard to sup with him, and made them all drunk. This end achieved, he seized the captain's dagger from his belt, and dispatched all four of his captors. Though he had gained in France the title of "Father of Chivalry," he treated most barbarously the corpses of his enemies. With the assistance of his attendant he threw all the bodies into the fire which blazed high in the great fireplace, "and there in their armour they broiled and sweltered like tortoises in iron shells."

He had previously secured the keys of the tower, and locked all the external doors. The rope was made fast to the top of the tower, and the attendant insisted on going down first. As the rope was twenty feet too short, he fell and broke his leg. Albany heard his groans, and rushed back for the sheets of his bed, which he tied to the rope, and came safely to the ground.   There he found the hapless attendant, raised him on his shoulders, and carried him all the way to Leith, whence they took ship to Dunbar and thence to France. Meanwhile the awful stench from the burning bodies had caused the tower to be broken into, but the prisoner was beyond recapture.

Albany now proved himself a traitor indeed, by bargaining with Edward IV to hold Scotland of him if assisted to gain the crown. James set out with an army to meet the English, but took all his favourites with him. His principal nobles took matters in their own hands, hanged the favourites, and committed James to Edinburgh Castle as a prisoner. The Dukes of Gloucester and Albany, meeting no resistance, entered Edinburgh, and Gloucester spared the town at Albany's entreaties, " only taking such presents as the merchants genteelly offered him."   Gloucester signed a treaty most unfair to his brother, by which Albany acknowledged James's authority, and was pardoned, and also made Lieutenant-General and Earl of Mar.   James was released from his imprisonment, but Albany immediately sent to England and renewed his contract of the previous year, using as a messenger Angus, " Bell-the-Cat."   James again retired to the castle, and by the help of the citizens, was saved from danger. Albany and his allies were outlawed. But a few years later, another conspiracy drove James north from Edinburgh to death at Sauchieburn.

In the troublous minority of James V the castle was alternately a refuge and a prison for him, while unruly nobles strove for the command of the government, but the history of the castle for many years is almost devoid of interest. It twice successfully resisted the attacks of the English under Hertford and Somerset, when the town was burnt and sacked, in 1544 and 1547.

In 1560 the Regent, Mary of Guise, died in the castle, and her body, wrapped in lead, lay there for some months before it was conveyed to France.

Less than a year afterward Mary Stuart decided to return to Scotland, her husband the Dauphin having died. In August, 1561, she arrived at Leith, and three days later made her entry to her capital. For the first time she saw her great rock-borne castle, and that day she dined there. Thereafter she often resided there, and after her marriage to Darnley, and the murder of Rizzio, she took up her residence in the castle for security. Here, on

June 19th, 1566, was born her son, James VI
of Scotland and I of England.

Darnley was at this time residing in the
castle, apparently on the most amicable terms
with his wife, and on this occasion he sent the
following letter to the Cardinal de Guise: —

" From the Castle of Edinburgh, 19th day
of June, 1566, in great haste: —

" Sir — my Uncle,

" Having so favourable an opportunity of
writing to you by this gentleman, who is on
the point of setting off, I would not omit to
inform you that the Queen my wife has just
been delivered of a son, which circumstance, I
am sure, will not cause you less joy than ourselves; and also to inform you how, on this
occasion, I have on my part — as the Queen
my said wife has also on hers — written to the
King, begging him to be pleased to oblige and
honour us by standing as sponsor for him, by
which means he will increase the debt of grat-
itude I owe him for all his favours to me, for
which I shall always be ready to make any
return in my power.

" So, having nothing more agreeable to inform you of at present, I conclude, praying

God, Monsieur my uncle, to have you always in His holy and worthy keeping.

" Your very humble and obedient Nephew,
" HENRY R.

" Please to present my commendations to Madame the Dowager de Guise."

The little room in which James was born is still shown in Edinburgh Castle; like all the rooms shown as abiding places of Mary, it is of extremely small dimensions.

Very little of Mary's tragic history is associated with the Castle of Edinburgh. She preferred Holyrood, when she was not visiting in other parts of the kingdom.

After Mary's escape in 1568, Kirkcaldy of Grange seized the castle in her behalf, and held it for three years. The town was bombarded, and the attacks of the various regents who followed each other in quick succession had little effect. At last Elizabeth sent Sir William Drury, with a siege battery and a well equipped force, to reduce the castle. Kirkcaldy had supplied himself with provisions by an underground passage into the town, but this had been discovered and blown up some time before, so that he was already short of provisions when the siege commenced. He might have surrendered on easy terms; the dying John Knox had sent him a letter of prophetic warning; but he waited in hope of relief from France.

Batteries were erected all around him, but he held out for thirty-three days. One by one the towers fell, the walls crumbled, the wells were choked. Provisions gave out, and finally the garrison mutinied. Kirkcaldy sued for terms; receiving the promise of favourable treatment, he surrendered, and was hanged at the town cross. His companion, Maitland of Lethington, Mary's secretary, had preferred suicide to the mercy of Elizabeth. The castle was so ruinous that James never lived there, preferring Holyrood.

In the reign of Charles I the castle was still in ruins, so that he did not visit it when making his progress. Six years later he sent a command to the citizens to put the castle into a good state of defence, but they voted fifty thousand pounds Scots to aid the Covenanters in besieging it, and it was forced to surrender to General Leslie.

Cromwell besieged the castle in 1650, and after two months' resistance it honourably capitulated. At the Revolution it was held for

James VII by the Duke of Gordon. At the Rebellion of 1715, the insurgents made an attempt to capture it by surprise, but failed. Prince Charles Edward, in 1745, although he occupied the city, made no attempt to get possession of the castle, in spite of the fact that it bombarded the city, because of his presence.

Since the union of the crowns the castle has been kept in good repair, this being guaranteed by the terms of the document. The only event of historical importance was the discovery of the regalia of Scotland by Sir Walter Scott, which will be described later.

CHAPTER X

(*Continued*)

THE usual approach to the Castle of Edinburgh is from the Princes Street side, crossing the valley of the beautiful gardens, once the Nor' Loch, by the Mound or Waverley Street Bridge. Both routes lead into the Castlehill, from which we enter the Esplanade in front of the castle.

Here was of old the place of execution for witchcraft, a bloodstained spot where, during the fifteenth, sixteenth and seventeenth centuries, no less than two thousand persons were " worryit at the stake." This process implies strangling and burning, and was inflicted on the most slender evidence. Frequently a dozen persons suffered at once, and the victims included those of all ranks and stations. Naturally, here as elsewhere, the old, the ill-tempered, the invalid, the ugly or useless man or woman was the usual sufferer, but the highest of Scotland were not exempt. Lady Jane Douglas, young and beautiful, faithful to the memory of her dead husband, John, Earl of Glamis, was revengefully accused by a rejected suitor of attempting to compass the death of the king by witchcraft, convicted, and here burned alive.

James VI took a great interest in the witchcraft trials, and even applied the torture with his own hands. In 1590-1 an unfortunate maid-servant was tortured by her master, and confessed that she and several others whom she named were guilty. They were all tried, condemned and burnt on the Castlehill. One of them, Agnes Sampson, told the story of her intercourse with the devil as follows:

" The devil in man's likeness met her going out into the fields from her own house in Keith, between five or sax at even, being alone, and commanded her to be at North Berwick kirk the next night. She passed there on horseback and lighted down at the kirkyard. A little before she came to it, about eleven hours at even, she and others danced alang the kirkyard; Geilie Duncan playing to them on a trump, John Fian missalit (masked) led all the rest, the said Agnes and her daughter fol-

lowed next, and some others, in all about ane
hundred persons, whereof sax were men, and
all the rest women. The women first made
their homage, then the men. The men turned
nine times withershins about (*i. e.* counter-
clockwise). The witches then took hands and
danced a reel to the music of Geilie Duncan's
Jew's trump, singing the while —

> "'Cummer, go ye before, Cummer go ye,
> Gif ye will not go before, Cummer let me.'

" John Fian touched the doors with his staff
and they opened; he then with his breath blew
in the lights, which were like muckle black
candles sticking round the pulpit. The devil
then started up in the pulpit, like ane muckle
black man, and callit everyane by his or her
name, and they answered, ' Here, Master.'
. . . On his command they openit up the
graves, two within and ane without the kirk,
and cut off the joints of the fingers, toes and
knees of the dead, and partit them amang
them, so that having ground them to a powder
they might work mischief therewith. They
also put to sea on the day James was expected
back from Denmark with his bride, and threw
a cat into the water, pronouncing at the same

time an invocation to the devil. This was intended to raise such a storm that the vessel would be wrecked and the king drowned. [James stated that he could vouch for the truth of this, for his vessel had been greatly troubled by storms and contrary winds, while the other vessels of the fleet were bowling along before a favourable wind.] The witches added that they asked the devil why they could not work the king any evil. And the Prince of Darkness replied, ' Because he is such a good man, I have no power over him. He is my greatest enemy.' "

The king regarded this statement as a high compliment, but it did not mollify him enough to prevent the unfortunate woman from being burned on the Castlehill.

The space before the castle, the Esplanade, was, during the seventeenth and eighteenth centuries, a favourite promenade of the citizens of the town. It was not levelled until 1753, when the earth excavated from the foundations of the Royal Exchange was employed to remedy the former inequalities of the hillside. The walls and railings were added about the middle of the nineteenth century. It contains two monuments, one to the Field Marshal the Duke of York and Albany, the other

in memory of members of the 78th Ross-shire
Highlanders who fell in the Indian Mutiny.

Before entering the castle we may recall
that the Castlehill possesses a certain interest
to students of American history, because during the reign of Charles I it was officially a
part of the province of Nova Scotia. In September, 1621, Sir William Alexander, who
later became Earl of Stirling, was granted by
James VI a charter which conferred upon him
and his successors most of what is now the
northern United States and Canada, as well
as the adjacent islands. This charter conferred on him almost royal authority over a
country two or three times as large as the
whole realm of Great Britain. Besides giving
him the proprietorship of the land and all its
products, the charter allowed him to appoint
legal tribunals, coin money and grant lands.
Charles I renewed the charter in 1625, and
thereupon Alexander began to create baronets.
From each he received one hundred and fifty
pounds, in return for which he transferred to
each new lord a tract of six square miles of
land, with right of pit and gallows thereon.
In order that these baronets might be conveniently enfeoffed in their new estates, the
king issued a royal mandate declaring the soil

of the Castlehill to be that of Nova Scotia. In the ensuing twenty-five years, sixty-four American baronets took seizin on this spot. But this, the first attempt to create a hereditary American aristocracy, met with little success.

To enter the castle we must cross the old moat, which was formerly filled with water from the Nor' Loch. It is now dry and laid out for recreation grounds. The gateway is modern, but contains an ancient door impressively studded with iron bolts. This is known as the Outer Port. The cobbled road leads under the rock wall on the left, and passes through the Portcullis Gate in the base of the Argyle Tower. This slit in which the iron grate descended is still to be seen.

The Argyle Tower is possibly the one formerly known as St. David's Tower, which was battered to pieces during the siege of 1573, when Kirkcaldy of Grange upheld the cause of Mary. The walls are of enormous thickness and show under the later ashlar work masonry of great antiquity, so that Blanc considers this undoubtedly some of David's work. Other authorities, however, place David's Tower about in the centre of the Half Moon Battery, just within and above the Outer Port.

The present name of the tower comes from
the two Argyles, father and son, one of whom
was imprisoned here in 1661, the other in 1685.
Both were executed for their religious prin-
ciples.   The last day of the younger Argyle
has been commemorated by a great fresco in
the lobby of the House of Commons in London, based on the following description by
Macaulay: —

" So effectually had religious faith and hope,
co-operating with natural courage and equa-
nimity, composed his spirits that on the very
day on which he was to die, he dined with appe-
tite, conversed with gaiety at table, and after
his last meal, lay down, as he was wont, to
take a short slumber, in order that his body
and mind might be in full vigour when he
should mount the scaffold.   At this time one
of the lords of the council (supposed to have
been Middleton), who had probably been bred
a Presbyterian, and had been seduced by interest to join in oppressing the church of
which he had once been a member, came to
the castle with a message from his brethren
and demanded to see the earl.   It was answered that the earl was asleep.   The privy
councillor thought that this was a subterfuge
and insisted on entering.   The door of the cell

was softly opened, and there lay Argyle on the bed, sleeping in his irons, the placid sleep of infancy. The conscience of the renegade smote him. He turned away, sick at heart, ran out of the castle, and took refuge in the dwelling of a lady of his family who lived hard by. There he flung himself on a couch and gave himself up to an agony of remorse and shame. His kinswoman, alarmed by his looks and groans . . . prayed him to tell her what had disheartened him. He replied, ' I have seen Argyle within an hour of eternity sleeping as sweetly as ever man did. But as for me — ! ' "

Passing through the archway of the Argyle Tower, we see on the left a staircase, formerly the only means of access to the citadel, which may now be more easily reached by the broad roadway which circles around the base of the upper platform. On the right of this roadway is first the Argyle battery, and then various buildings pertaining to the internal economy of the garrison. Behind them on the west side is the location of the old sallyport through which the body of St. Margaret was conveyed, and up to which Dundee climbed in 1689 for his historic conference with the Duke of Gordon, governor of the castle, on the possibility of raising the Highland clans in support of the deposed James. A tablet over the postern records this interview.

Following the roadway we reach the upper platform, on which are the parts of the castle open to the public. Immediately before us is the old bomb battery, from which a most extensive prospect is visible in clear weather. The most conspicuous object here is the old cannon, famed as Mons Meg. Sir Walter Scott affirms that this gun was made by Kim of Mollance or Mons in Kirkcudbrightshire, and presented by the McLellans of that county to James II, when he arrived at Carlingwark in 1455, on his way to besiege Threave Castle, belonging to William, Earl of Douglas. This story has been much disputed. Mr. Burnet, who edited the Exchequer Rolls, thinks it very unlikely that a country smith in West Scotland would be skilled enough to build such a piece of ordnance, even if he had the needful tools and appliances. He finds in the Rolls proof that the king imported his bombards from Flanders, and an entry covering the expense of conveying the king's great bombard from Linlithgow to the siege of Threave Castle. It therefore seems most likely that the gun was forged at Mons in Flanders, as affirmed in the inscription on the gun, though perhaps earlier than 1476, as there asserted.

Whenever it was made, it was used at the siege of Dumbarton in 1489, when the treasurer's books reveal the payment of eighteen shillings Scots for drink money to the gunners. It was again used in Edinburgh on April 24th, 1558, when the marriage of Mary, Queen of Scots, to the Dauphin was being celebrated. The treasurer's accounts on this date contain the following entry: — " By the Queenis precept and speciale command to certain pyonaris, for their laboris in the mounting of Mons furth of her lair to be schote, and for the finding and carrying of her bullet after she wes schot, frae Weirdie mure to the Castell of Edinburgh." In 1682 the gun burst while firing a salute to the Duke of York. In 1745 it was removed to the Tower of London, whence it was brought back in 1829 on the prayer of Sir Walter Scott.

Nearby stands St. Margaret's Chapel, the oldest building in Edinburgh and the oldest church in Scotland. This without doubt dates back to the time of the good queen, and is the only building on the rock which was not destroyed by Bruce. It is only twenty-eight feet long and ten wide, and is architecturally Early

Norman, with some Saxon details. The chancel is sixteen feet long, and is separated from the circular apse by a wall pierced by an enriched Norman arch. The chapel has been restored in recent years as nearly as possible to its original appearance. By tradition it is the place where Edward I received the fealty of the Abbot of Holyrood and other ecclesiastics.

On the right is the doorway to the Argyle Tower, from which the two noblemen of that name, Marquis and Earl, went forth to death. The younger man was twice imprisoned here, escaping once, even as his father might have done, had not his courage failed at the last moment. The earl was visited on a stormy night by his step-daughter, Lady Sophia Lindsay of Balcarres, who came to bid him farewell. When she left, the earl, disguised as her footman, held her train. At the outer gate, the sentinel seized his arm, and the agitated earl dropped the train. As if incensed with his clumsiness, the quick-witted woman slapped the muddy train across his face, and the sentinel was so amused at the comical spectacle that he forgot his suspicions and let them pass. The earl escaped to Holland, and was not recaptured until 1685. In this chamber also the wraith of " bloody Claverhouse " appeared to his comrade and friend, Lord Balcarres, on the night when Dundee died at Killiecrankie.

Passing the Half Moon Battery, we enter the Palace Yard, historically the most interesting part of the castle.   On the east is the entrance to the Crown Room, an oak-panelled apartment where are kept under heavy bars the Regalia of Scotland.   The crown, which possibly dates back to the time of Bruce, though added to in the time of James V, is richly adorned with precious stones.   The sceptre was made in Paris for James V, of silver gilt, and is richly adorned with carvings and a great beryl taken from an ancient Egyptian sceptre.   The sword of state, five feet long, was presented by Pope Julius II to James IV, together with the golden rose.   The collection also contains the royal jewels bequeathed by Cardinal York, the last of the Stuarts, to George IV, including the jewels of the Garter and the Thistle belonging to James VI and the coronation ring of Charles I.

Oliver Cromwell had the Regalia of England destroyed during the Commonwealth, and the Scotch Privy Council was apprehensive lest the same fate should befall those of Scotland. So they were sent to Dunnottar Castle, and afterwards conveyed from there to safe concealment, as is more particularly related elsewhere. After the Restoration they came back to Edinburgh, and at the Union, the Council, fearful lest they should be conveyed to England, ordered them concealed once more. They were placed in a huge chest in one of the vaults of the castle, the door sealed, and stringent orders given that the room should never be opened. There they remained for a hundred years and ten, and faded from the memory of living men. The room was entered in 1794, when certain valuable papers were being searched for, and the huge chest shaken. As it gave forth no sound, it was believed to be empty, and the legend that the jewels were there concealed was put down as an idle fable. It then came to be believed that the English Government had had the Regalia secretly conveyed out of the kingdom and melted down.

Sir Walter Scott made researches which convinced him that there was truth in the ancient legend, and in 1818 obtained an order from the regent allowing him to enter the Crown Room and break open the chest. So, on the 4th of February, a commission consisting of some of the principal officials of the kingdom, of which Scott was a member, visited the Crown Room with a smith, who broke open the chest. The dust was thick inside the chest, but the jewels were there, wrapped in a cloth and uninjured. A salute was immediately fired from the castle batteries to communicate the good news to the populace, and great joy was everywhere manifested. They are still preserved in the room in which they were found, where stands the chest which preserved them safely. A passage from Lockhart shows Scott's feeling about the precious relics: —

" On the 5th February, Scott and some of his brother commissioners revisited the castle accompanied by several of the ladies of their families. His daughter tells me that her father's conversation had worked her feelings up to such a pitch that when the lid was again removed, she nearly fainted and drew back from the circle. As she did so she was startled by his voice exclaiming in a tone of deepest emotion: ' No, by God, no! ' One of the commissioners, not quite entering into the solemnity with which Scott regarded this business, had, it seems, made a sort of motion as

if he meant to put the crown upon the head
of one of the young ladies near him; but the
voice and aspect of the great poet were more
than sufficient to make the worthy gentleman
understand his error."

On the ground floor at the northeast angle
is a doorway, over which is the date 1566 and
the initials H and M, standing for Henry
Darnley and Mary, father and mother of
James VI, who was born here in that year.
These ornaments were probably inserted by
James VI, as the buildings date from the fifteenth century. The queen's mother, Mary of
Guise, died in this room in 1560. The most
remarkable thing about Mary's bedroom is its
small size, — not more than eight feet in its
longest dimension. In this it is like every
room shown in any Scotch castle as a chamber
of the queen. She seems to have had a fond-
ness for tiny apartments, and according to the
traditions of many castles, always slept on a
camp bedstead of her own when outside her
palace of Holyrood.

The wainscoting of this room is older than
the date of James's birth, having been brought
here from the Guise Palace in Blyth Close.
The panelled oaken ceiling, with royal crowns
and the initials I. R. and M. R., remains un-

changed from Mary's day. The famous inscription, surmounted by the Scottish arms, is still to be read on the wall: —

"Lord Jesu Chryst, that crounit was with Thornse,
Preserve the Birth, quhais Badgie heir is borne,
And send Hir Sonne successione, to Reigne stille,
Lang in this Realme, if that it be Thy Will;
Als grant, O Lord, quhat ever of Hir proceed,
Be to Thy Honer, and Praise; Sobied.
        19th IVNII, 1566."

The south side of the quadrangle is occupied by the old Parliament or Banqueting Hall. Long neglected, it has in recent years been restored by the munificence of an Edinburgh citizen, William Nelson, and now houses a fine collection of arms and armour. This was the meeting-place of many parliaments; here was proclaimed king the six year old James II; here Crichton and Livingstone feasted the Douglases, when the fatal Black Bull's Head ended the meal with a sentence of death; here banqueted the peers of Scotland at all the coronations down to the time of Charles I; and here the Earl of Leven entertained Cromwell in 1648.

From the windows of this gallant hall, fair ladies and proud knights watched the tilting

in the Grassmarket below. The Stuart kings
were very fond of this exercise, and such was
the renown of the tiltings of Edinburgh that
knights came from all parts of Christendom
to break a lance with the kings or their lords.
Pitscottie tells of a combat which was witnessed by James IV in 1503 from one of these
windows: —

" A famous cavalier of the Low Countries,
Sir John Cochbevis, challenged the best knight
in Scotland to break a lance or meet him in
combat *à l'outrance*. Sir Patrick Hamilton of
the House of Arran took up his challenge.
Amid a vast concourse, they came to the bar-
riers, lanced, horsed and clad in tempered mail,
with their emblazoned shields hung around
their necks. At sound of the trumpet they
rushed to the shock and splintered their spears
fairly. Fresh ones were given them, but as
Hamilton's horse failed him, they drew their
two-handed swords and fought on foot. They
fought thus for a full hour, till the Dutchman,
being struck to the ground, the king cast his
plumed bonnet over the castle wall to stay
the combat, while the heralds and trumpeters
proclaimed the Scottish knight victorious."

The northern and western buildings of the
quadrangle are of no importance, architectural

or otherwise. They include the hospital, into the walls of which are built the stones of an old church which formerly stood on the spot. As we pass out of the castle, the sentimental will be inclined to take a peep at the dogs' cemetery in a corner of the ramparts, where are buried the pets of the regiments that have been quartered here.

Below the north side of the castle, in the gardens, may be seen the ruins of the Wellhouse Tower, the starting point of the first wall of the city, where for centuries gushed forth a spring which was the principal reliance of the garrison in time of siege. On the side of the rock may be seen the lines of a built-up arch. This may have been the lion's den, but is more probably a remnant of the subterranean passage which once connected the castle with St. Giles and Holyrood and through which Kirkcaldy of Grange was provisioned during his long defence of the castle for Mary.

CHAPTER XI

Holyrood Palace

ALTHOUGH no castle in the strict sense of the word, the Palace of Holyrood demands some mention, more especially because linked with so many events in the life of Mary, Queen of Scots. The legend of the foundation of the abbey by David I has already been related. Although we have told it as it has been handed down for centuries, there is little doubt that it was invented many years after the death of the king; nevertheless, it is interesting, and a fair sample of the legends which have attached themselves to many abbeys in various parts of Europe.

The abbey was endowed for the canons regular of the Augustinian order, a colony of whom was transferred from St. Andrews. The financial resources of the establishment were large from the outset, and in addition it was gifted with the privileges of trial by wager of battle, by water, by red-hot iron, etc., and also possessed the right of sanctuary, which still exists, though no longer useful since the abolition of imprisonment for debt. It soon became one of the most splendid establishments in the kingdom, and, like all monasteries, contained numerous apartments for the entertainment of visitors of all ranks. Nobility and royalty were frequent guests within its walls, and it became one of the favourite residences of Scotland's kings.

Robert Bruce and Edward Baliol held parliaments within its walls. Robert III resided here when he came to Edinburgh. James I and his queen preferred it to any of their palaces, and in Holyrood the queen gave birth to twins, one of whom was afterward James II, and was crowned in the abbey. The same king was married and buried here, and spent much of his life in residence within its walls.

Just when a royal residence was erected in connection with the abbey is not clear. Probably the accommodations were extended at various times, as the needs of the royal family crowded the original quarters designed for guests. James IV, however, began the erection of a truly royal palace which henceforth subordinated the monastery, and it was finished by the fifth James.

The abbey did not escape the storms of war which rolled over the Lowlands. In August, 1332, the army of Edward III, on its return to England, laid waste the grounds and buildings of the abbey, and carried off its treasures. In 1385, during the furious raid of Richard II, it was burnt. It was wholly dismantled during Hertford's invasion in 1545, and the roofs were stripped of the remaining lead three years later by Somerset, after the battle of Pinkie. Some repairs were made for the Scottish coronation of Charles I, but final ruin was accomplished by a mob at the time of the Revolution, when the roofs were again stripped, the monuments destroyed, the vaults desecrated, and the bones of kings and nobles scattered in the most disgraceful manner. The head of Queen Magdalen, still retaining its lifelike appearance and much of its beauty, and the skull of Darnley were stolen, and the other bones were piled promiscuously in heaps, where they long remained a show for sightseers and a prey for thieves. The church was roofed again in 1758, with heavy stone flags, but the weight was too much for the shattered walls, and the structure succumbed and assumed its present ruinous state.

The original palace was destroyed by Hertford at the same time as the abbey, but was rebuilt. Again it was partially destroyed by the soldiers of Cromwell. At the orders of Charles II it was reconstructed in its present form by Sir William Bruce, who incorporated the whole western front of the old palace, including the two castellated towers, so that the architectural appearance is not wholly homogeneous. This older portion, to the north, contains the apartments which are of the deepest interest to all visitors, those of Mary, Queen of Scots.

Here she resided during almost all of that period of her life which was so crowded with passionate and tragic incidents, her two marriages with Darnley and Bothwell, the murder of Rizzio in her presence, and of Darnley with her knowledge or at least approbation.

After visiting some public rooms of indifferent interest, we enter the apartments of Darnley. The most interesting thing here is the little private stair from the turret room, by which access was gained from the courtyard to Mary's apartments. By this stair the assassins of Rizzio entered the palace, and were con-

ducted by Darnley to Mary's rooms above.
This is now closed, and entrance is made by
a stair from the audience room to Queen
Mary's audience chamber. Here stands the
bed of Charles I, used also by Prince Charles
Edward in 1745, and by the Duke of Cumberland, his conqueror, in the following year. In
this room Mary disputed with John Knox.

From this room we enter the bedchamber of
Mary, panelled and tapestried as befitted a
royal apartment. Fenced from the devastating touch of the relic-hunter, made up with
the mouldering linen and rotted damask under
which the queen slept on her last night here,
her bed is the most pathetic memorial of past
greatness which can be. imagined. As one
stands in the presence of this tangible evidence of the bodily presence of the queen in
this historic spot, the centuries vanish, and the
imagination easily repeoples these bare and
decaying chambers with the ghosts of the past;
the passionate and changeable queen; the four
Maries, attendants of her youth, desolating her
as they one by one married and left her;
Chastelard, poet of love and gentleman of
France, loser of his own head from inflated
vanity; Rizzio, the murdered secretary; Secretary Maitland; the awkward and lascivious

king, Henry Darnley; Bothwell, seducer,
murderer and pirate, invincible with women;
John Knox, the Reformer; Ruthven; George
Douglas; Ker of Faldonside; gentlemen and
ruffians, nobles and churchmen, courtiers and
retainers, a motley crowd, all intent on their
own petty purposes, and dragging the des-
tinies of a nation through their coils of in-
trigue, passion and violent death.

The queen's supper room, at the head of the
spiral staircase, is the culminating point of the
visit. Here occurred the tragedy whose visible evidence is the dark stain in the audience
room which a doubting public requires to be
renewed yearly, against the wish of the authorities, that it may be assured that the vital fluid
of some unfortunate sheep is the very life-
blood of the Piedmontese secretary. The murder of Rizzio has been depicted over and over
again, but who could do it better than Mary
herself. Here it is as she testified to it: —

" Upon the 9th day of March, we being, at
even, about seven hours, in our cabinet at
supper, sociated with our sister the Countess
of Argyle, our brother the Commendator of
Holyrood House, the Laird of Creich, Arthur
Erskin, and certain other our domestic servi-
tors, in quiet manner, especially by reason of

our evil disposition (illness), being counselled to sustain ourselves with flesh — having then passed almost to the end of seven months in our birth — the king, our husband, came to us in our cabinet, and placed himself beside us at our supper. The Earl of Morton and Lord Lindsay, with their assisters, bodin (armed) in warlike manner, to the number of eighteen persons, occupied the whole entry of our palace of Holyrood House, so that they believed it was not possible for any person to escape forth out of the same.

" In the meantime the Lord Ruthven, bodin in like manner, with his complices, took entry per force in our cabinet; and there seeing our secretary, David Riccio, among others our servants, declared he had to speak with him. In this instance we required the king, our husband, if he knew anything of that enterprise, who denied the same. Also we commanded the Lord Ruthven, under the pain of treason, to avoid him forth of our presence. He (Riccio) then for refuge took safer guard, having retired him behind our back; but Ruthven, with his complices, cast down our table upon ourself, put violent hands on him, struck him over our shoulder with whinyards (daggers), one part of them standing before our face, with bended dags (cocked pistols), most cruelly took him out of our cabinet, and at the entry of our chamber gave him fifty-six strokes with whinyards and swords. In doing whereof we were not only struck with great dread, but also by sundrie considerations were most justly induced to take extreme fear of our life.

" After this deed immediately the said Lord Ruthven, coming again into our presence, declared how they and their complices were highly offended with our proceedings and tyranny, which was not to them tolerable; how we were abused by the said David, whom they actually put to death, namely, in taking his counsel for maintenance of the ancient religion, debarring of the lords who were fugitives, and entertaining of amity with foreign princes and nations with whom we were confederate; putting also upon Council the Lords Bothwell and Huntly, who were traitors, and with whom he (Riccio) sociated himself."

Mary was not deceived by Darnley's protestations of innocence in the matter, more especially as his bloody dagger was found in the hastily made grave of Rizzio, and this terrible invasion of her chamber, regardless of her rights as a queen, a woman, and an approaching mother, combined with Darnley's indiscriminate amours with the most debased companions, effectually killed her love for him. The manly Bothwell succeeded to her favour, and less than a year later the house where Darnley was staying, in the Kirk o' Field, was blown up at night, and the king killed. Then followed the secret marriage with Bothwell in the hall of Holyrood, not the Chapel Royal, where Darnley had been espoused. The beginning of the end; few and short were her hours of ease thereafter. Secrecy, evasion, flight, defeat, imprisonment, in varied sequence, were her lot, and finally came death by behest of that Elizabeth depicted with bloody hands in Mary's bedchamber at Holyrood.

In the registers of Holyrood these entries relate to some of the important events of Mary's life.

On July 21st, 1565: proclamation of marriage between Mary and Darnley:

" Ye quhilk daye, Johnne Brand, Mynister, presented to ye Kirk ane writtin writin be ye Justice-Clerk's hand, desyring ye Kirk of ye Cannogait and Mynister thairof to proclaime Harie, Duk of Albayne, Erle of Roiss, etc., on ye ane pairt, and Marie, be ye Grace of

God, Queene of Scottis, Soverane of this Realme, on ye ather pairt. The quhilk ye Kirk ordains ye Mynister so to do wi. invocationne of ye Name of God."

And on the 29th of July of the same year, stands the entry of the said parties having been proclaimed: "Harie, Duk of Albayne, Erle of Roiss, Marie, be ye Grace of God, Queene Soverane of this Realme, 1. 2. 3." with the note, "Mar. in ye Chappell."

The two murders are thus entered: "Monsr. Singnior Dauid wes slaine in Halyruidhous ye ix. daye o' Merche anno 1565. (Old style.) " "The King's Grace blaun up wi' pudr. in ye Kirk o' Field, ye x. day o' Februar, 1566."

Craigmillar Castle

Three miles south of Edinburgh, in the parish of Liberton, there stand on a wooded hill the well preserved ruins of Craigmillar Castle. The nucleus of this castle was probably erected in the latter part of the fourteenth century. It was a keep of L-plan, four stories high, with a flat roof well adapted for purposes of defence. Two of the floors were vaulted, the others were formed of wood midway in the height of the vaults. This keep was provided with a courtyard which has probably always retained the same dimensions. Entering the castle by the gateway on the north side, which formerly had a guardhouse and a portcullis, it

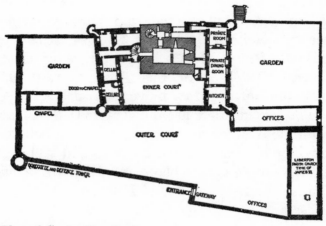

Plan of Craigmillar Castle

was necessary to pass around two sides of the keep, through a narrow passage between it and the south wall of the courtyard, and across a chasm in the rock provided with a movable bridge, before reaching the entrance door. This was consequently deemed to be well enough defended to be placed on the ground floor. Inside there is a lobby below the outside level, commanded by a guardroom above. To get to the stairs, an abrupt turn through a narrow door is necessary. The stair contains a provision for defence, in that it does not continue straight up, but leads into a guard-room at the hall level, and makes a new start upward several feet to one side. It would hardly be possible to make a more tortuous and difficult entrance for an enemy to win.

The walls of the enceinte are about thirty feet high, and provided with turrets at each corner. They are corbelled out to make a continuous rampart with open machicolations, embrasures and loopholes. Some parts of the curtain had also wooden hoardings outside, the beam-holes for which are still visible.

In the sixteenth century, after the ravages of Hertford, the castle was restored, and a range of buildings erected around the east and south sides of the wall, thus converting this into a courtyard castle. A new staircase was built at this time for easier access to the keep. The west wing was added later, perhaps in the seventeenth century, to replace earlier buildings on this side.

This castle is almost unique in having intact the outer bailey, which contained the farm buildings, chapel, and gardens. The whole enclosure is over three hundred feet long and about two hundred wide. This outer court is not extended around the south side, where the castle stands on the edge of a precipitous cliff some thirty feet high, and needed no additional defence.

Craigmillar is mentioned in a charter of Alexander II as early as 1212. It was purchased from Sir John de Capella by Sir Simon Preston in 1374, and remained in the Preston family for almost three hundred years. In 1477 it was the prison of John, Earl of Mar, younger brother of James III, who was confined here on the charge of conspiring against his brother's life. It was the residence of James V during his minority, when he left Edinburgh on account of the plague; and by the favour of his guardian, Lord Erskine, the queen dowager was allowed to visit him here while the Duke of Albany, the governor, was absent in France. The castle was burned and plundered by the English in 1554, and most of the present buildings are of later date, as stated above. The castle was a favourite residence of Queen Mary after her return from France in 1561. Her French retinue were lodged in the little village which still exists to the east of the castle, and is known as Petit France. Mary's room, in the south wing of the keep, is only seven feet by five, but never-

theless contains two windows and a fireplace.
Mary was residing here in November, 1566,
when the " Conference of Craigmillar " was
held, at which Bothwell proposed her divorce
from Darnley. Here also was signed and
dated the " bond of blood " for the murder of
Darnley, by Maitland, Morton and the other
conspirators.

The castle has been much repaired in recent
years, and is in good preservation. It may be
visited on application to the custodian in the
village to the east, the fee to the guide being
optional.

Borthwick Castle

Borthwick Castle, now unfortunately absolutely closed to visitors, is the finest keep in
Scotland. The building is in good preservation and stands almost in its original form.
Its date of erection is exactly known, as Sir
William Borthwick was created Lord Borthwick in 1430, and was granted, by James I,
a license to erect upon the spot called the
Mote of Locherwart a castle or fortalice, to
surround it with walls and ditches, to defend
it with gates of brass or iron, and to place
upon the summit defensive ornaments, that is,
battlements and turrets; he was further em-

powered to place in the castle so erected a constable, a porter, and all other persons and things necessary for the defence thereof.

The castle stands on a slight eminence between two streams, towards which the ground slopes precipitously. It is defended by outer walls, forming an irregular courtyard about two hundred and forty feet long and one hundred and twenty broad. At the bottom of the steep slope crowned by these walls is a ditch. The wall is defended by towers, of which that at the corner by the gate is very strong, and had a fair-sized apartment within.

The castle is perhaps the largest simple keep in Scotland. It is seventy-four feet by sixty-eight, and ninety feet high, exclusive of the battlements. It consists of an oblong block containing the great hall, and two wings on the west side, with a deep recess between. It is built of polished sandstone, which has resisted the weather remarkably well, and gives it an unusual appearance of freshness in spite of its great age.

The basement comprises several vaulted rooms, as is usual, and access from it to the hall is gained by a spiral stair opening into the guardroom. The great hall, fifty-one feet by twenty-three, occupies the entire first floor of the main building. To enter from without it was necessary to go around two sides of the keep, and mount a stair to the parapet of the enceinte on which rested a drawbridge from the entrance. The first floor walls are twelve to fourteen feet thick and a guardroom in them defends the entrance.

The hall is vaulted and twenty-nine feet high. It contains a lofty hooded fireplace, somewhat ornamented, and a music gallery. In the north wing is the kitchen, containing an enormous fireplace, in which are three windows. The south wing contains a parlour. The rooms above in each wing are bedrooms. In the main block are a drawing-room and chapel on the second floor, and bedrooms on two more floors.

The roof was defended by parapets supported on bold corbels with open machicolations all around and round bartizans at the corners. These parapets are gone on the east side, where they were destroyed during Cromwell's bombardment in 1650.

The land on which this castle was built was purchased by its builder from William Hay of Locherwart, and was on the extreme edge of his property. This was a common custom, the reason for which was well expressed by a

northern laird who did the same thing. One
of his friends warned him of the inconvenience
of such a procedure, as removing him too far
from the other side of his estate. The laird
significantly answered, "We'll brizz yont."
Translated, this signifies, "We'll press forward," and is indicative of the habit of the
feudal barons to extend their domains upon
every pretext.

Hay of Locherwart looked with envy on
the magnificent castle rising on the land he had
so lately parted with, and vented his spleen
by building just below the tower, in the valley
which was still in his domain, a mill, declaring
that the pride of Borthwick should never cease
to be wounded by the clack of his neighbour's
mill.

William, Lord Borthwick, the builder, was
a man of note in his time, and was a member
of the assize which sat at Stirling on Murdoch,
Duke of Albany, builder of Doune, and his
sons. His descendants were also men of merit,
ambassadors overseas, and forward in Parliament. The third lord, with his neighbour of
Crichton, fell on the fatal field of Flodden.
His last descendant died in 1672, and ninety
years later the peerage became extinct. It had
been one of the greatest in Scotland, its lands

in 1538 comprising no less than thirteen domains, in five counties. The last lord, on being confirmed in his title by Parliament, claimed the title of First Baron of Scotland.

Sir Walter Scott relates the following curious incident which occurred at Borthwick in 1547, having found an account of it in the ecclesiastical records of St. Andrews. In consequence of a process betwixt Master George Hay de Minzeane and the Lord Borthwick, letters of excommunication had passed against the latter, on account of the contumacy of certain witnesses. William Langlands, an apparitor or macer of the see of St. Andrews, presented these letters to the curate of the church of Borthwick, requiring him to publish the same at the service of high mass. It seems that the inhabitants of the castle were at this time engaged in the favourite sport of enacting the Abbot of Unreason, a species of *highjinks,* in which a mimic prelate was elected, who, like the Lord of Misrule in England, turned every sort of lawful authority, and particularly the Church ritual, into ridicule. This frolicsome person with his retinue, notwithstanding the apparitor's character, entered the church, seized upon the primate's officer without hesitation, and, dragging him to the mill-

dam on the south side of the castle, compelled
him to leap into the water. Not contented
with this partial immersion, the Abbot of Unreason pronounced that Mr. William Langlands was not yet sufficiently bathed, and
therefore caused his assistants to lay him on his
back in the stream, and duck him in the most
satisfactory and perfect manner. The unfortunate apparitor was then conducted back to
the church, where, for his refreshment after
his bath, the letters of excommunication were
torn to pieces, and steeped in a bowl of wine;
the mock abbot being probably of the opinion
that a tough parchment was but dry eating.
Langlands was compelled to eat the letters,
and swallow the wine, and dismissed by the
Abbot of Unreason with the comfortable as-
surance that if any more such letters should
arrive during the continuance of his office,
" they should a' gang the same gait."

The authorities of St. Andrews, owing to
the progress of the Reformation, appear to
have been unable to avenge the insult by anything more serious than threats of excommunication against the perpetrators when discovered. This species of license grew so fast,
that a few years later an act of Parliament
not only prohibited the choosing of Abbots

of Unreason, but ordered that women singing around summer-trees or May-poles were to be taken, handled and put upon the ducking-stone.

This same John, fifth Lord Borthwick, who allowed the license of the Abbot of Unreason, was a loyal friend and adherent of Queen Mary. The Earl of Bothwell was proprietor of Crichton Castle, only two miles away, and Mary often visited Borthwick to be near him. As shown by Cecil's diary on the 7th of October, 1566, when the queen heard that Bothwell had been hurt in Liddesdale, she rode to Borthwick. She was also there on June 6th, 1567, with Bothwell, to whom she had been married little more than three weeks.

Less than a week later, on the eleventh, Mary and Bothwell were again here, fear having driven them from Holyrood. A letter of James Beaton, Archbishop of Glasgow, states that, in this morning, "my Lords of Morton, Mar, Hume, Lindsay, etc., with sundry odderis barronis, to the nommer of nine hundredth or a thousand horsemen, arryvit in the morning about Borthwick, in deliberation to comprehend and tak my Lord Duk, wha was in the said place with the Queen's Majestie. My Lord Duk hearing of this enterprize, thinking well he could be in mair securitie in the field than in ane house, passit forth and red away.

"Her Majestie, in mennis claithes, butit and spurrit, departit that samin nicht of Borthwick to Dunbar, quhairof na man knew saif my Lord Duk and sum of his servants, wha met her Majestie a myll off Borthwick, and conveyed her hieness to Dunbar."

The insurgent nobles had not yet felt themselves able to touch the person of Mary, so, finding Bothwell flown, they returned to Edinburgh, where they beat down the gates of the castle, without opposition from the provost and town officers. There they captured Mary's friends, who had retired there for safety. Beaton, the writer of the letter just quoted, conveyed these tidings to Mary, whom he found "so quiet at Borthwick, that there was none with her, passing six or seven persons." This small garrison probably determined her to ride forth, "butit and spurrit, and in the guize of a page," to Cakemuir Castle, where she passed a night, and where Bothwell's servants met her, to escort her to Dunbar.

During the Civil War, the eighth Lord Borthwick was a follower of the king. Borthwick Castle, as well as all the other strongholds in the vicinity of Edinburgh, was garrisoned for the royal side, which fact was greatly instrumental in causing the retreat of Cromwell from Edinburgh. After the disastrous battle of Dunbar had caused the surrender of the capital, these fortresses fell gradually into the possession of the English. Borthwick Castle held out persistently and its garrison harried the victorious army on every occasion. Cromwell soon determined to put an end to this wasp-like annoyance, and sent from Edinburgh on the 18th November, 1650, a letter endorsed " For the Governor off Borthwick Castle — These." Its terse and emphatic contents were as follows:

" SIR,

" I thought fitt to send this trumpett to you to let you know, that if you please to walk away with your company, and deliver the house to such as I shall send to receive it, you shall have libertie to carry off your arms and goods, and such other necessaries as you have. You harboured such parties in your house as have basely and inhumanely murdered our men; if you necessitate me to bend my cannon against you, you must expect what I doubt you will not be pleased with. I expect your present answer, and rest

> " Your servant,
> > " O. CROMWELL."

The governor, supposed to be Lord Borthwick, chose to remain, whereupon the artillery was duly brought into position on the east side, and the garrison soon found their defences tumbling about their ears. They then surrendered on honourable terms. Thus closes the history of Borthwick's wars.

Of the name of Borthwick, not in the line of succession, one or two men have passed into history. Of these was Robert Borthwick, gun founder and gunner in the infancy of great guns, master of artillery to James IV. He cast the beautiful guns called the Seven Sisters, a greatly admired prize of the English on the bloody field of Flodden.

Another of the name spoke on his last bed the sentence proverbially called " David Borthwick's Testament." He was a lawyer, and became rich; all his estates he gave to his son, Sir James Borthwick, who spent prodigally what came so easily. As the old advocate lay dying he was told that Ballencrieff, the last estate, was sold. He merely replied: " What can I say? I bequeath every man to the devil that begets a fool, and does not make a fool of him."

Crichton Castle

Crichton Castle, two miles from Borthwick, is a fine specimen of a structure begun as a simple fourteenth-century keep, and afterward extended into a castle surrounding a courtyard. It was until recently accessible to the public, but entrance is now forbidden, as the present owner has again made it into a dwelling house.

The keep contained the usual hall, with a vaulted basement below, there being no communication between the floors. The dungeon was in one corner of the basement, in the thickness of the wall and the haunch of the basement vault, a cramped apartment communicating with the hall by a stair. The door of the dungeon is less than three feet high, and is nine feet above the floor. It has no windows but an air-slit.

On the north and west sides of the courtyard are fifteen-century additions, including new halls, kitchens, etc., as at Doune and Tantallon. Two halls are included, one above the other, each with its own kitchen and serving-room.

The latest portion of the buildings is the finely decorated north side, erected about 1600. The lower floor is an arcaded corridor, and the stonework above is cut into square facets, so that the whole aspect of this side is rather that of a Venetian palace than a Scottish castle.

The first recorded proprietor of Crichton was Sir William Crichton, chancellor to James I and guardian of his son. In 1445 the castle was stormed and destroyed by For-rester of Corstorphine, a follower of Living-stone. In 1488 the estate was given to Pat-rick Hepburn, first Earl of Bothwell, and descended from him to the famous earl of Mary's time. Forfeited by him to the Crown, it was given by James VI to Francis Stu-art, Earl of Bothwell. Later it passed through numerous changes of proprietorship, and was until lately a crumbling ruin. Scott thus describes it in " Marmion: " —

> "That castle rises on the steep
>   Of the green vale of Tyne:
> And far beneath, where slow they creep,
> From pool to eddy, dark and deep, —
> Where alders moist and willows weep, —
>   You hear her streams repine.

The towers in different ages rose;
Their various architecture shows
   The builders' various hands;
A mighty mass that could oppose,
When deadliest hatred fired its foes,
   The vengeful Douglas bands.

Crichton! though now thy miry court
   But pens the lazy steer and sheep;
   Thy turrets rude, and totter'd keep,
Have been the minstrel's loved resort.
Oft have I traced within thy fort,
   Of mouldering shields the mystic sense,
   Scutcheons of honour, or pretence,
Quarter'd in old armorial sort,
   Remains of rude magnificence.
Nor wholly yet has time defaced
   Thy lordly gallery fair;
Nor yet the stony cord unbraced
Whose twisted knots, with roses laced,
   Adorn thy ruin'd stair.
Still rises unimpaired below
The court-yard's graceful portico;
Above its cornice, row on row
Of fair hewn facets richly show
   Their pointed diamond form;
Though there but houseless cattle go
   To shield them from the storm;
And, shuddering, still, may we explore,
   Where oft whilom were captives pent,
The darkness of the Massy-More;
   Or from thy grass-grown battlement,

May trace, in undulating line,
The sluggish mazes of the Tyne."

Roslin Castle

Roslin Castle stands on a high promontory
lying above the North Esk, twelve miles south
of Edinburgh. To the ordinary visitor it is
an unimportant incident of the visit to the
wonderful Roslin Chapel, one of the gems of
Gothic architecture, which stands hard by.
The castle is indeed but a shapeless mass of
ruins, with a house of late date built over part
of them, but it possesses some unusual architectural features. The approach to the castle
was over a narrow promontory of rock. This
has been cut through at its narrowest part,
and the gap was formerly crossed by a drawbridge, but is now filled with a stone arch.
The road under this once crossed the river,
but the bridge has long vanished.

The entrance to the castle was anciently
guarded by a gatehouse with round towers,
and by a square tower, both of which are now
utterly ruinous. The keep, the oldest part of
the castle, was at the southwest corner, on the
highest part of the site. It was fifty feet long,
of unknown width, and is now represented

only by the walls of one side and part of
another. No vestige of the internal arrangements is left. It was built in the thirteenth
century. Continuing its wall to the northward
is what is apparently a wall of the fifteenth
century. This is unique in Scotland, and its
construction is both curious and hard to describe. It is composed of eight buttresses or
rounds, wedge shaped in plan, with rounded
outer ends. Father Hay, the historian of the
family, gives a description which makes it
probable that arches were thrown across the
tops of these buttresses, to form a parapet.
He calls them the wall of the chapel, but
there is no present indication that they ever
formed part of a building.

The buildings on the southeast side of the
court are seventeenth century. Three stories
are built below the level of the courtyard,
vaulted in stone, and reached by a wide stone
stair. These buildings rise two stories above
the courtyard level, containing the dining-
room, great hall, etc., while the lower rooms
were used as kitchen, bakery, and store rooms.
They overlook the tilting ground to the south
in the valley. Though surrounded by trees of
great age, this is still clear, and bears evident
marks of its original purpose.

" The lordly line of high St. Clair " has been
domiciled in Scotland since the time of Malcolm Canmore.   This monarch gave William,
son of Waldernus, Comte de St. Clair, one
of the Norman barons who came with the
Conqueror, the lands of the barony of Roslin.
This was about 1100, and there has probably
been a castle on the spot ever since.   His
castle was doubtless incorporated in the present keep, built by William de St. Clair, who
set out with Lord James Douglas to carry the
heart of the Bruce to Palestine.   The line
prospered, and its titles extended until the St.
Clairs were Barons of Roslin and several other
lands in Lothian, Earls of Orkney and Caithness, and Dukes of Oldenburg.   They were at
the head of the baronage of Midlothian, and
rich to an extent unusual for Scotland.   Their
glory culminated in Earl William, who flour-
ished in the middle of the fifteenth century,
and founded Roslin Chapel.   He maintained
his court at Roslin Castle with a state and
magnificence even greater than that of many
of the Scotch monarchs..   He was served at
his own table from vessels of silver and gold,
by great nobles; Lord Dirleton was the master of his household, Lord Borthwick his cup-
bearer, and Lord Fleming his carver.   If

these were absent their deputies were respectively Stuart, Laird of Drumlanrig, Tweedie,
Laird of Drumerline, and Sandilands, Laird
of Calder, each of which six owned a castle of
his own. As to the state of his remaining
equipage, let us quote Father Hay: —

"His Countess, Margaret Douglas, was
waited on by seventy-five gentlewomen,
whereof fifty-three were daughters of noblemen, all cloathed in velvets and silks and with
their chains of gold and other pertinents;
together with two hundred rideing gentilmen,
quho accompanied her in all her journies. She
had carried before hir when she went to Edinburgh if it were dark eighty lighted torches.
So that in a word none matched her in all the
contrey save the Quene's Majesty."

The castle was destroyed by fire in 1452,
and again demolished during the English invasion of 1544, along with Craigmillar. It
was partially restored in 1580, but Monk
knocked it to pieces again in 1650, and it was
never rebuilt. What he left, the mob tore
down and carried away when they ravaged
Roslin Chapel in 1681.

Roslin is the scene of more than one picturesque legend, some of which have been the
subjects of Scott's poetic genius. The most

famous is that which relates how the earl of the time of Bruce obtained from that monarch his broad baronies in the Pentlands. It seems that Robert Bruce was in the habit of hunting in the dense forest which then covered all this region, and that his hounds had often started a beautiful white deer, which regularly outran them and escaped. On a certain day William St. Clair boasted that his dogs were better than the king's, and offered to wager his head that Help and Hold, for so they were named, would pull down the white hind before she should cross the March burn. The king, incensed, accepted the wager, but saying that the head of a Scottish nobleman was too valuable to be risked for nothing, he staked against it the broad forest of Pentland.

So the wager was joined, and all the hounds were called to leash save Help and Hold, and the slowhounds used to raise the deer. St. Clair was allowed to post his animals as he pleased, and all awaited the result. The slow-hounds did their work, and the white deer flashed by Earl William, seeming to cast a reproachful glance upon him as she passed. He released his dogs, urging them on with his voice and galloping close at their heels. Fleet as they were, the white hind was faster,

and reached the burn long before them. Into
the stream she plunged, and the spectators
felt that St. Clair's head was lost. But in the
middle of the stream the deer paused, and in
an instant the hounds were upon her. Their
terrible fangs tore her throat, and they
dragged her upon the bank just as the hunting
party rode up. The deer reproachfully turned
her fast-glazing eyes on the earl, and from
that moment neither the saving of his head
nor the increase of his possessions could drive
away the impression that a misfortune had
befallen him in the death of the white deer.

In the night in a vision he saw again the
chase of the white deer. This time he was
aware that it foreboded disaster, but could not
avert it. When he again saw before him the
dying deer, a whisper came to him: " O day
of infinite sorrow! You have slain the guardian of the brightest jewel of the house of
Roslin!" The vision passed and he awoke.
A storm was impending. The clouds rolled
across the sky, the wind howled, the lightning
flashed. A terrible tempest burst over Lothian
and the Firth of Forth, and not only devastated the lands of Roslin, but swamped the
barge in which his only daughter Rosabelle
was returning from a visit to her aunt in Fife.

The barons of Roslin were anciently buried in a vault in the chapel, each in his armour, without coffins, and before the Revolution, the vault contained the remains of ten of the line thus interred, and perfectly preserved by the dryness of the situation. A superstitious belief arose that on the night before the death of any of the family, the chapel appeared to be in flames, and this, with part of the legend of Rosabelle, has been woven into the verses of Scott: —

"O'er Roslin all that dreary night,
    A wondrous blaze was seen to gleam;
 'Twas broader than the watch-fire's light,
    And redder than the bright moonbeam.

"It glared on Roslin's castled rock,
    It ruddied all the copsewood glen;
 'Twas seen from Dryden's groves of oak,
    And seen from cavern'd Hawthornden.

"Seem'd all on fire that chapel proud,
    Where Roslin's chiefs uncoffin'd lie;
 Each baron, for a sable shroud,
    Sheathed in his iron panoply.

 Seem'd all on fire, within, around,
    Deep sacristy and altar's pale;
 Shone every pillar foliage-bound,
    And glimmer'd all the dead men's mail.

" Blazed battlement and pinnet high,
    Blazed every rose-carved buttress fair, —
So still they blaze, when fate is nigh
    The lordly line of high St. Clair.

" There are twenty of Roslin's barons bold
    Lie buried within that proud chapelle;
Each one the holy vault doth hold —
    But the sea holds lovely Rosabelle !

" And each St. Clair was buried there,
    With book, with candle, and with knell;
But the sea-caves rung, and the wild waves sung,
    The dirge of lovely Rosabelle ! "

Hawthornden

A mile down the glen of the Esk from
Roslin Castle stands the house of Hawthornden on a high crag rising from the south bank
of the stream. The walk hither from Roslin
is one of the most beautiful and romantic in
all of Scotland, and in the perfumed air of
spring a delight to all the senses.

". . . The spot is wild, the banks are steep,
With eglantine and hawthorn blossomed o'er,
Lychnis, and daffodils, and harebells blue:
From lofty granite crags precipitous,
The oak, with scanty footing, topples o'er,
Tossing his limbs to heaven; and, from the cleft,

Fringing the dark-brown natural battlements,
The hazel throws his silvery branches down:
There, starting into view, a castled cliff,
Whose roof is lichened o'er, purple and green,
O'erhangs thy wandering stream, romantic Esk,
And rears its head among the ancient trees."

The age of Hawthornden is usually over-
stated. The modern house dates only from the
seventeenth century. Attached to this are fragments of a small square keep whose age is difficult to determine, but which is probably of the
fifteenth century. That there was a castle
here much earlier we know, as also that the
perpendicular cliff under the house was carved
into caves used as habitations and places of
refuge in very early times. One room is arranged as a dovecot, and is popularly called
King Robert Bruce's library, but as a Scotchman cannily remarked, "There wadna be
mony bund books then." These caves were
used as refuge by Sir Alexander Ramsay of
Dalhousie during the reign of David II, when
the English were in possession of Edinburgh.

The most celebrated owner of the house was
the poet, William Drummond, friend of
Shakespeare and Ben Jonson, and the first
Scotchman who wrote good English verse.
The incident of his visit from Ben Jonson,

who walked all the way from London, is well-known.

Though of old Edinburghshire boasted a hundred castles, the number is now sadly reduced. Many of those which remain have been so changed by rebuilding as to lose whatever architectural interest they have possessed, while others have been removed by the march of progress. So, though we might enumerate many other structures in Midlothian called by the title of castle, we will pass on to other fields.

CHAPTER XII

CASTLES OF EAST LOTHIAN

Dunbar Castle

THE fragmentary ruins of the once magnificent Castle of Dunbar stand on a reef of trap
rock projecting into the sea, which makes its
way through many fissures and caverns of the
crags to the base of and even under the massive walls.

The buildings were once of considerable
extent. The main body of the castle was
about one hundred and sixty-five by two hundred and seven feet, stretching its length
from north to south. Southwest of the main
building was what Grose supposes to have
been the citadel or keep, an octagonal building sixty feet in diameter on a perpendicular
rock accessible only on one side, and connected
with the main building by a defended passage.
On the other side of the ruins is a large natural cavern of black stone, called the dungeon,
which, as Pennant says, " the assistance of a

little art had rendered a secure but infernal prison." It is perhaps more likely to be the postern gate through which Sir Alexander Ramsay and his band succoured the garrison in the famous siege of 1337-8.

The age of Dunbar goes far back of history. The name in Gaelic means " the fort on the height," but the legend asserts that Kenneth I defeated the Picts at Scoon through the aid of one of his most valiant soldiers, whose name was Bar. On him was bestowed the stronghold as a reward; hence the name Dun-Bar, " Castle of Bar." However this may be, in 961 two leaders named Dunbar and Graeme led the men of Lothian against the Danes at Cullen.

In 856 Kenneth II burned the castle, but it speedily rose again, for it was justly considered one of the keys of the Lowlands.

The founder of the family of Dunbar, which for four centuries maintained an almost regal authority in the east of Scotland, was Cospatrick, great-grandson of Uthred, Prince of Northumberland. After the Norman conquest in 1066, he, with other northern nobles, fled to Scotland, carrying with him Edgar Atheling, the heir of the Saxon line, together with his mother and sisters. One of the latter,

Margaret, became the queen of Malcolm Canmore, and Cospatrick was created Earl of Dunbar. For his exploit in defeating a formidable band of robbers, of whom he killed six hundred and hanged eighty, later presenting the head of their leader to the king, he was created Earl of March and granted arms of a bloody head. He was also granted Cockburnspath on the unusual tenure of keeping the March and East Lothian free of robbers. His successors prospered, and rendered their castle so strong that Henry III and a great army, after reducing the powerful fortress of Berwick in 1214, were unable to capture Dunbar, and retired to England. Patrick, earl at this time, in 1231, after assembling all of his family and neighbours to celebrate Christmas, entertained them most sumptuously for four days. At the end of this time he summoned the Abbot of Melrose, received extreme unction at his hands, and assumed the monastic habit.

He died a year later and was succeeded by his son Patrick, who became the most powerful lord in Scotland, and was the leader of the twenty-four barons who guaranteed the treaty with England in 1244. He was the head of the faction which caused the downfall of the

Bissets in 1242, when the king was powerless.
This was the outcome of a royal tournament
held at Haddington, where the Earl of Athole
bore down Walter Bisset, head of the family.
In revenge, the earl's lodgings were fired that
same night, and the earl and a number of his
party perished.

The sixth Earl Patrick died in 1248, while
besieging Damietta in Egypt. His son Patrick was a leader of the English party during
the troublous minority of Alexander III. In
1285 he was visited at Dunbar by Thomas
Learmouth of Ersildown, known for his gift
of prophecy as Thomas the Rhymer. Arriving at the castle in the evening, the earl jocu-
larly asked him what strange thing would occur
on the morrow. The prophet's face immediately became grave, and he replied: " Alas for
to-morrow, a day of calamity and misery!
Before the twelfth hour shall be heard a blast
so vehement that it shall exceed those of any
former period, — a blast which shall strike the
nations with amazement, — shall humble what
is proud, and what is fierce shall level with the
ground! The sorest wind and tempest that
ever was heard of in Scotland! " Thereafter,
refusing all entertainment and conversation,
he retired to his apartment. The next fore-

noon, the earl and his friends watched the weather until nearly noon, but without discovering anything untoward. Summoning the Rhymer, they upbraided him as an impostor, and prepared to partake of their dinner. As they sat down at the table, and the shadow on the dial reached the noon mark, a messenger on a horse covered with foam dashed up to the door and demanded instant admittance. Brought before the earl and asked as to his message, he replied: " I do indeed bring tidings most lamentable, and to be deplored by the whole realm of Scotland. Alas, our renowned king has ended his fair life on yonder coast near Kinghorn! " The Rhymer advanced with an air of conscious triumph. His reputation was sustained by the king's fatal fall from his horse. Loudly he exclaimed, " This is the scaithful wind and direful tempest which shall be such a calamity and trouble to the whole kingdom of Scotland! "

Patrick, the eighth earl, was a partisan of the English. When Edward I entered Scotland in 1296, the earl, together with the Bruces, joined him, leaving his countess, Marjory, daughter of Alexander Comyn, Earl of Buchan, in the Castle of Dunbar. She patriotically delivered it to the Scotch leaders, who garrisoned it with the flower of the nobility. Edward despatched Warrenne, Earl of Surrey, with twelve thousand men to recover the fortress. Conscious of the impossibility of withstanding such a force, the Scots agreed to surrender unless relieved in three days. The main army of Scotland, forty thousand men, commanded by the Earls of Buchan, Lennox, and Mar, advanced to its support. On the third day they took their position on Doon Hill, — in the same spot occupied in 1650 by General Leslie before his defeat by Cromwell, — and waited for an attack. Despite the disparity of the forces, the Earl of Surrey left part of his army to blockade the castle and advanced to meet the Scotch. In order to reach them, the English had to cross a valley, and, in doing so, seemed to waver. The Scotch, believing victory already won, charged from their well-chosen position with shouts and trumpetings. Warrenne faced them undismayed, and the undisciplined troops broke and fled, being pursued with great slaughter to Selkirk forest. Many of the fugitives sought shelter in the castle, but on the next day Edward appeared, and Seward, the governor, surrendered. The Earls of Athole, Ross, and Menteith, four barons, thirty-one knights, one hundred esquires, and many men of lesser rank were taken. Later the king gave Earl Patrick two hundred pounds to furnish the castle with military stores and provisions.

The ninth earl, also named Patrick, succeeded on the death of his father in 1309. He was also English in his sympathies, and in 1314 sheltered Edward II after the annihilation of his army at Bannockburn. The king, with a small body of horsemen, was in flight toward Berwick, but was followed so closely by Sir James Douglas and eighty picked riders, that he was very glad to find refuge in Dunbar. The earl " full gently received him," entertained him hospitably, and caused him to come by boat safely to Berwick, a very honourable proceeding, as he was well aware how advantageously he might make peace with his cousin, King Robert Bruce, by delivering to him the person of the King of England. Shortly after the earl submitted to Bruce, and later demolished his castle to prevent it from falling into the hands of the English. In 1333, however, he submitted to King Edward III and rebuilt the fortress at his own cost, to shelter an English garrison. The next year he was present at Edinburgh at the parliament at which Baliol ceded all south Scot-

land to the English king. Thereafter he
changed sides again and retired to the Highlands with the friends of Bruce. His castle
was left in charge of his wife, daughter of
Randolph, Earl of Moray, and grandniece of
King Robert Bruce, called " Black Agnes "
from her dark complexion.

On January 28, 1337, William de Monta-
gue, Earl of Salisbury, commenced the most
famous siege in the history of the castle. The
English placed their engines in position and
hurled massive stones against the walls.
Agnes stood on the battlement, and when a
great bullet struck the stones just below her,
she scornfully ordered one of her handmaidens
to wipe off the marks of the impact with her
clean handkerchief, gaily observing that it was
scarcely gentlemanly on the part of Salisbury
to throw dust in a lady's eyes.

The earl, with infinite pains, advanced to
the foot of the walls an immense shed covering
battering rams, called a sow. The lady taunt-
ingly cried out:

> " Beware, Montagow,
> For farrow shall thy sow ! "

and caused to be hurled an immense fragment
of rock, which utterly demolished the roof, and

caused the inmates who remained alive to
scatter in all directions, thus speedily fulfil-
ling the prophecy.

Having exhausted his resources in this direction, the earl tried the power of gold, and
attempted to bribe the keeper of the gate to
open to him in the night. The canny guardian
assented and took the purse, but then laid the
whole story before the countess. At the appointed time Salisbury and his men approached and found the gate indeed open.
The earl pressed forward to enter first, but
John Copeland, one of his officers, rushed
before him and reached the courtyard. As he
did so the portcullis fell, but failed to trap
the earl. Agnes was watching from a high
tower, and jeeringly exclaimed: " So, Monta-
gue! We had hoped to-night to have received
the noble Salisbury as our guest, and con-
sulted with him on the best means to defend
a Scottish fortress against an English army;
but as my lord declined the invitation, we will
e'en take counsel of ourselves. Farewell, Mon-
tague! With truth within, we fear no treason
from without! "

The earl was disheartened by this failure
and sat down to a close blockade of the castle,
every avenue to which by sea or land was

closely watched. When the garrison was at
the last extremity, Alexander Ramsay of Dalhousie determined to succour it. Embarking
at midnight with forty determined men, he
eluded the English flotilla, and landed at the
water postern. The garrison, freed from danger of famine, received him most joyfully, but
Ramsay was satisfied with no half-relief. He
immediately sallied forth from the main gate,
surprised and cut to pieces the enemy's advanced guard, and returned in safety. Salisbury was so discouraged by this new reverse,
and the length of the siege, that he broke
camp on June 10th, after nineteen weeks
blockade, and retired to England.

George, eleventh Earl of Dunbar and
March, quarrelled with the Duke of Albany,
and fled to England. While he sojourned in
the English camp, his castle and titles were
sequestrated, and passed nominally to the
Crown, actually to Albany, who was created
Earl of March. When Earl George made
peace with his sovereign it was at the expense
of Dunbar, which remained a fief of Albany.

The Duke of Albany, brother and chief
counsellor of James III, is thus depicted by
Lindsay of Pitscottie: " He was hardy and

manly, and wise so that they [the barons of
Scotland] stood in more awe of him than of
the king's grace, for his manhood. This Alexander was of a mid stature, broad shoul-
dered, and well proportioned in all his members, and specially in his face; that is to say,
broad-faced, red-nosed, great-eared, and of
very awful countenance, when he pleased to
show himself to his unfriends." He was as
ambitious as he was bold, and almost as strong
in the kingdom as the king himself.

In 1475, not for the first time, he became
the object of his brother's suspicions, and was
cast into Edinburgh Castle, fated to death.
His friends helped him to escape, as is elsewhere more particularly related, and he fled
by sea. On the way he stopped at Dunbar,
and put his castle in order, then resumed his
journey to France, where he married the
Duchess of Bouillon, and remained until 1482.
Meanwhile the castle was taken, the garrison
escaping by sea. On his return at the head
of an English force, in 1482, he recovered his
estates, but the next year was forced to flee
again from Scotland, leaving an English garrison in Dunbar, who were able to hold it
against all the efforts of the Scotch.

On September 21, 1484, a truce of three

years between England and Scotland was concluded at Nottingham. By a singular clause in the agreement, Dunbar was to have six months truce only, after which, by giving six weeks' notice, the Scottish king was to be at liberty to recover the castle by force, if his strength were sufficient. Although his parliament repeatedly advised James to give notice, and besiege this castle, he did not feel strong enough to do so until 1486, when he laid siege to it in the depth of winter, and soon recovered it, without causing the English to feel that the truce was broken.

In 1488 an Act of Parliament was passed, directing the Castle of Dunbar to be " casten down and utterly destroyed, in such manner as to render repairs utterly impossible," " because it has done great skaith in time bygane, and it were great danger to the realme if it were negligently kepit or reparit again." By bitter experience the Scots had found that the English were far more skilled in sieges than themselves, and their own captured fortresses had more than once been thorns in the flesh. Nevertheless it was not until 1567 that this ordinance was actually put into execution.

During the regency of Mary of Guise, Dunbar was garrisoned by her French troops.

This was a source of much annoyance both to Scotch and English, and in the treaty of 1560, between Queen Elizabeth, and Francis and Mary, it was agreed that all the French garrisons should be dismissed, except sixty men each in Dunbar and Inchkeith, and that the new works at Dunbar should be demolished. The English army, marching to Berwick, took good care to see that this was done.

Dunbar is a name especially associated with the troublous years of Mary, Queen of Scots. In 1566, after the murder of Rizzio, Bothwell aided her escape from Holyroodhouse, and after a short sojourn at Seton, she moved to Dunbar. Here she was speedily joined by so many of her friends that she gained a temporary ascendance over the authors of her secretary's death. Again, in November of that year, she sojourned six days in Dunbar. In April, 1567, Bothwell, who had been constable of Dunbar, obtained a " ratification " of the " Queen's Castle and Strength of Dunbar " and the " Captaincie " of the fortress, in part recompense of his " great service and exorbitant expenses," and also because his friends, kinsmen, tenants and servants for the most part dwelt adjacent to the said castle and strength. Under his guardianship, Mary was twice more here. The last time was when she fled from Borthwick, disguised as a page, and barely escaped Home's troopers by refuge in its walls. Here her proclamation called together the feeble and unwilling army which dissolved in panic at Carberry Hill, leaving her a prisoner destined for Lochleven Castle.

The Laird of Whitelaw still held Dunbar for Bothwell, but the regent brought cannon from Edinburgh, and the place surrendered on favourable terms. Then came the resurrection of the act of 1488, and the margin of the record of the Council contains this incomplete note: " 26th December, 1567. Ordains the Inche and Dunbar to be demolished and taken down, in respect of K. Jas — ." By this politic move, the regent destroyed Bothwell's strength by virtue of an ancient statute, without incurring hostility for his own government.

It stands to-day, the ruins of that wrecking, and was until lately free to all visitors. But it is now used as a rifle range, and in consequence much closed to sightseers. Even this year of 1907, great tumult has been caused in the town by further restrictive measures, and it may soon be entirely closed to the public.

Innerwick Castle

Innerwick Castle, in the parish of the same name, and five miles from Dunbar, seems to be a ruin of great antiquity and was formerly of considerable extent. The earliest portion was a simple keep, but this was later added to on the east, where originally was an open court. It was a position of considerable strength, standing on a high sandstone cliff, with sheer faces on three sides. On the fourth was a deep ditch cut in the rock.

Of its history little is known. It belonged successively to the Stuarts and Hamiltons. Together with Thornton, a keep of Lord Home's, and Dunglas, a tower a few miles off, it was destroyed by Somerset's expedition in 1548. Patten's diary gives an account which, modernized in the spelling, I quote as a good picture of the savage warfare of that period:

" Tuesday, the 6th of September.

" Our Pioneers were early at their work again about the castle [Dunglas, which had been taken the day before]; whose walls were so thick and foundation so deep, and thereto set upon so craggy a plot, that it was not an easy matter soon to underdig them.

" Our army dislodged and marched on. In the way we should go, a mile and a half from Dunglas northwards, there were two Piles or Holds, Thornton and Anderwick [Innerwick], both set on craggy foundation, and divided, a stone's cast asunder, by a deep gut, wherein ran a little river.

" Thornton belonged to the Lord Home, and was kept then by one Tom Trotter. Whereunto, my Lord's Grace, over night, for summons, sent Somerset, his Herald. Towards whom, four or five of this Captain's prickers, with their gads ready charged, did right hastily direct their course: but Trotter both honestly defended the herald, and sharply rebuked his men; and said, for the summons, ' he would come and speak with my Lord's Grace himself.'

" Notwithstanding, he came not; but straight locked up sixteen poor soldiers, like the soldiers of Dunglas, fast within the house, took the keys with him, and commanding them they should defend the house and tarry within (as they could not get out) till his return, which should be on the morrow with munition and relief; he, with his prickers, pricked quite his ways.

" Anderwick pertained to the Lord of Ham-

bleton [Hamilton] and was kept by his son
and heir (whom, of custom, they call, the Master of Hambleton), and eight more with him;
gentlemen, for the most part, we heard say.

" My Lord's Grace, at his coming nigh,
sent unto both these Piles; which upon summons, refusing to render, were straight assailed. Thornton, by a battery of four of our
great pieces of ordnance, and certain of Sir
Peter Mewtys's hackbutters to watch the loopholes and windows on all sides; and Anderwick, by a sort [company] of these hackbutters alone. Who so well bestirred them, that
where these keepers had rammed up their outer
doors, cloyed and stopped up their stairs
within, and kept themselves aloft for defence
of their house about the battlements; the
hackbutters got in, and fired the underneath,
whereby being greatly troubled with smoke
and smother, and brought in desperation of
defence, they called pitifully, over their walls.
to my Lord's Grace, for mercy: who, notwithstanding their great obstinacy and the en-
sample others of the enemy might have had
by their punishment, of his noble generosity,
and by these words, making half excuse for
them, ' Men may sometimes do that hastily
in a gere [business], whereof, after, they may

soon repent them,' did take them to grace, and therefore sent one straight to them. But, ere the messenger came, the hackbutters had got up to them, and killed eight of them aloft. One leapt over the walls, and, running more than a furlong after, was slain without, in a water.

"All this while, at Thornton, our assault and their defence was stoutly continued: but well perceiving how on the one side they were battered, mined at the other, kept in with hackbutters round about, and some of our men within also occupying all the house under them, for they had likewise shopped [shut] up themselves in the highest of their house, and so to do nothing, inward or outward, neither by shooting of base [small cannon], whereof they had but one or two, nor tumbling of stones, the things of their chief annoyance, whereby they might be able any while to resist our power or save themselves; they plucked in a banner that afore they had set out in defiance, and put out over the walls a white linen clout tied on a stick's end, crying all, with one tune, for 'Mercy!' but having answer by the whole voice of the assailers, 'They were traitors! It was too late!' they plucked in their stick, and sticked up the banner of defiance again, shot off, hurled stones, and did what else they could, with great courage on their side, and little hurt of ours. Yet then, being assured by our earnesty that we had vowed the winning of their hold before our departure, and then that their obstinacy could deserve no less than their death, they plucked in their banner once again, and cried upon 'Mercy!' And being generally answered, 'Nay, nay! Look never for it! for ye are arrant traitors!' then, made they petition that 'If they should needs die, yet that my Lord's Grace would be so good to them, as they might be hanged: whereby they might somewhat reconcile themselves to God, and not to die in malice, with so great danger of their souls!' A policy, sure, in my mind, though but of gross heads, yet of a fine device. Sir Miles Partridge being nigh about this Pile, at the time, and spying one in a red doublet, did guess he should be an Englishman; and, therefore, the rather came and furthered this petition to my Lord's Grace. Which then took effect. They came and humbled themselves to his Grace: whereupon, without more hurt, they were but commanded to the Provost Marshal.

"It is somewhat here to consider, I know

not whether the destiny or hap of man's life. The more worthy men, the less offenders, and more in the Judge's grace, were slain; and the beggars, the obstinate rebels that deserved nought by cruelty, were saved.

" To say on now. The house was soon after so blown with powder, that more than one half fell straight down to rubbish and dust, the rest stood, all to be shaken with rifts and chinks. Anderwick was burned, and all the houses of office, and stacks of corn about them both.

" While this was thus in hand, my Lord's Grace, in turning but about, saw the fall of Dunglas, which likewise was undermined and blown with powder.

" This done, about noon, we marched on, passing soon after within gunshot of Dunbar, a town standing long-wise upon the seaside: whereat is a castle, which the Scots count very strong, that sent us divers shots as we passed; but all in vain."

Seton Palace

Not far from Prestonpans, a mile and a half inland from the fishing village of Cockenzie, stood for centuries Seton Palace, the architectural pride of East Lothian. Not one stone now remains upon another; the beautiful gardens and terraces, a favourite resort of monarchs in the heyday of its owners' pride, are utterly obliterated, and the ruined walls of one of the most magnificent mansions of Scotland have long since been built into other and meaner fabrics.

A castle of the Setons occupied the site for centuries, but was destroyed in Hertford's invasion in 1544. The famous palace was erected by George, fourth Lord Seton, a zealous supporter of Queen Mary. It was the finest mansion in Scotland in the seventeenth and eighteenth centuries, and was a favourite resort of royalty, having been visited by Mary, Queen of Scots, James VI, and Charles I.

The spot has many historical associations. Cardinal Beaton was imprisoned there for a while and was released by Maitland of Lethington, father of Queen Mary's famous secretary. Mary herself often visited here, and Mary Seton, one of her four maids, was connected with the house.

On the 16th of February, 1566-7, Mary, who had been at Bothwell's castle of Dunbar, arrived at Seton, accompanied by Archbishop Hamilton of St. Andrews, the Earls of Bothwell, Argyle, and Huntly, Lords Fleming and

Livingstone, Secretary Maitland and others, to the number of a hundred. The queen, though her murdered husband was but six days dead, evinced no grief, nor showed any while she remained at Seton. She played with Bothwell in shooting at the butts against Huntly and Lord Seton. These latter, losing, paid forfeit by furnishing a dinner one day at Tranent. Time fled away pleasantly, and Mary remained at Seton until the 7th of March. On the 8th she was in Edinburgh, but the next night she rode to Seton again and slept there. On the 29th or 30th she came again and stayed a week, entering on the 5th of April into a nuptial contract with Bothwell, as her enemies allege. The document was written by the Lord Chancellor, the Earl of Huntly, to whose sister Bothwell was married; Huntly thus consenting to the divorce of his own sister on pretence of consanguinity.

Another frequent visitor to Seton was James VI. As he left Edinburgh, on another 5th of April, in the year 1603, on his way to ascend the throne of England, he passed the palace at the very moment when there issued from the house the funeral procession of the first Earl of Winton, one of his mother's most devoted adherents. The king halted his train and seated himself on a fragment of masonry still standing, to watch the passage to the tomb. He wept profusely and declared that he had lost a faithful and loyal friend. The king returned to Scotland in 1617, and spent the night at Seton, being greeted most loyally by the third earl and his adherents. His reception included the reading of an English poem of four hundred and twenty-two lines by Drummond of Hawthornden, and a Latin one of two hundred and eighty-six lines by John Gillie of Gillieston. Truly even a prince has trials!

A few years later this same earl entertained Charles I on a progress. The second earl, who, for some unexplained reason, had resigned title and estates to his younger brother, was still alive, and his second son, twelve years old, welcomed the king in a Latin oration. Charles was so pleased with this that he knighted the boy, and then said, " Now, Sir Alexander, see that this does not spoil your school; by the appearance you will be a scholar." The boy stammered, " No, please your Majesty," and returned to his studies with increased diligence.

In 1715 a party of the Adventurers under Brigadier McIntosh of Borlum, who had oc-

cupied Cromwell's citadel at Leith, moved by
the threats of the Duke of Argyle, retired
from that position and entrenched themselves
at Seton. They drove back troops sent from
Edinburgh to expel them, and had determined
to hold the house permanently. This did not
suit the Earl of Mar, who ordered them to
march into England. General Wightman
thereupon occupied the place and demolished
the courtyard walls. The earl had joined the
Adventurers, but refused to march into England with them, urging the folly of leaving
the Duke of Argyle in their rear, and desiring
them to reduce the duke and thus gain Scotland. He afterwards reconsidered his decision,
entered England and was captured at Preston.
He was condemned to be beheaded, and re-
mitted to the Tower of London with forfeit
of his honours and estates. Refusing to make
any application for mercy, he succeeded in
cutting the bars of his cell and escaped to
Italy, where he died more than thirty years
later.

This earl and his brother were born several
years before the marriage of their parents.
He was of a fiery disposition, and quarrelled
so bitterly with his father when less than twelve
years of age, that he ran away to France and

had no communication with family or friends for many years. During this time he earned his living as a bellows-blower and blacksmith's helper. His brother and then his father died, and he knew nothing of it. A relative took possession of the estates, alleging that the son was illegitimate, and kept them till 1707, when the earl returned and brought an action against the usurper. The Supreme Court finally gave him possession in 1711, but his enjoyment was short, as he was attainted of treason five years later, when only twenty-five years old.

The estate was sold to a company of real estate speculators, with many other confiscated estates. Overloaded with mansion-houses for which they could find no outlet, they went bankrupt, and the lands were sold in lots. The ruinous palace was torn down by the purchaser and built into a house of no pretension. We may gain some idea of it from Pinkie house, which was built as a reduced model of Seton Palace.

Preston Tower

Preston Tower is an L-keep of the fifteenth century. It contains the usual basement vault, connected with the upper floors only by a trap in the roof. The main entrance was on the

first floor, guarded by a projecting wooden
structure and staircase, the corbels and joist-
holes of which still remain. Above this was
another wooden projection carried on immense corbels, which further protected the
door of access. The wing contained private
apartments. Under the floor of the lord's
room, off the main hall, was a prison, the stair
to which was gained through a trap in the
floor. Under this prison was a dungeon,
reached only by a hatch in the prison floor,
and without light, but ventilated by flues in
the walls. The present doorway to this dungeon is of recent date.

In the seventeenth century, the house being
too small, two stories, smaller in diameter, were
added to the top. The castle has for ages
belonged to the Hamiltons. It was burned
by Hertford in 1544, by Cromwell in 1650,
and again accidentally in 1666, when it was
abandoned.

Hailes Castle

Hailes Castle, near East Linton, stands on
a rocky point between the Tyne and another
small stream which flows into it from the
north. The castle dates from the thirteenth
century, and is very large, being two hundred

and forty feet long and ninety feet wide. It has a square keep at the point of the promontory and a very long quadrangular courtyard, with walls about nine feet thick. The courtyard contains a roofless hall of the sixteenth century. Great portions of the walls have disappeared, and the remains, though imposing, are very ruinous. A remarkable feature is a postern staircase leading down to the river. This had a trap in the middle in the shape of a deep pit crossed by a drawbridge. The castle belonged to the Hepburns, and many parts of the building were erected by James, Earl of Bothwell, husband of Queen Mary. Here she was conducted by him, after he had seized her near Linlithgow.

Whittingham Tower

About two miles from East Linton, and in the immediate vicinity of Hailes Castle, from which it is hidden by Traprain Law, stands Whittingham Tower, a well preserved and rather ornamental L-keep of the fifteenth century. It is quite small, the main building being only thirty-one by twenty-three and one half feet, and about forty feet high. A square wing for the staircase projects to the east from

one of the narrow sides, contrary to the usual
custom of placing the wings on the long sides.
The doorways, windows, and parapets are all
ornamented with moldings similar to many
English Tudor structures. The parapets have
embrasures, and a complete walk inside.
South of the castle are some ruined vaults, perhaps powder magazines, and a long platform
for cannon.

In the Tower of Whittingham was laid the
plot for the murder of Darnley. Here, in
January, 1566-7, came the Earl of Morton to
visit his cousin, Patrick Douglas, whose arms
are still visible on the lintel of the entrance
door. From the castles of Hailes and Lethington near by came their owners, Bothwell
and Secretary Lethington, and the murder was
then planned. Tytler says, writing of a later
occasion, " It was only a year and a half before
that in this fatal house, the conference had
been held between Lethington, Bothwell and
Morton, in which the king's murder was determined. Bothwell was now a fugitive and
an outlaw; but his associates in guilt, the
same Lethington and Morton, now received
Moray at Whittingham, and cordially sympa-
thized with him when he expressed his horror
for the crime, and his resolution to avenge it."

Stoneypath Tower

Stoneypath Tower is two miles from Whittingham, on the Papana Burn. It is a very dilapidated structure, but occupies a most picturesque location, standing on a high and wooded bank above the brook. The tower is L-shaped, and offers few peculiarities of construction. The staircase in the angle is inside the wall instead of being projected into the angle. The fireplace in the hall is about eight by ten feet and served also as the kitchen, being furnished with a window, and a stone sink and drain. The entrance was through the fireplace arch. The building may be early sixteenth century, but there is little to determine this fact. The tower belonged first to the Lyles and later to the Douglases.

Elphinstone Castle

Two miles south of Tranent, on a hill overlooking Ormiston and the Tyne valley, stands Elphinstone Castle, a simple keep of the fifteenth century, and one of the most remarkable of its kind. Thanks to a modern roof, it is well preserved and bids fair to remain so.

It is an oblong keep, fifty feet by thirty-five, and about sixty feet high. Inside it contains a round vaulted basement which originally had a loft resting on corbels, a hall with a high pointed vault, and two stories above with wooden floors. The walls are about ten feet thick and contain a most remarkable maze of staircases, passages and chambers. To such an extent are the walls honeycombed that they resemble those of the Pictish brochs, and it is probable that this is due to a revival of this architectural tradition. Stairs, kitchen, servants' rooms and guest-rooms, with fireplaces, wall-closets and dressing-rooms, are all to be found in these walls. Alongside the fireplace in the great hall are two private rooms, one above the other. From the upper one a passage leads behind the fireplace flue, and in this is a window into the flue. As there is another window in the front of the flue, this gives a most unusual form of spy-hole into the hall. These spy-holes are common in Scotch castles, and there is another one into this same fireplace from a spiral stair in the wall. The upper part of the fireplace was probably also used for curing hams, etc., and access was gained by the passage mentioned.

Falside Castle

Seven miles east of Edinburgh, overlooking a plain which stretches along the shores of the Forth, stands the Castle of Falside. Under its walls, in September, 1547, was fought the battle of Pinkie, between the troops of Somerset and the Regent Arran. That the castle stands at all to-day is simply due to its solidity of construction, for the accounts of the battle state that its total demolition was averted only " through its first floor and roofs being arched over with stone."

The castle consists of an original keep about forty feet by thirty, to the south of which an L-shaped structure has been added, making a compact block with a reëntrant angle at the southwest. The keep is fourteenth or fifteenth century work, and the additions were made before the battle of Pinkie. The ruins are rather picturesque, with their round staircase tower, and remains of turrets.

Yester Castle

Yester Castle, on Hopes Water, in the parish of Yester, belonged to the Gifford family and was erected, according to Cosmo Innes, in

1268. It was originally triangular in shape
and stands on a high promontory between
two streams. The third side is defended by
a ditch fifty feet wide and twenty deep. It
has been a lofty structure. The remaining
walls are over six feet thick and about forty
in height. No traces of the internal arrangements can be found.

The most remarkable feature of the castle
is a subterranean chamber known as "The
Goblin Hall," referred to in "Marmion." It
is situated under the northern side, the rear of
the original castle, and lies mainly outside the
walls. It is thirty-seven feet long, thirteen
wide, and nineteen high, with a pointed vault
as a roof. It is entered from the castle by a
staircase defended by three barred doors. At
the north end is a sloping vaulted passage
thirty-three feet long, at right angles to the
hall. This also is defended with three barred
doors, one of which had a portcullis. The
outer door opens on the steep bank of the
stream, half way down the slope. Opposite
this passage is another similar one, but it was
never completed. Instead the builders cut
under it a steep stair, descending forty-four
feet into the rock to a well, now filled with
stones. Between these two passages in the

main chamber is a fireplace with a sloping flue running upwards. This chamber is undoubtedly a military post, and may possibly have been intended as a place of last resort, with means for escape into the stream bed.

CHAPTER XIII

CASTLES OF EAST LOTHIAN

(*Continued*)

Tantallon

THE fortress of Tantallon occupies a bold promontory at the mouth of the Firth of Forth, about three miles east of North Berwick. It is, like Doune, a magnificent specimen of the quadrangular castles built about the end of the fourteenth and the beginning of the fifteenth centuries. By the nature of its site, a precipitous point surrounded on three sides by the German Ocean, it was necessary to defend it artificially only on its fourth or western front. The entrance was over a drawbridge and through a strong deep gateway leading under a central tower, which formed an independent castle or keep. On each side of this is a huge battlemented curtain wall twelve feet thick and fifty feet high, falling back at an angle and flanked by the project-

ing keep. At the north and south extremities
are large round towers on the brink of the perpendicular rocks. The buildings forming the
other three sides of the quadrangle have been
undermined and fallen into the sea, save at
the north, where ruins still remain. The interior is a maze of broken staircases, ruined
chambers and dismal subterranean dungeons.

Before the west front lies a deep ditch cut
in the rock, and in front of this is a large level
court five hundred feet long and two hundred
wide, protected by an elaborate series of
ditches and mounds. The roadway runs for
a considerable distance between these outworks
and a burn which flows through a rocky ravine
to the south. It is thus completely commanded
by the outworks, as well as the towers of the
castle itself. The entrance archway passed
completely through the keep as at Doune. On
one side was a guardroom, on the other a
straight stair leading to the upper stories.
The interior of the keep is entirely gone. The
curtain walls make an angle with and are commanded by the projecting keep, as well as by
towers at each end. The staircases and passages in their thickness, which were filled in
solid by James V, have now been cleared out.

On the north side of the enceinte were the

hall and other apartments, with vaults below
and bedrooms above. The angle towers also
contained numerous rooms. Traces of structures erected against the curtains still remain,
and they were probably continued all round
the quadrangle. The new work done by
James V in 1528 is still visible in some of its
details. His object was to make the walls as
solid as possible, to prevent them from being
breached by artillery. To this end he filled
solid all the stairways and passages in the curtains, and they have but recently been cleared
out. The entire west front of the centre tower
was cased in new masonry of soft green tufa,
probably chosen as less liable to splinter under
the impact of cannon balls than the original
freestone. The fine ancient gateway was
blocked up, and only a narrow passage was
left in the wall in front of it. Embrasures for
guns at each side sweep the ditch and flank
the curtains. Other provisions for guns were
made at the gateway at the south end of the
main outer ditch, where they would sweep the
road of approach.

The exact date of the erection of Tantallon
is unknown. Scott says that it " is believed to
have belonged in more ancient times to the
Earls of Fife, the descendants of Macduff.

It was certainly in the possession of Isabel, the last countess of that renowned line, and was comprehended in the settlement which she made of her honours and estates upon Robert Stuart, Earl of Menteith, whom she recognized by that deed as her lawful and nearest heir in 1371." This Robert, the third son of Robert II, became afterwards Earl of Fife, Duke of Albany and Regent of Scotland. His son Murdoch, second duke, and also regent while James I was a prisoner in England, succeeded in 1419. In 1424 he was arrested at Doune with his whole family and all his adherents. His duchess, Isabella, daughter of the Earl of Lennox, was taken as a prisoner from her hall to the dungeon beneath it, and afterwards committed to Tantallon, while he was hurried away to Stirling. With two of his sons and the Earl of Lennox, he was beheaded the next year.

Two years later these dungeons became a prison for Alexander, Earl of Ross and Lord of the Isles, who had headed a rebellion in the Highlands. Unsuccessful, he submitted to James I, appearing in St. Giles Church in Edinburgh on Easter Day clothed only in his plaid, and delivering up his naked sword in token of unreserved submission. Nevertheless he was incarcerated in Tantallon in charge of George, fourth Earl of Angus, the king's nephew. This nobleman was granted the castle and the adjacent lands, which were constituted a barony in 1452. His son, Archibald " Bell-the-Cat," was confirmed in their possession in 1479. Later castle and barony passed to the younger branch of the family and with the growth of its power became a constant menace to the throne.

James V, a youth of fifteen, escaped from the power of the Douglases in June, 1528, as related elsewhere, and began war on the family. After the passage of a bill of attainder, which forfeited Tantallon, as well as the other possessions of the house of Douglas, twenty thousand men were sent to invest Tantallon. This castle was almost the only one in private possession which was strong enough to resist artillery, and was itself equipped with great guns, the embrasures for which are in striking contrast to the small musketry loopholes of most of the Scotch castles which belonged to private owners.

The great strength of the castle, which was indeed impregnable at the time of its erection, is indicated by the old proverb of the district, " Ding doon Tantallon? Big a brig to the

Bass." On this occasion the first half of the
saying proved true enough, for after twenty
days' siege, the thunders of " thrawin-mouthed
Meg and her Marrow," and other great guns,
proved unavailing, and the besiegers withdrew.
These guns, including " two great botcards
and two moyans, two double falcons and four
quarter-falcons," were borrowed from the
Duke of Albany, and to ensure their return,
three of the king's noblemen were impignorated at Dunbar. James withdrew to Edinburgh, leaving a small detachment to protect
his artillery. Earl Archibald had not been
present during the siege, for he declined to
trust himself within walls in war, holding to
the maxim of his ancestors that " it was better
to hear the lark sing than the mouse cheep."
Emerging from his retirement in Berwickshire, he crushed the detachment, captured the
leader, and then escorted him and his artillery
some distance towards Edinburgh, giving him
a message to the king that he was loyal to
the throne and hostile only to its evil advisers.
Despite this magnanimity, war against him
was successfully prosecuted and he was forced
to flee to England. In December of the same
year Tantallon surrendered for lack of supplies. James immediately put the castle into

a good state of defence. Says Lindsay of Pitscottie: " The King gart garnish it with men of war and artillery, and put in a new captain, to wit, Oliver Sinclair; and caused masons to come and ranforce the walls, which were left waste before, as trances and thorow passages, and made all massey work, to the effect that it should be more able in time coming to any enemies that would come to pursue it." This work is very evident to-day, as previously stated.

After the death of James in 1542, the Earl of Angus was allowed to return from exile and given back his possessions. He made the castle stronger than ever, but never regained his own power, though he lived here till his death in 1558. He was so meagrely furnished with necessities that he was unwilling to receive the English Ambassador, Sir Ralph Sadler, who sought personal safety in the castle during the progress of his unpopular negotiations on behalf of the young Prince Edward and infant Mary. He sent his servant to the castle and received the report that it was " cleanly unfurnished both of bedding and all manner of household stuff, and none to be bought or hired, nor no manner of provision to be made thereof, nor any kind of victual nearer than this town, which is twenty miles off." Sadler, however, went there, and observes that though Tantallon is poorly furnished, and " slendour lodging in it, yet, I assure you, it is of such strength as I must not fear the malice of mine enemies, and therefore do I now think myself to be out of danger."

In 1572 another English ambassador resided there, Killegrew, who came with secret instructions from Queen Elizabeth to cause the execution of the captive Queen Mary in such a manner as not to create a dangerous popular commotion.

In 1639 William, eleventh Earl of Angus, first Marquis of Douglas, here made stand for king and church against the Covenanters, and for the first time a hostile force " dang doon Tantallon," and garrisoned it against the king. In 1651 the Captain of the Bass captured an English store-ship bound for Leith and immured its crew in Tantallon. General Monk decided to reduce the fortress, with three regiments of horse and foot. He planted his artillery on high ground to the southwest and summoned Alexander Seton, commandant of the garrison, to surrender. Seton elected to resist. Two days' bombardment with mortars had no effect, and heavy siege guns were brought into operation. After twelve days continuous battering a breach was made in the curtain, the stones filling the ditch. The besiegers entered, only to find the garrison safe in the central tower, which was so impossible of reduction that they were allowed to capitulate on favourable terms. This was the last appearance of Tantallon in history. It remained habitable until the beginning of the eighteenth century, when it was dismantled by Sir Hew Dalrymple, who bought it of the Duke of Douglas, and left it a ruin for his heirs, who still own it. Scott has admirably described its former condition in " Marmion ": —

> " Tantallon vast,
> Broad, massive, high, and stretching far,
> And held impregnable in war.
> On a projecting rock it rose
> And round three sides the ocean flows,
> The fourth did battle walls enclose,
>   And double mound and fosse;
> By narrow drawbridge, outworks strong,
> Through studded gates, and entrance long,
>   To the main court they cross.
> It was a wide and stately square,
> Around were lodgings fit and fair,
>   And towers of various form,
> Which on the coast projected far,
> And broke its lines quadrangular;

Here was square keep, there turret high,
Or pinnacle that sought the sky,
Whence oft the warder could destroy
The gathering ocean-storm."

Though now long ruinous, there was a period in the last century when the castle was for a short time inhabited. A gang of thieves, under the leadership of a sailor whose vessel had come to grief on the island of Fidra, chose it as a place of refuge. They made entrance and exit by a rope ladder, which was carefully concealed when not in use. Sallying forth under cover of darkness, they obtained necessary supplies and provisions by plundering farmhouses, stealing sheep, and similar practices. Notwithstanding the ease of this mode of life, the members of the band deserted one by one, until only the sailor was left. He obtained employment in a neighbouring quarry, and might have lived in the castle indefinitely had he not been careless. Some girls working in the fields one evening saw a red cap at one of the upper windows. They thought they had seen a brownie, and told their story broadcast. As other people had seen lights at night, and a gardener engaged in planting ivy about the walls had been pelted by bits of mortar from above, the idea that the castle was haunted had gained ground. The tenant of the farm, however, believed in no such nonsense. He led a party of his workmen into the vaults, and soon discovered the offender, who was tried and sentenced to transportation.

The Bass

Nearly opposite Tantallon, and about two miles off shore, is the Bass, a stupendous insulated rock, a mile in circumference and four hundred and twenty feet high. Toward the north it is almost absolutely perpendicular, but on the south side the surface is conical, with steep slopes toward the sea. On the top there are about seven acres of short grass, which once afforded pasturage to twenty or thirty sheep. Under the rock there is a great cavern thirty feet high and five hundred feet long, which passes entirely through it from northwest to southeast. Within the cavern, the entrance to which is a hundred feet high, is a dark pool which holds water enough to drown an incautious visitor even at the lowest ebb of the tide. The only landing place is on the southeast side, and is commanded by the castle, which occupies the lowest of three terraces into which the slope of the top is divided.

Beague visited this castle during the regency of Mary of Guise and thus describes it in 1607: " Now, the island in which the castle stands is itself an impregnable rock, of a small extent and oval figure, cut out by the hands of nature; it has only one avenue that leads to it, and that is towards the castle, but so very difficult and uneasy, that by reason of the hidden sands that surround the rock, nothing can approach it but one little boat at a time. The island is so exorbitantly uneven, that till one reach the wall of the castle, he cannot have sure footing in any one place; so that — as I have often observed — those that enter it must climb up by the help of a strong cable thrown down for the purpose, and when they have got with much ado to the foot of the wall, they sit down in a wide basket, and in this posture are mounted up by strength of hands. There is no getting into this wonderful fortress by any other means. Formerly, it had a postern-gate which facilitated the entry, but it is now thrown down, and fortified in such a manner as is incredible." The tale of " hidden sands " is altogether untrue, as the channels all about the rock are of enormous depth.

The landing is now easier, as steps have been cut in the rock, but it is always difficult and often dangerous.

The earliest stories of the rock are religious. At the end of the sixth century it is said to have been selected as a refuge by St. Baldred, " Doctor of the Picts " and apostle of East Lothian. He is reputed to have been a pupil of St. Mungo of Glasgow, and his successor. When he retired to the Bass, his parish embraced wide districts of the mainland and he performed numerous miracles. When he died the representatives of three mainland parishes, Aldhame, Tynninghame and Preston, came to bury his remains. Unable to agree, they were instructed to pray for illumination over night. When morning came, they found three biers in place of one, each with a body decently covered, all so similar that no man could tell the difference. All strife being thus miraculously settled, each party joyfully bore off a body to solemn interment in its own church. However we may regard the stories of St. Baldred, a chapel undoubtedly existed on the rock in very early times. The Bass formed a parish by itself, and the " kirk in the Crag of the Bass " was dedicated to the saint in 1542 by order of Cardinal Beaton. This was the same

one which to-day stands as a ruin midway
between the castle and the top of the rock.
It stands on the traditional site of St. Baldred's cell, and was used for divine service
until after the Reformation, falling into disuse
because the number of inhabitants became so
small as to render it unnecessary. The Bass
is now included in the parish of North Berwick, to the incumbent of which is annually
due from it a stipend of twelve solan geese
" entire with feathers."

The Bass has long been famous for these
birds. Says Grose, " This rock is more particularly famous for the great flock of sea fowls
which resort thither in the months of May and
June, the surface of it being almost covered
with their nests, eggs and young birds. The
most esteemed among these birds is the Solon
Goose and the Kittie Waicke, there being only
one other place, that is an island in the west
of Scotland, called Ailscy, where these geese
breed; and from these two places the country
is furnished with them during the months of
July and August." Of these geese Defoe
has given us the following account: " They
feed on the herrings, and therefore 'tis observed they come just before, or with them,
and go away with them also; though 'tis evi-

dent they do not follow them, but go all away
to the north, whither none knows but themselves, and He that guides them. As they
live on fish, so they eat like fish, which, together with their being so exceeding fat, makes
them, in my opinion, a very coarse dish, rank,
and ill-relished, and soon gorging the stomach.
But as they are looked upon there as a dainty,
I have no more to say; all countries have
their several gusts and particular palates.
Onions and garlick were dainties, it seems, in
Egypt, and horse-flesh is so to this day in
Tartary, and much more may a solan goose
be so in other places. It is a large fowl,
rather bigger than an ordinary goose; 'tis
duck-footed, and swims as a goose; but the
bill is long, thick and pointed like a crane or
heron, only the neck much thicker, and not
above five inches long. Their laying but one
egg, which sticks to the rock, and will not fall
off, unless pulled off by force, and then not to
be stuck on again, though we thought them
fictions, yet, being there at the season, we
found true; as also their hatching by holding
the egg fast in their foot. What Nature
meant by giving these singularities to a crea-
ture that has nothing else in it worth notice,
we cannot determine."

For at least five centuries this rock belonged to the family of Lauder of the Bass.   Part of it was claimed by the Priory of St. Andrews, but in 1316 William Lamberton, Bishop of St. Andrews, deeded this to Robert Lauder, one of the companions of Sir William Wallace.   The family tenaciously held on to its singular possession, and stubbornly refused to sell it to various Scotch monarchs who desired it.   James VI visited it in 1581, at a time when it appears to have been temporarily in his possession, and requested the laird to sell it to him, but the uncompromising answer was, " Your Majesty must e'en resign it to me, for I'll have the auld craig back again."   Not until 1671 was the Crown able to purchase it, at the high price of four thousand pounds.

For centuries the Bass was a place of the utmost security, used alike as a stronghold and a prison.   In 1405, Robert III placed his son, the Earl of Carrick, afterwards James I, on the Bass in order to protect him from the designs of his brother, the Duke of Albany. A vessel being prepared to convey the young prince to France, where he was to receive an education, he embarked together with the Earl of Orkney and a small suite.   There was a truce at the time between England and Scotland, so that no danger was apprehended from the voyage; yet off Flamborough Head an armed merchantman of Wye captured the prince's vessel and bore him off to an incarceration which lasted for nineteen years. This misfortune — the very one the anxious father had wished to avoid — caused his death in Rothesay Castle when informed of it in 1406. James I returned from his long captivity in 1424, when Walter Stuart, eldest son of Murdoch, Duke of Albany was committed a prisoner to the Bass.

About 1570 the Earl of Morton attempted to secure the rock and his designs were exposed to the Regent Moray by Wishart of Pitarrow in the following words: " I hear say my Lord of Morton is trafficking to get the house of the Bass, which, if he does, he will stop some devices your Grace knows, and therefore were I in your Grace's stead, I would go between the cow and the corn. I tell you the auld Crag is a good starting hole, at least it will serve to keep them that you would be sure of."

This opinion was later acted on, for when the government obtained the rock a century later, it was constituted a state prison, the chapel becoming the magazine for the garrison. In the reigns of Charles II and James II numbers of the turbulent Covenanters were consigned to safe custody here. The names of thirty-nine are preserved, beginning with Robert Gillespie in 1672 and ending with John Spreul, a fanatical apothecary of Glasgow, who entered in July, 1681, and was released in May, 1687. In this month was also released Major Learmouth, a Covenanting officer, who was pardoned on account of failing health. Other well-known prisoners of this character were Sir Hugh and Sir George Campbell of Cessnock and Alexander Gordon of Earlston, while the best-known of all was John Blackadder, the elder, minister of Troqueer, father of Colonel John Blackadder. He was outlawed in 1674 and fled to Flanders, but later returned. On April 5th, 1681, he was " made prisoner in his house at Edinburgh " and after a form of examination, sent to the Bass. After four years of rigid imprisonment his health finally gave way. The Privy Council, in hot haste, gave permission to him to leave, on condition of confining himself to Edinburgh, but it was too late, and he died on the Bass in January, 1686. His grave, with a poetical inscription, is in North Berwick churchyard, while his gloomy cell on the western side of Bass Castle, with three small iron-barred windows, is still shown to curious visitors.

Other noted Covenanters confined here were James Mitchell, who attempted to assassinate Archbishop Sharp of St. Andrews in the High Street of Edinburgh in July, 1667, and Fraser of Brae, a noted preacher. Both were brought here on January 30th, 1677, in charge of a guard of twelve horse and thirty foot. Curious to relate, all these " martyrs of the Bass," as their co-religionists designate them, stayed in prison sometimes for years of their own accord or obstinacy, as all were offered liberty if they would promise not to molest the government.

There were prisoners on the Bass who were not Covenanters. A Quaker of Leith was sent here for railing at his parish minister; George Young, a Roman Catholic priest, was immured for an unknown offence. A third was John Philip, Episcopal curate of Queensferry, who lost his position for refusing the " Test." On his arraignment before the Privy Council in 1683 he was accused of denouncing the Duke of York as a " great tyrant detestable to the subjects; " for asserting that the Bishop of Edinburgh and the Lord Advocate were "bloody and cruel men, and that he hoped to see them suffer for it;" and for saying that the Earl of Argyle had been unjustly forfeited. For these heinous offences he was fined two thousand pounds sterling, to be paid within a fortnight, declared infamous and sentenced to life imprisonment on the Bass.

The garrison of the Bass refused to submit at the Revolution, and the deputy-governor, Charles Maitland, held out for James II until 1690, when he surrendered. The Stuart garrison held possession for only a few months, however. The Jacobite prisoners mutinied and gained possession of the rock. By the aid of friends on shore they obtained provisions and fitted out a galley, by means of which they plundered merchant vessels, exacted tribute from every ship which came within reach of their guns, and maintained themselves against the Crown for four years. In 1694, two ships of war sent by William III, assisted by numerous small vessels, destroyed their galley and blockaded the rock. Although reduced to extremities, they obtained easy terms of surrender through a stratagem of their leader, David Blair. A deputation having been sent to treat with him, he ranged about the walls all the hats and coats of the garrison, placed on muskets, leading the enemy to believe that the place was well garrisoned. He happened to have a few bottles of excellent French wine and brandy and some biscuits, with which he regaled his visitors. Convinced that the castle was well manned and provisioned, the Privy Council granted him easy terms, and thus obtained possession of the last Jacobite stronghold.

The fortifications were dismantled in 1701 and now only one corroded cannon remains. The buildings, though roofless, are externally entire, and may be entered by three flights of steps, formerly guarded by gates, now gone. The garden of the castle still produces some flowers, though the cherry trees mentioned by Fraser of Brae are gone. Visitors were formerly made " burgesses of the Bass " by drinking the disagreeable water of the well and receiving a flower out of the garden. Now its only citizens are the rabbits, the sheep, and the innumerable wild fowl, whose sudden flight when disturbed fills the air like the snow of the wintry storm.

In 1902 a lighthouse was erected at the top of the castle ruins, but all damage done at this time was scrupulously repaired, so that the castle, with the exception of the governor's house, has practically the same appearance as before the Northern Lights Commissioners began their operations. Access to the island is now much easier than formerly, as not only is there a good landing for the supply of the light, but the hotel-keeper at Canty Bay owns a launch, which carries parties to the island at a charge of ten shillings per trip, irrespective of the number of passengers. It is therefore quite feasible to visit Dirleton, Tantallon and the Bass in one day from Edinburgh.

Dirleton Castle

Two miles from North Berwick, and easily reached from there by a service of motor omnibuses, lies the little village of Dirleton, clustered at the foot of its castle. The scene is romantic; before the gray and battered ruins, standing in their beautiful gardens, lies the velvety village green, and about this, under tall trees and in pleasant little gardens, stand the houses of the feudal village.

The date of erection of Dirleton Castle is unknown. It was a strong place in 1297, when Edward I invaded Scotland. It then belonged to the family of De Vaux or De Vallibus, barons powerful in both kingdoms.

In July, 1298, it was besieged by Anthony
Beck, the martial Bishop of Durham, on the
part of Edward I. It made such an obstinate
resistance that the English troops exhausted
their supplies, and only escaped starvation by
subsisting on the beans and peas which they
found growing in the fields: a proof that agriculture was at that early date in a forward
state in southern Scotland. After a long siege
the castle surrendered, and was for a while an
English stronghold. Many entries regarding
its disposal and upkeep are found is the English records. The battle of Bannockburn sum-
marily cut short their occupation of it.

For several centuries afterward, history is
silent regarding the castle. The line of De
Vallibus became extinct in the fourteenth century, the castle passing in 1340 to Sir John
Haliburton by marriage. In 1440, Sir Walter
Haliburton, Lord High Treasurer of Scotland, was created a peer as Lord Dirleton.
A century later the male line again failed,
and the castle passed into the line of Ruthven. The last Earl of Gowrie here hospitably
entertained James VI, a fugitive from the
plague, and treated him to a histrionic repre-
sentation of Robin Hood's adventures. Then
followed the Gowrie conspiracy, when it was

alleged that a plot was made to seize the person of James at Perth on August 5, 1600.

The possession of Dirleton was the bribe held out by the unhappy earl to Logan, his principal associate. This person seems to have exceedingly coveted the estate, as he wrote to a friend, " I care not for all the other land I have in the kingdom, if I may grip of Dirleton, for I esteem it the pleasantest dwelling in Scotland." But it never came to him, for it was part of Ruthven's forfeit, and " James VI," says Camden, " gave it to Sir Thomas Erskine, Captain of the English Guard, for his happy valour in preserving him from the traitorous attempts of Gowrie, first creating him Baron Dirleton, afterwards, in 1606, Viscount Fenton, — the first viscount that ever was in Scotland."

In the Civil War, Dirleton was occupied by a party of Scottish moss-troopers. Against them in 1650 came Monk with five guns; joined by Lambert, the siege was entered on in form; after a gallant defence, the place fell, and the commandant, Waite, with two officers, were executed under martial law. The English demolished the castle and it was never occupied again.

The castle stands on a rock, which, though

not high, is well defined in its extent, and gave a firm foundation, proof against mining operations. Around this was sunk a deep moat at least fifty feet wide. This strength may account for the scanty records of siege, as only a great army, well equipped, could hope for success against so strong a place.

Of the thirteenth-century castle destroyed by Beck, there remain only a square and two round towers at the southwest and a foundation at the southeast. These were lighted only by small loops, and the rooms in the great round tower are polygonal vaults, with enormously thick walls.

The fifteenth-century castle was reached by a bridge on piers across the moat. The last eleven feet were spanned by a drawbridge, and when this was raised it left no doorsill visible on the castle front. Besides this, the entrance had gates and a portcullis, with machicolations above and a defensive opening in the floor of the portcullis room. On the east side of the castle there is a great range of ruinous buildings. The great hall was enormous, seventy-two feet by twenty-five, but one wall has fallen out. The cellar has the usual storerooms, and a prison. Beneath this, entered only by a hole in the floor, is a dungeon for the most important prisoners.

The north wing is entirely gone. On the southwest are buildings intended as private apartments, built in the sixteenth century. At some distance to the northeast, fronting on the village green, are a fine circular dovecot and an arched gateway, with some parts of the old outer wall. These are in the line of the boundary walls of the present estate.

The castle is shown to visitors, but the attendant is not always to be found, and I was unable to obtain any reliable information as to the times at which admission could be gained.

CHAPTER XIV

CASTLES OF THE BORDER

Fast Castle

THE insignificant ruins of this once impregnable fortress, the prototype of Scott's Wolf's Craig, stand on a bold peninsulated crag some seventy feet above the German Ocean, near St. Abb's Head in Berwickshire. The platform on which the castle stands is about two hundred and fifty feet long and a hundred wide, and absolutely inaccessible cliffs descend to the ocean level throughout its entire periphery, except on the west, where a deep chasm separates it from the mainland. This was twenty-four feet wide, and crossed by a drawbridge. While Fast Castle was impregnable to early weapons, it became untenable on the introduction of artillery, as the whole platform is commanded by the cliffs of the mainland, which tower high above it. The remains of the castle are very small, as it was destroyed by lightning in 1871.

The castle was a government fortress in 1333, but changed hands often, as was the case with Border holds in general. In 1410 it was in the hands of the English, under command of Thomas Holden, and was a scourge to the whole surrounding country by reason of the pillaging excursions which they made. Patrick, Earl of Dunbar, with a hundred men, surprised and captured the place. In 1548, being again in English possession, it was captured by the following stratagem: " The captain of Fast Castle had commanded the husbandmen adjoining to bring thither, at a certain day, great store of victuals. The young men thereabouts having that occasion, assembled thither at the day appointed, who taking their burdens from their horses, and laying them on their shoulders, were allowed to pass the bridge, which joined two high rocks, into the castle; where laying down that which they brought, they suddenly, by a sign given, set upon the keepers of the gate, slew them, and before the other Englishmen could be assembled, possessed the other places, weapons, and artillery of the castle, and then receiving the rest of the company into the same, through the same great and open gate, they wholly kept and enjoyed the castle for their countrymen." Sir Nicholas Throgmorton, writing in 1567, characterizes it as a place "fitter to lodge prisoners than folks at liberty."

In 1570, Sir William Drury, Marshall of Berwick, after taking Home Castle, besieged Fast Castle with two thousand men, and after capturing it, passed on to besiege Edinburgh, "leaving in it a garrison of ten, or, according to some, fourteen men — a force which was considered adequate for holding it out against all Scotland." The castle belonged at that time to the Homes, but passed by marriage in 1580 to Logan of Restalrig.

"In the reign of James VI," says Scott, in his "Provincial Antiquities," "Fast Castle became the appropriate stronghold of one of the darkest characters of that dark age, the celebrated Logan of Restalrig. There is a contract existing in the charter-chest of Lord Napier, betwixt Logan and a very opposite character, the celebrated inventor of the logarithms, the terms of which are extremely singular. The paper is dated July, 1694, and sets forth, 'Forasmuch as there were old reports and appearances that a sum of money was hid within John Logan's house of Fast Castle, John Napier should do his utmost diligence to search and seek out, and by all craft and ingine to find out the same, and, by the grace of God, shall either find out the same, or make it sure that no such thing has been there.' For his reward he was to have the exact third of what was found, and to be safely guarded by Logan back to Edinburgh. And in case he should find nothing, after all trial and diligence taken, he refers the satisfaction of his travel and pains to the discretion of Logan." Logan was afterwards a participant in the mysterious plot known as the Gowrie conspiracy. It was proposed to abduct the king in a boat from the garden of Gowrie House and carry him by sea to Fast Castle, which has a water gate. In this stronghold he was to be held at the disposal of Elizabeth or the plotters. That Logan was implicated in this affair was not known until he had been buried nine years, when his correspondence with the Earl of Gowrie was discovered in the hands of Sprott, a notary, who had stolen it from John Bour, its custodian. Sprott was executed, and the bones of Logan were disinterred and brought into court for trial on the charge of high treason, of which they were duly convicted. As attainder of treason implied confiscation of

property, this process was not as foolish as
it might appear.

Home Castle

Home or Hume Castle, one of the oldest
fortresses of the Border, stands on the summit
of a hill nine hundred feet above the level
of the sea, near Kelso, in the valley of the
Tweed. The walls which are now visible
merely serve to show the extent of the ancient structure, having been built on the old
foundations in the last century. The plan
proves, however, that castles of enceinte were
built in the Lowlands as well as the west, for
the castle dates from the thirteenth century.

The Homes, first barons, and later earls,
played a very prominent part in Scottish history. They were in all times powerful in the
Border, and occupied great offices in court
and council, enjoying at times almost regal
power. More than one of them was guilty
of treason, and one was executed for this
crime. The fifth Lord Home signed the order for imprisoning Mary in Lochleven Castle, and when she escaped, his six hundred
troops turned the fortune of the battle of
Langside against her. He died under con-
viction of treason for this.

The Castle of Home sustained many memorable sieges. More than once taken in civil war, it first fell to a foreign foe when Somerset captured it in 1547 after a stout resistance by Lady Home. Two years later its owner regained it. Again in 1569 it was reduced by the Earl of Sussex, and its last capture was in the Civil War.

In 1650, Cromwell, after he had captured Edinburgh, sent two regiments under Colonel Fenwick to reduce Home. The colonel sent in to Cockburn, the governor of the castle, a peremptory message to surrender. He got back the following communications: " Right Honourable, I have received a trumpeter of yours, as he tells me, without a pass, to surrender Hume Castle to the Lord General Cromwell. Please you, I never saw your general. As for Home Castle, it stands upon a rock. Given at Home Castle, this day, before 7 o'clock. So resteth, without prejudice to my native country, your most humble servant, T. COCKBURN." This was accompanied by the following doggerel verse:

> " I, Willie Wastle,
>   Stand firm in my castle;
>   And a' the dogs o' your town
>   Will no pull Willie Wastle down."

The roar of cannon, and the sight of Fenwick's troops drawn up ready to assault the breach, changed Cockburn's spirit, and he was very glad to be allowed to march out, leaving the castle to the ruin from which it never rose.

Cessford Castle

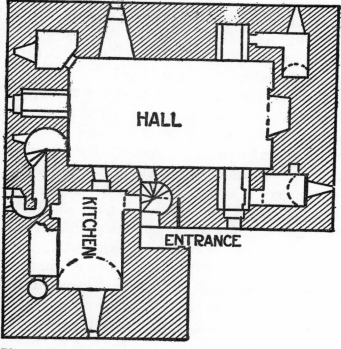

Plan of Cessford Castle

Cessford Castle, a Border fort of massive construction and great strength, stands between Kelso and Jedburgh on the Kale Water. It formerly belonged to the Kers, ancestors of the Duke of Roxburgh, and was built in the fourteenth century. It was besieged by Surrey in May, 1523, and he wrote thus to Henry VIII after its surrender, "I was very glad of the same appointment (capitulation) for in maner I sawe not howe it wolde have been won if they within wold have contynued their deffending." Jeffrey gives this account of the siege:

"In the month of May, 1523, the castle was besieged by Surrey, in the absence of its owner, with a numerous army, well provided with powerful ordnance, with which he battered the donjon with little effect. While the guns were playing against the castle, the Lord Leonard, Sir Arthur Darcy, Sir William Parr, and others, by means of scaling ladders, entered the barnkin, where they suffered severely from the iron guns of the castle and stones cast down upon them. They then attempted to scale the donjon, while the archers and ordnance kept the besieged engaged; but notwithstanding all the efforts of the besiegers, they could not prevail against the castle, which was gallantly defended. At last, when Surrey was despairing of success, the warden came within a mile of the castle, and not knowing how matters stood within the castle, but fearing the worst, offered to give up the place on his men being allowed to leave with their bag and baggage, to which Surrey was but too glad to accede, as he could not have taken the castle by force of arms. On the castle being delivered up, it was thrown down by the ordnance, and, while the destruction of its walls was going on, another party went on to Whitton Fort and cast it down." In 1545 it was again taken by Hertford. It ceased to be a dwelling house in 1650, but was used as a prison for Covenanters in 1666.

Smailholm Tower

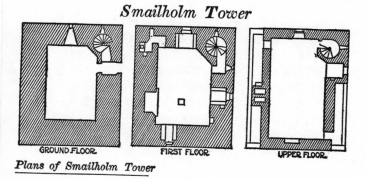

GROUND FLOOR.   FIRST FLOOR.   UPPER FLOOR.

Plans of Smailholm Tower

On the north side of the Tweed, in the parish of Smailholm, not far from Melrose,

stands the Border keep known as Smailholm
Tower. This is on the farm of Sandyknowe,
which was the property of the paternal grandfather of Sir Walter Scott, and one of the
homes of the poet's boyhood. Hence this
plain keep, of no importance in itself, has
thrown over it the glamour of the poet's description in " Marmion: " —

> "It was a barren scene, and wild,
>   Where naked cliffs were rudely piled;
>   But ever and anon, between,
>   Lay velvet tufts of loveliest green.
>   And well the lonely infant knew
>   Recesses where the wall-flower grew,
>   And honeysuckle loved to crawl
>   Up the low crag and ruined wall.
>   I deemed such nooks the sweetest shade
>   The sun in all its round surveyed;
>   And still I thought that shattered tower
>   The mightiest work of human power,
>   And marvelled as the aged hind
>   With some strange tale bewitched my mind,
>   Of forayers who, with headlong force,
>   Down from that strength had spurred their horse,
>   Their southern rapine to renew,
>   Far in the distant Cheviots blue,
>   And home returning filled the hall
>   With revel, wassel-rout, and brawl."

The tower stands on a rocky knoll which
well protects all sides save the west, where is

the entrance door, and remains of a barmkin or fore-court. The tower is absolutely plain externally, with a gabled roof, which has battlements on the sides and not on the ends, a late arrangement. Internally there are four stories, two of which are vaulted.

For two hundred years after the beginning of the fifteenth century, the tower belonged to the Prestons of Whytbank, from whom it passed to Scott of Harden. It now belongs to Lord Polwarth, his descendant. Sir Walter Scott, in a note prefixed to "The Eve of St. John," says that he wrote that poem about Smailholm Tower and its vicinity.

Darnick Tower

The visitor to Abbotsford by coach from Melrose, a very common way, will see between the two places, at a turn in the road, a very good example of the Border peel in Darnick Tower. This is a four-story structure erected in 1569, to which has been added for more room an ell of later date. The tower is about thirty feet by twenty-two, with walls about four feet thick. On the south front is a square turret which carries a wheel stair to the battlements, and is then continued a story higher than the main tower to form a watch-tower. The entrance door is in the base of this tower, and seems to have been well guarded by double doors. It gives into the kitchen, formerly a vaulted apartment, but now with a square ceiling. Above this is the hall, occupying the whole of the first floor. On the floor above are bedrooms, and in the roof, with an entrance from the battlements, which run almost around the roof, is an armoury. The battlements are carried on corbels, as is the watch-tower. Embrasures and numerous gargoyles add to the picturesqueness of the roof.

Darnick has continuously belonged to and been inhabited by the Heitons. It is built on the site of an older tower, which was destroyed by Hertford, in 1545. The present building was erected by virtue of a charter given by Mary and Darnley in 1566.

Branxholm Castle

Three miles from Hawick, on a bold bank overhanging the river Teviot, still stands Branxholm Castle, now no more a feudal fortress, but a noble mansion of the sixteenth century, with few relics of its earlier strength.

The lands of Branxholm were acquired by the Scotts in 1420 by exchange for their own estate in Lanarkshire. "One-half of the barony of Branxholm belonged to Sir Thomas Inglis. This gentleman was a lover of peace, ill able to bear the excitements and conflicts and perils of the Border warfare; and, happening one day to meet Sir William Scott of Buccleuch, who was then proprietor of the estate of Murdiestone in Lanarkshire, he strongly expressed to him his disgust at being obliged to sleep every night in boots and shirt of mail, and to hold himself in constant readiness for action with English freebooters, and his envy of the quiet and security and continual ease which the lairds of Clydesdale enjoyed at a distance from the Border, and behind the ramparts of the Leadshill mountains. Scott loved frolicking and feud as much as Inglis hated them; and he abruptly answered, 'What say you to an exchange of estates? I like that dry land of yours much better than this stretch of wet clay.' 'Are you serious?' replied Inglis. 'If you be, take the dry land with all my heart, and let me have the clay.' They made short work of the bargain; and Scott soon found himself laird of Branxholm, and significantly re-

marked as he got possession of it that the
cattle of Cumberland were as good as those
of Teviotdale. He promptly gathered around
him a strong body of hardy, active, resolute,
unscrupulous, well-mounted retainers, and
rode so often and vigorously at their head
across the Border, and made such smart reprisals upon the English for any occasional
injury they did him, that he soon and permanently made the balance of account between
Cumberland and Teviotdale very much in his
own favour; and his successors, for several
generations, rivalled his energy and closely
followed his example, — so that they rendered
all the country round them resonant with the
clang of arms, and rich with well-defended
or rapidly augmented flocks."

In 1463, Sir Walter Scott and his son, who
had by now acquired the whole of the lands
of Branxholm, surrendered them to the king
and received them back as a barony, to be
held on rent of a red rose. The castle now
became the chief seat of the Buccleuch family,
was enlarged and strengthened, and became
one of the strong posts of the Border. Sir
Walter thus sings its pride: —

" Nine-and-twenty knights of fame
  Hung their shields in Branxholm Hall;

Nine-and-twenty squires of name
Brought them their steeds to bower from stall;
    Nine-and-twenty yeomen tall
    Waited duteous on them all;
    They were all knights of mettle true,
    Kinsmen to the bold Buccleuch.

"Ten of them were sheathed in steel,
  With belted sword, and spur on heel;
  They quitted not their harness bright
  Neither by day, nor yet by night;
    They lay down to rest
    With corselet laced,
  Pillowed on buckler, cold and hard;
    They carved at the meal
    With gloves of steel
  And they drank the red wine through the helmet
      barred.

"Ten squires, ten yeomen, mail-clad men,
  Waited the beck of the wardours ten;
  Thirty steeds, both fleet and wight,
  Stood saddled in stable day and night,
  Barbed with frontlet of steel, I trow,
  And with Jedwood-axe at saddle bow;
  A hundred more fed free in stall;
  Such was the custom of Branxholm Hall."

Branxholm Hall was such a thorn in the
flesh of the English that it was burned by the
Earl of Northumberland in 1532, and in 1570
a force under the Earl of Sussex and Lord

Hounsdon was sent to completely destroy it. When they arrived, they found that the Scotts had burnt their own tower. This did not satisfy the English troops, who " cawysed powder to be sett, and so blew up the on halfe from the uther." Rebuilding was immediately undertaken by Scott, and finished by his wife in 1576, after his death. These buildings still stand.

Goldielands

Goldielands, a Border peel, famed in Border balladry, stands above the Teviot, a mile or so above Hawick. It is a typical keep of late date, and offers nothing of especial interest to the visitor, aside from its associations. It was owned by a branch of the Scotts of Branxholm, the last of whom was hanged over his own doorway for his maraudings and plunderings.

Dryhope Tower

The home of Mary Scott, the " Flower of Yarrow," is a dismantled and ruinous keep overlooking St. Mary's Loch. It is arranged much as all other simple keeps in Scotland, but is in extremely dilapidated condition. It

was destroyed in 1592 by Scott of Goldielands, because the owner had been "art and
part in the late treasonable attempt against
the king at Falkland." The chief interest of
the castle lies in the legends and ballads of
the "Flower of Yarrow," famous for her
beauty, and the heroine of a tragic combat
when seven Scott brothers and seven Douglas
brothers fought for her and perished to the
last man. She was eventually married to
Scott of Harden, as famous for his freeboot-
ing as she was for her beauty, and in this
career she heartily encouraged him. The story
is that when the larder of their home was
empty, the laird and his sons got nought for
dinner but a pair of spurs instead of a roast;
upon the uncovering of this significant but
unsatisfying dish, they were accustomed to
quit the table and ride across the Border, soon
driving back their dinner before them.

Newark on Yarrow

Four miles from Selkirk stands the strong
and ancient pile of Newark Castle, once a
royal hunting seat in Ettrick Forest and later
the hold of the Scotts of Buccleuch. It is the
scene of the "Lay of the Last Minstrel:"

" He paused where Newark's stately tower
Looks out from Yarrow's birchen bower:
The Minstrel gazed with wishful eye —
No humbler resting-place was nigh.
With hesitating step, at last,
The embattled portal-arch he passed,
Whose ponderous gate and massy bar
Had oft rolled back the tide of war,
But never closed the iron door,
Against the desolate and poor.
The Duchess marked his weary pace,
His timid mien, and reverend face,
And bade the page the menials tell
That they should tend the old man well:
For she had known adversity,
Though born in such a high degree;
In pride of power, in beauty's bloom,
Had wept o'er Monmouth's bloody tomb! "

The keep is quite large, sixty-five feet by forty, with walls ten feet thick, and is surrounded by a barmkin or courtyard. It was built in the fifteenth century. In 1548 it was captured by the English. In 1645 a hundred prisoners from the battlefield of Philiphaugh were executed in the courtyard. In 1650 it was occupied by Cromwell. Anna, Duchess of Monmouth and Buccleuch, resided here after the execution of her husband, the Duke of Monmouth, under James VII, and is the duchess of Scott's poem.

Hermitage Castle

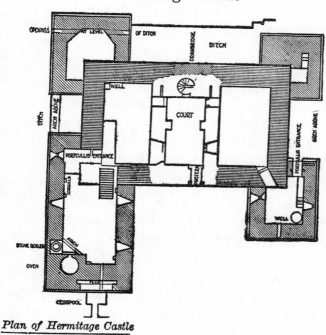

Plan of Hermitage Castle

Hermitage Castle in Liddesdale, four miles from Riccarton Junction, was one of the largest and strongest on the Border, and remains in an exceptionally good state of repair. It stands on the Hermitage Water, between two other small streams, which gave plenty of water for filling the ditches. It was built in the thirteenth century by Walter Comyn, Earl of Menteith, and its erection was one of

the causes given by Henry III, in 1243, for
the assembling of an army to invade Scotland.
He claimed that the fortress was too near the
Liddel Water, the boundary between England and Scotland, and that it was a standing
menace to the English frontier.   The castle
was intended as a royal possession, but passed
into the hands of the lords of the district.
From the family of de Soulis, who acquired
it from Comyn, it was forfeited to the Crown,
and was granted by David II to William of
Douglas, Knight of Liddesdale.   From him
it passed to the Earls of Angus, and by them
was enlarged about the beginning of the fifteenth century.   In 1492, Archibald, sixth
Earl of Angus, exchanged Hermitage Castle
and Liddesdale for Bothwell Castle on the
Clyde, which had belonged to Hepburn, Earl
of Bothwell.   While in the possession of the
Douglases, the valiant Sir Alexander Ramsay of Dalhousie was confined in its dungeon
without food or water; and although he managed to subsist for a time on the grains of
corn which fell through the floor from the
granary above, he eventually starved to death
in his prison.

The most famous episode in the history of
Hermitage is the visit made by Queen Mary

to the Earl of Bothwell. He had been severely wounded in an attempt to capture a desperate freebooter called Elliott of the Parke, and lay seriously ill in the castle. When the news was conveyed to Mary, she made the journey to Hermitage and back to Jedburgh, forty-eight miles over roadless wastes and barren hills, in drenching rain, in a single day, nearly paying with her life for her foolhardiness. When the Hepburn titles and lands were forfeited by Francis Stuart, the castle passed to the Buccleuchs, who still hold it.

The earliest portion of the castle is the wall surrounding the small central court. Only one story of this remains, but it is evident that this keep originally had wooden floors. What the plan of this oldest castle was cannot now be told, as all other traces of it have disappeared. When the castle was enlarged, probably by William Douglas, Knight of Liddesdale, in the beginning of the fourteenth century, a keep on the prevalent rectangular plan was built, with the unusual result of producing a double tower with a central courtyard.

The final change took place in the fifteenth century. This was the time when keeps were enlarged into courtyard castles, but Hermitage was extended by building on a tower at each angle. Thus the extra accommodation was provided while the towers furnished additional security by flanking all sides of the keep. The castle was now extremely strong, both in situation and artificial defences. It was surrounded by ditches and a mound, and access was gained only by very small gateways, the most important of which was defended by a portcullis.

The two eastern and the two western towers were mutually united many feet above the ground by pointed arches. These resemble the arched gateway at Dirleton, but were not intended for that purpose, as there is no doorway in either arch. The probable reason for this construction is that the castle was defended at the top by wooden hoardings outside the ramparts, and these arches enabled them to be carried entirely around the castle, while the spaces between the towers would otherwise have been too narrow to allow them to be conveniently carried into the recess. The holes for the beams are still to be seen, and also doorways from which the hoardings could be reached. There is also provision for two or three levels of wooden defensive platforms in the recesses under the great arches,

with more doorways. The castle was altered
for artillery by Lord Maxwell in 1540, when
a number of windows and doorways were built
up to form embrasures for guns.

Neidpath Castle

Neidpath Castle, near Peebles, is more familiar because of the facility with which it
can be photographed, and its picturesqueness
of situation, than for its history. It stands
on a high bank, overlooking a bend in the
Tweed, and is a most conspicuous object in
the landscape. It is a keep built on the
L-plan, and probably dates back to the fourteenth century, although the time of its erection is difficult to determine. It is built with
a very peculiar hard mortar, which has caused
the assertion that it is of Norman construction, like the Tower of London. So hard is
the cement, that a staircase was dug out of
the thickness of the wall in the seventeenth
century, without injuring the structure.

The walls of the tower are about eleven feet
thick. The original door was on the basement
floor, on the side facing the river. Access was
had to the upper floors by a spiral stair in the
wall. The tower was divided vertically into

three vaults, each of the lower two being sub-divided by a wooden floor. It thus contained five floors. The corners are all rounded, and the parapets had no projecting bartizans.

In the seventeenth century it was altered somewhat by placing the principal entrance on the eastern front and adding a forecourt, in which were a number of domestic buildings.

The castle was for centuries the property of the Hays of Yester. In 1686 it was sold to the Duke of Queensberry, and given by him to his son, the first Earl of March. The new proprietors beautified the estate by lay-ing out gardens and planting trees until it became the most beautiful estate in Peebles-shire. The third earl, who became Duke of Queensberry, despoiled the estate by cutting all the ornamental trees, and allowed the gar-dens to become a grassy sward. Wordsworth condemned this act in one of his sonnets, " Composed at ——— Castle: "

"Degenerate Douglas! Oh, the unworthy lord!
   Whom mere despite of heart could so far please,
   And love of havoc (for with such disease
   Fame taxes him), that he could send forth word
   To level with the dust a noble horde,
   A brotherhood of venerable trees,
   Leaving an ancient dome, and towers like these

> Beggared and outraged! Many hearts deplored
> The fate of those old trees; and oft with pain
> The traveller, at this day, will stop and gaze
> On wrongs which Nature scarcely seems to heed:
> For sheltered places, bosoms, nooks, and bays,
> And the pure mountains, and the gentle Tweed,
> And the green silent pastures, yet remain."

Of history, Neidpath Castle has little. Almost its only historical event was its capture by Cromwell after a short defence. It seems to have been visited at various times by several Scotch monarchs.

A touching legend of the castle is told by Scott as follows: — "There is a tradition that when Neidpath Castle was inhabited by the Earls of March, a mutual passion subsisted between a daughter of that noble family and a son of the Laird of Tushielaw, in Ettrick Forest. As the alliance was thought unsuitable by her parents, the young man went abroad. During his absence the lady fell into a consumption; and at length, as the only means of saving her life, her father consented that her lover should be recalled. On the day he was expected to pass through Peebles on the road to Tushielaw, the young lady, though much exhausted, caused herself to be carried to the balcony of a house in Peebles belonging to her family, that she might see him as he rode past. Her anxiety and eagerness gave such force to her organs that she is said to have distinguished his horse's footsteps at an incredible distance. But Tushielaw, unprepared for the change in her appearance, and not expecting to see her in that place, rode on without recognizing her or even slackening his pace. The lady was unable to support the shock, and, after a short struggle, died in the arms of her attendants." This account is quoted from the introduction to Scott's poem, "The Maid of Neidpath," of which the last verse is as follows: —

> "He came — he pass'd — a heedless gaze,
>   As o'er some stranger glancing;
> Her welcome, spoke in faltering phrase,
>   Lost in his courser's prancing —
> The castle arch, whose hollow tone
>   Returns each whisper spoken,
> Could scarcely catch the feeble moan
>   Which told her heart was broken."

CHAPTER XV

Johnny Armstrong's Tower

IN the valley of the Esk, between Canonbie and Langholm, stands the most famous of all the Border keeps, Hollows or Gilnockie Tower. It is exactly like many other peels internally and externally, except that it has a beacon lantern on the top of the gable. These were frequent along the Border, but existing examples are very rare. The law of raising the countryside by fire was well understood, and continually practised. In 1570 the Earl of Sussex promulgated an order to the English wardens of the Border as follows:— " Everie man that hath a castle or a tower of stone shall upon everie fray raysed in thie night, give warning to the countrie by fire in the topps of the castle or towre in such sort as he shall be directed from his warning castle."

The Armstrongs first appeared in this part

of Scotland early in the sixteenth century, when the redoubtable Johnny built himself this tower against the laws, which stringently forbade the erection of any strength in the debatable lands without license from the Crown. They soon became one of the most powerful clans on the Scottish side, and built themselves numerous keeps, the ruins of which are scattered all through Liddesdale.

" The habitual depredations of this Border race had rendered them so active and daring, and at the same time so cautious and circumspect, that they seldom failed either in their attacks or in securing their prey. Even when assailed by superior numbers, they baffled every assault by abandoning their dwellings, and retiring with their families into thick woods and deep morasses, accessible by paths only known to themselves. One of their most noted places of refuge was the Terras-moss, a frightful and desolate marsh, so deep that two spears tied together could not reach the bottom."

Several of the Scottish monarchs tried in vain to end their raids, but it remained for James V, after escaping from the power of the Earls of Angus, to break the power of the Border raiders. Knowing that to curb the followers, he must overawe the chieftains, he forfeited or imprisoned the whole of them, except Cockburn of Henderland and Scott of Tushielaw, commonly called the "King of the Border," who were publicly executed.

In June, 1529, the king at the head of his army marched from Edinburgh through Ettrick Forest, and into the southern border. During this expedition, Johnny Armstrong presented himself to the king, with thirty-six followers, in the hope of being pardoned. Pitscottie says that he "was the most redoubted chieftain that had been for a long time on the borders either of Scotland or England. He ever rode with twenty-four able gentlemen, well-horsed; yet he never molested any Scottish man." It was said that from the Border to Newcastle, every Englishman, of whatever state, paid him tribute.

He "came before the king with his foresaid number (thirty-six), richly apparelled, trusting that, in respect of this free offer of his person, he should obtain the king's favour. But the king, seeing him and his men so gorgeous in their apparel, frowardly turned himself about and bade them take the tyrant out of his sight, saying, 'What wants that knave

that a king should have?' John Armstrong
made great offers to the king, that he should
sustain himself with forty gentlemen ever
ready at his service, on their own cost, without wronging any Scottish man. Secondly,
that there was not a subject in England, duke,
earl, or baron, but, within a certain day, he
should bring him to his majesty, either quick
or dead. At length he, seeing no hope of
favour, said very proudly, ' It is folly to seek
grace at a graceless face: but, had I known
this, I should have lived on the borders in
despite of King Henry and you both; for I
know that King Harry would down-weigh
my best horse with gold to know that I were
condemned to die this day.' "

In spite of his entreaties, he and all his followers were hanged on trees and buried at
Ceanlarig chapel. The rest of the family continued in their high-handed life, and were
never suppressed until James VI made a cam-
paign against them in which their leaders were
brought to the scaffold, their houses razed,
and their estates conferred on strangers, so
thoroughly that the very name of Armstrong
was exterminated from the whole district
where they had held sway.

Lochmaben Castle

Lochmaben, the hereditary home of the Bruces, which, with its outworks, covered sixteen acres, was the most powerful castle on the Border, and was, before the invention of gunpowder, all but impregnable. By its location it was the key to southwestern Scotland, and the scene of many conflicts. It stands on a flat peninsula which juts into Loch Maben. Across the isthmus are the remains of a deep ditch, through which flowed the waters of the loch, converting the site into an island. Within this ditch are a second, third and fourth, all of which except the last were crossed by movable drawbridges. The fourth ditch, about twenty feet wide, flowed under the two side walls of a forecourt through arched openings which were presumably defended by bars or gates. Thus access to the castle was had only by boats, and the main gate, opening on the ditch, was commanded by all the four walls of the court. Within the courtyard of the castle proper there are a few remains of buildings, probably of late date, but so ruinous that nothing can certainly be said about them The castle itself is wholly in ruins, having long been used as a quarry.

It was a square courtyard of typical thirteenth-century plan, and originally had walls which were very thick and high.

The present building is not the original castle of the Bruces, which stood on an eminence called the Castlehill on the other side of the loch.

Robert de Brus was the son of a noble knight of Normandy who came into England with William the Conqueror, and was given the manor of Skelton. Having become a friend of David I before that king came to the throne, he was granted by him in 1124 the lordship of Annandale, with right to enjoy his castle there, with all the customs appertaining to it. A charter of William the Lion of about 1170, dated at Lochmaben, confirms to the third Lord of Annandale all the property possessed by his father. The Bruce who was competitor for the throne and grandfather of Robert I died at Lochmaben in 1295. He was the builder of the present castle. Edward I took possession of the castle in July, 1298, strengthened and provisioned it, and placed a garrison there. When Bruce left London in 1304, he directed his course toward Lochmaben. Near the west marches he met a foot traveller, whom he questioned and found to be a bearer of messages from Comyn to the English king. He seized and read the letters, which urged his imprisonment or death. After beheading the messenger, he went on to Lochmaben, where he found shelter. Later he proceeded to Dumfries to see Comyn, and the result was the death of the latter.

When Bruce obtained the throne he gave the castle of Lochmaben to Randolph, Earl of Moray. The English conferred it on the Bohuns, Earls of Hereford, and when Randolph returned from captivity in France in 1335, he " found William Bohun in his own castle of Lochmaben, and bearing sway over all his own lands of Annandale." In 1342 the Scots made a vigorous attempt to capture the castle from the garrison placed there by Edward III, but their efforts were unsuccessful. The next year David II imprudently led his forces into England, and was severely harassed by the garrison of the castle. In 1346 he besieged and took it, and executed the governor. After the Battle of the Standard, the castle again opened its gates to an English garrison, who held it for years, though continually at war with the surrounding population. The garrison's sallies and forages led to frequent reprisals by raids into England, particularly one into Westmoreland in 1380, when the fair of Penrith was plundered with great booty. In 1384 the Earl of Douglas and Archibald Douglas, Lord of Galloway, raised a formidable force to take vengeance on the garrison, who had wasted their lands, and, capturing it, drove the English out of Annandale.

In 1409 the Earl of March resigned the castle to the Regent Albany, who gave it, with the lordship of Annandale, to the Earl of Douglas. The Douglases defied the king's authority in 1450, and James II besieged and took Lochmaben, which was confiscated five years later, at the attainder of the Earl of Douglas. Thereafter, until the Union, it remained a Crown possession.

James IV built a great hall in the castle, and visited it during a royal progress. In 1511 he appointed Lauder of the Bass governor for seven years. In the minority of James V, Robert, Lord Maxwell, was appointed governor for nineteen years. Queen Mary visited it in 1565, when pursuing rebels in Dumfriesshire. In 1588, James VI besieged the castle and took it from Lord Maxwell, and thereafter the governorship was conferred on the Earl of Annandale.

The governor of the castle had a salary of three hundred pounds Scots, and the right of fishing in the lochs with boats and nets. For the support of the garrison, he had from every parish of Annandale, the fattest cow that could be produced, thirty-nine meadow geese, and " Fasten's e'en hens." The privileges were claimed long after the castle was dismantled, and anger for these exactions had much to do with the stripping of the castle of all its cut stone by the people of the vicinity.

Torthorwald Castle

Torthorwald Castle, the wreck of a massive keep of the fourteenth century, stands four miles east of Dumfries, on a ridge between Nithsdale and Annandale. It stands on a mound surrounded by ancient earthworks, probably the defences of a primitive fortification of an era before castles were built of stone. The tower, one end of which has fallen out, much resembles Dundonald Castle on a smaller scale. The castle belonged to the Carlyles, long inhabitants of this district.

Thomas Carlyle was of this stock, and says, "What illustrious genealogies we have; a whole regiment of Thomas Carlyles, wide possessions, all over Annandale, Cumberland, Durham, gone all now into the uttermost wreck, — absorbed into Douglasdom, Drumlanrigdom, and the devil knows what."

Caerlaverock Castle

Seven miles south of Dumfries, where the river Nith flows into the Solway Firth, stands the magnificent and ancient Castle of Caerlaverock. It occupies a situation which must have been very strong, being placed at the edge of an extensive marsh, which surrounds the castle on all sides except the north. About the base of the castle walls runs a wide and deep moat which is still full of water. Outside of this is a great earthen mound seventy feet wide. The approach to the castle is from the north, where it is joined by a drawbridge to firm ground.

The castle as it stands to-day shows the work of several generations of builders. The triangular walls of enceinte belong to a very early period, and were probably standing when Edward I besieged the castle in 1300.

The castle at this period was like all the early castles, a simple enceinte, probably provided with towers similar to those now standing. The description written at this time by Walter of Exeter would serve fairly well to-day. The castle was finally taken and the towers demolished. It was soon rebuilt, and the front erected at this time, identified by the shape of an Edwardian splayed loophole, is about ten feet behind the present front. The round towers were rebuilt at a later period on the stumps of those destroyed by Edward, and at the same time the round towers at the southern corners were erected.

The buildings of the courtyard were built at two or three different times, first those on the west, and last of all, about 1620, the fine Renaissance structures on the east and south sides.

The entrance to the castle is admirably defended. The entrance passage passes between the two great towers, with a guard room on each side, and is considerably contracted before its opening into the courtyard. At the outer end was a portcullis, worked by very elaborate machinery in a room overhead. The twin front towers are twenty-six feet in diameter and provided with gun-holes. As these

were built with the towers, their date is thus
fixed as not earlier than the fifteenth century. They contain three stories, the lower
vaulted, and the upper one domed at the
top. They are finished with corbelled parapets.

The west range was probably built in the
first half of the sixteenth century. The original wall of enceinte was raised to give sufficient height to the rooms within, and the
masonry is much inferior to the original stonework. One external window only was made
to light these rooms. In this building there
were a hall and retiring room on the ground
floor, and the library and a smaller apartment
on the floor above. Later a circular stairway
was built between this block and the entrance
doorway, and the high archway inside the
entrance was erected. The last building at
Caerlaverock was the fine Renaissance range
on the east and south sides. This still stands
in its full height, three stories, on the east,
and is highly ornamented. The windows have
shafts at the sides, with Ionic caps, and the
pediments are filled with sculpture portraying
classic myths and heraldic emblems. The
rooms are lighted by windows on both sides,
as the necessity for serious defence had passed

away, and so it was deemed safe to cut up
the curtain wall to any desired extent. This
side of the court contains service rooms on
the ground floor and chambers above. The
fireplaces are richly carved. On the south
side was the banqueting hall, a most magnificent apartment, now entirely ruined, and
with its walls fallen in many places. The
doorway by which it was entered is a splendid
and finely decorated arch. The chapel is said
to have been over the hall.

The Romans possessed a station here, and
the remains of one of their camps may be
seen a little to the west of the castle. The
barony of Caerlaverock belonged to the family of Maxwell as early as the time of Malcolm Canmore. Herbert, the eleventh baron
of the line, fell under the banner of Bruce
at Bannockburn. In his time the castle was
besieged and taken by Edward I in person,
after a protracted siege. This was prosecuted
with all the knowledge of the period, but so
inadequate were the means of attack as com-
pared with the defensive powers of the massive walls, that it was discovered, on the surrender, that the garrison had consisted of only
sixty men. Edward demolished the towers,
but seems to have put the castle into a state

of defence again, for it was held against the Scots, and being later taken by them, was again besieged and captured.

In 1355, Roger Kirkpatrick of Closeburn, faithful to the Scottish Crown, captured this castle and Dalswinton from the English, and by his firm loyalty kept the whole of Nithsdale for Scotland. Two years later he was atrociously murdered in his own castle by Sir James Lindsay, because Kirkpatrick had won the lady whom Lindsay desired for his wife. The murderer was executed for his crime by order of David II. The castle was given back to the Maxwells, who have been its owners through all of recorded history.

In 1425 Murdoch, Duke of Albany, convicted of high treason, was brought here and confined in Murdoch's Tower, until the time came for him to be taken back to Stirling, where he died on the Heading Hill. Lord Maxwell had been arrested with him, but was liberated, to be later one of the conservators of the truce concluded with England in 1438. Robert, the next Lord Maxwell, was slain near Bannockburn with James III in 1488. Another Maxwell, Robert, " made a road into England, and spoiled all Cumberland," in

1526. With his two brothers, he was made a prisoner at the rout of Solway Moss, in November, 1542. He was imprisoned in the Tower of London, and ransomed a year later for one thousand merks. King James was at this time residing in Caerlaverock, and he was so mortified at the defeat of the Scots, that he retired to Falkland Palace and died of grief within a month. Henry VIII was desirous at this time of obtaining the mastery of the castles of Caerlaverock, Lochmaben, and Langholm, and ordered Lord Wharton, his envoy, to examine them, " and knowe their strength and scituations; " if he found them tenable, he was " ernestly to travaile with Robert Maxwell for the delyverie of the same into his majestie's hands, if with money and reward, or other large offers, the same may be obtayned."

Sir John Maxwell, son of Robert, known as Lord Herries, was a faithful follower of Queen Mary, and fled with her from Langside. He afterward wrote a history of her reign. He was forfeited in parliament, but died a natural death in 1594. His son was placed in possession of his estates in 1569. In 1570 the Earl of Surrey led fifteen thousand men into Scotland by command of

Queen Elizabeth to support James VI after the death of the Regent Moray. His army " took and cast down the castles of Caerlaverock, Hoddam, Dumfries, Tinwald, Cowhill, and sundry other gentlemen's houses, dependers on the house of Maxwell; and having burnt the town of Dumfries, they returned with great spoil into England."

The castle does not seem to have been seriously injured, and was fully restored by Robert, first Earl of Nithsdale, after his accession in 1620. During the civil war, he expended his whole fortune in behalf of the cause of Charles I. In 1640 Lieutenant-Colonel Home attacked the castle and besieged it for thirteen weeks. The owner refused to surrender until he had received letters from the king, authorizing him to deliver up Caerlaverock and Threave on the best terms he could obtain. This was the end of the castle as a place of defence or habitation, the Maxwells removing to another house.

Threave Castle

Threave Castle, a fourteenth-century keep of the Douglases, stands on an island in the River Dee, about two miles from the town of

Castle-Douglas. The only access to the island is by fording the river at the south end. The castle consists of a tower, about forty feet by sixty, surrounded by portions of a wall which formerly had round turrets at each corner. The entrance was by a gate tower, from the top of which a drawbridge gave access to the second floor of the keep. There is also a doorway at the ground level. The basement was vaulted, and above this were three wooden floors, and a wooden flat roof, supported by strut beams, the recesses for which in the walls may still be seen. The main defence of the castle was by wooden hoardings which were supported on projecting beams all around the castle. The double row of holes for the reception of these beams may still be seen, and all around the walls there is a tunnel just large enough to crawl through, intended to give access to the inner ends of the beams to fasten them in place. This is the best preserved example of this kind of defence to be seen in Scotland.

Threave Castle was built by Archibald Douglas, an illegitimate son of the good Sir James Douglas, about the end of the fourteenth century. In spite of the fact that he was a bastard he was created Lord of Gallo-

way, and later succeeded to the earldom of
Douglas. He served in both home and foreign wars, taking part in the battles of Hali-
don in 1333 and Poitiers in 1356. His cruel
and hard-hearted oppression of his tenants
and peasants in Galloway earned him universal execration and the title of " Archibald
the Grim." He died at Threave in 1401. In
1455 the castle was forfeited to the Crown
by Earl James Douglas, and was afterwards
transferred to the custody of the Maxwells.
In 1640 the Earl of Nithsdale held this castle
for Charles I, as well as Caerlaverock, and
armed, paid and fed a garrison of eighty men;
nor did he surrender except on written orders
from the king. Thereafter the War Council
" ordaines the hows of Threave to be plighted,"
" the sklait roofe of the hows and battlement
thairof be taken downe, with the lofting
thairof, dores and windows of the samen, and
to tak out the haile iron worke of the samen."
Power is further given the Laird of Bal-
maghie " to work his will with the castle, and
to put sex musqueteires and ane sergand
thairin, to be enterteanit upon the public."
Since that time the elements have had full
sway in the ruined tower.

Dunskey Castle

Dunskey Castle, on the high and rocky seaboard in the town of Portpatrick, is an ancient seat of the Blairs. The present building was erected in the sixteenth century, and is now very ruinous. It occupies a strong site, cutting off with its eastern front a rocky neck, which is further cut across by a deep moat. The building is an L-shaped keep, with a long wing stretching northward. It does not figure in history to any extent, but makes an attractive addition to a desolate landscape.

Ayrshire is full of castles, numbered by hundreds, a single parish on the west coast being able to enumerate fifteen. In spite of this multiplicity, few of them possess any particular interest except as picturesque adjuncts to the landscape. The western provinces were far removed from the capital, and all the great families had their seats in more convenient parts of the country. Far from the Border, foreign war scarcely disturbed the peaceful current of agricultural life in the west, and Ayrshire is happy in that it has no history. Our survey of these castles is therefore limited to a bare half-dozen.

Turnberry Castle

This famous fortress, situated at the end of a promontory, six miles north of Girvan, is reduced to a few insignificant fragments, but possesses great historic interest. It is one of the oldest castles of Scotland, and was the seat of the Celtic Lords of Galloway. Later it became the seat of the Earls of Carrick. In 1274, Margaret, Countess of Carrick, was married here to Robert Bruce of Annandale, and the castle later became the property of King Robert the Bruce. On September 20th, 1286, there was held here the first recorded association or assembly of the nobles of Scotland, the object of which was to lay plans to support the claim of Robert Bruce, competitor for the Scottish Crown. In 1306 it was held for the English by Earl Percy, while King Robert Bruce lay in exile in the Isle of Arran. His friends were to give him signal by fire when the hour was propitious for him to return and attack the English, and he was brought over prematurely by an accidental fire, referred to in " The Lord of the Isles: "

" Wide o'er the sky the splendour glows,
   As that portentous meteor rose,

Helm, axe, and falchion glitter'd bright;
And in the red and dusky light,
His comrade's face each warrior saw,
Nor marvell'd it was pale with awe,
Then high in air the beams were lost,
And darkness sank upon the coast."

Returning, Bruce stormed the castle, drove out the English garrison, and obliged them to retire to Ayr. This incident gave him determination to keep up the struggle, and proved the turning point of his fortunes. Never after was the castle inhabited; its owner had passed to greater things.

Dunure Castle

Dunure Castle, the original residence of the Kennedies, Earls of Cassilis, stands on a high rock on the coast of Maybole, a town of which it has been said, "No fewer than twenty-eight baronial mansions, stately, turreted and strong, are said to have stood within its limits." Little is left of Dunure, except fragments of the keep, and vaults of the courtyard structures.

"The description of the means by which, in Queen Mary's disturbed reign, Gilbert, Earl of Cassilis, increased his domain is in-

teresting," say MacGibbon and Ross, " as a
specimen of the mode in which the church
lands were too often dealt with by the nobles
and lairds about the time of the Reformation.   The earl's proceedings are thus described: ' Gilbertt was ane particuler manne,
and ane werry greidy manne, and cairitt
nocht how he gatt land, sa that he culd cum
be the samin.'   This earl schemed with one
of the monks of Glenluce Abbey to counter-
feit the necessary signatures to a deed conveying to him the lands of the abbey.   Fearing
that the monk would reveal the forgery, he
employed a ' cairill ' to ' stik ' him; and then
in order to silence the latter, the earl persuaded his uncle, the laird of Bargany, to
accuse the ' cairill ' of theft and hang him.
' And sa the landis of Glenluse wes conqueist.'
The action of the same Earl Gilbert, for the
purpose of acquiring the lands of the Abbey
of Crosraguel, was even more horrible.   ' At
the alteratioune of the religioun, my Lord
deltt with the abbott,' but the feu, not having
been confirmed by the Crown, was disputed
by Allan Stuart, the succeeding abbot or
commendator.   The earl then carried him off
to his castle of Dunure, and ' Quhane he fand
him obstinatt, at last tuik him and band him

to ane furme, and sett his bair legis to ane
gritt fyr, and extreymly brunt him that he
was ewer thairefter onabill of his leggis.'
The laird of Bargany, hearing of this atroc-
ity, sent to rescue the abbot. His men concealed themselves at night in a chapel close
to the gate ' at the drawbrig-end,' and when
the gate was opened in the morning they
rushed in and took possession. The earl was
absent, but soon returned, and endeavoured
to retake the castle. His followers entered
the chapel above mentioned, and attempted
to mine the wall of the ' dungeone' which
adjoined it. ' Bot the Lairdis menne, that
was within, keist gritt staneis doune of the
heiche battelling of the dungeone: and sa
brak the ruiff of the chapell, in sik maner,
that thay war forssitt to leiff the samin.'
Bargany soon appeared on the scene with a
strong force, and removed the abbot to Ayr,
and after a time, and with some negotiation,
' all agreyitt. Me Lord gaiff the Abott sum
mony to leiff wpone, quhilk contentit him all
his dayis. And this way wes my lordis con-
queise of Corsragall; quhilk wes bot ane bad
forme.' "

The feud which arose from this event was
the cause later of a very tragical happening,

thus told by an anonymous writer: " In December, 1601, the Earl of Cassilis rode out from Maybole Castle at the head of two hundred armed followers to waylay the Laird of Bargany on a ride from Ayr to his house on Girvan-water; and on the farm of West Enoch, about half a mile north of the town, he forced on the Laird an utterly unequal conflict, and speedily brought him and several faithful adherents gorily to the ground. The Laird, mortally wounded, was carried from the scene of the onset to Maybole, that he might there, if he should evince any symptom of recovery, be despatched by the Earl as ' Judge Ordinar ' of the country; and thence he was removed to Ayr, where he died in a few hours. Flagrant though the deed was, it not only — through manœuvring and state influence highly characteristic of the period — passed with impunity, but was formally noted by an act of council as good service to the King. The Laird of Auchendrane, son-in-law of the slain baron, was one of the few adherents who bravely but vainly attempted to parry the onslaught, and he received some severe wounds in the encounter. Thirsting for vengeance, and learning that Sir Thomas Kennedy of Colzean intended to make a journey to Edinburgh, he so secretly instigated a party to waylay and kill him, that no witness existed of his connexion with them except a poor student of the name of Dalrymple, who had been the bearer of the intelligence which suggested and guided the crime. Dalrymple now became the object of his fears; and, after having been confined at Auchendrane, and in the island of Arran, and expatriated for five or six years a soldier, he returned home and was doomed to destruction. Mure, the Laird, having got a vassal, called James Bannatyne, to entice him to his house, situated at Chapel-Donan, a lonely place on the coast, murdered him there at midnight, and buried his body in the sand. The corpse, speedily unearthed by the tide, was carried out by the assassin to the sea at a time when a strong wind blew from the shore, but was very soon brought back by the waves, and lodged on the very scene of the murder. Mure, and his son who aided him in the horrid transactions, fell under general suspicion and now endeavoured to destroy Bannatyne, the witness and accomplice of their guilt; but the unhappy peasant making full confession to the civil authorities, they were brought up from an imprisonment

into which the King, roused by general in-
dignation, had already thrown them, and were
placed at the bar, pronounced guilty, and sum-
marily and ignominiously put to death."

Another of the fifteen castles of which the
town of Maybole boasts is Greenan, a tall
gaunt keep which occupies a picturesque
position in the bay of Ayr, about three miles
south of that town.

Dundonald Castle

Dundonald Castle, which stands in a most
conspicuous position on an isolated hill eight
miles north of Ayr, is a royal castle of the
fourteenth century. It was originally a very
extensive structure, as is evident from the
size of the keep, about eighty feet long and
forty feet wide, and the remains of the wall
of enceinte, which cover a large part of the
hilltop. The present castle, old as it is, is
built on the ruins of one still older, as appears from the base of an old round tower
which has been built into the west wall of the
keep. The interior of the keep contains only
two lofty pointed vaults. There was certainly at least one more floor, but its walls
have fallen out.

The castle has never been the scene of any historical events. Its sole claim to fame is that it was a favourite residence of some of the kings of Scotland. " The manor of Dundonald," says Chalmers, " belonged to Walter the son of Alan, the first Stuart, who held the whole of the northern half of Kyle, in the beginning of the reign of William the Lion; and it might have been granted to him by David I, or his successor Malcolm IV. Perhaps the castle of Dundonald was built by the first Walter, who had no appropriate house or castle when he settled in Scotland. It seems to have been the only castle which the Stuarts had in their extensive barony of Kyle Stuart; but several of their vassals had small castles in that district."

Robert II, after he ascended the throne, lived much in Dundonald, and died there in 1390. His son Robert III also resided here occasionally.

Dean Castle

Dean Castle stands some little distance northeast of the town of Kilmarnock, and is an excellent specimen of an early keep extended into a courtyard castle. It belonged

to the once powerful family of the Boyds.
Lord Boyd was created a peer by James II,
and his brother Alexander was tutor in horse-
manship to the boy James III.   Becoming
favourites, the Boyds became masters of the
king's person in 1466, and Lord Boyd received the highest offices of the kingdom.
His son was created Earl of Arran and married the Princess Mary, sister of the king.
Their fall was as rapid as their rise.   Found
guilty of treason in 1469, Sir Alexander was
beheaded, and the Earl of Arran fled to Denmark. His wife was confined in Dean Castle
as long as he lived. The castle was ruined
by fire in 1735. It consists of a massive keep,
another tower, and some buildings between.
The castle is similar to Doune.

A traditional rhyme of the district thus
alludes to the last Earl of Kilmarnock, who
lost his title and estates by joining in the
Rebellion of 1745, and whose crest was a
" loupen hand," that is, one with two fingers
folded in on the palm: —

> " The water of Carth runs by the Dean,
> That ance was Lord Boyd's lodgin':
> The lord wi' the loupen han',
> He lost his title and his lan'."

INDEX